LOCAL GOVERNMENT IN
SOUTHERN NIGERIA

LOCAL GOVERNMENT IN SOUTHERN NIGERIA

A MANUAL OF LAW AND PROCEDURE
UNDER THE EASTERN REGION
LOCAL GOVERNMENT LAW, 1955, AND THE
WESTERN REGION
LOCAL GOVERNMENT LAW, 1952

BY

PHILIP J. HARRIS, M.A.

Scholar of St Catharine's College, Cambridge
Senior Lecturer in Local Government at the
Nigerian College of Arts, Science and Technology

CAMBRIDGE
AT THE UNIVERSITY PRESS
1957

PUBLISHED BY
THE SYNDICS OF THE CAMBRIDGE UNIVERSITY PRESS

Bentley House, 200 Euston Road, London N.W.1
American Branch: 32 East 57th Street, New York 22, N.Y.

*Printed in Great Britain
by The Stellar Press Ltd., Barnet, Herts.*

FOREWORD

Local government of a modern kind is being established in Southern Nigeria and Mr Harris has written just the book that is needed by all those people who have to understand the work of a new system. Whilst the book is primarily concerned with law and procedure, it has much in it of wisdom derived from an intimate knowledge of practice and of the course of development over the last few years. The reason for that is the author's unique experience: he was an officer of the Overseas Service who turned teacher, at first temporarily and now permanently. He went to Nigeria as an administrative officer in 1948, becoming a District Officer in the Western Region. He was appointed Private Secretary to the Minister for Local Government, who later became Premier of the Western Region. Mr Harris was then posted as Assistant Secretary in charge of local government training and was for two years engaged in running training courses in the Extra Mural Department of the University College of Ibadan.

I went to Ibadan to take part in one of those courses and I can well understand anyone who has been engaged in that kind of teaching wanting to go on with it. It was a course that was immensely alive, with the men very keen to learn and looking forward to the new system. Yet with a staff who were themselves officials, and students who were secretaries and treasurers, either already or prospectively, it was close enough to the outside world to be realistic and down to earth. When Mr Harris told me that he had resigned from the Overseas Service in order to take an appointment as a Senior Lecturer in Local Government at the Nigerian College of Arts, Science and Technology, I was hardly surprised: for there is a great work to be done in training men for running the institutions that they have established for the government of their country.

Looking at the general scene of local government in Nigeria, it is a fair prospect. Of course there are troubles, not the least being the shortage of competent men to get the new system going. That is why so much importance must be attached to training courses and why Mr Harris' book is something of a landmark. A new system of government must have its own work-books, written round its own body of law.

Now with the training courses established and equipped with a good book, is it just a matter of a year or so before all will be well ? I have a large measure of enthusiasm for the progress that is being made, yet feel that a warning is needed. There is, I think, a definite danger that too much may be expected from the new kind of local government. We are right to regard democracy as a way of life and local government as one of the democratic forms, and so as being part of that way of life, but it is perhaps better to think of local government more as a tool or piece of machinery for getting a number of things done. The establishment of local government will not do anything by itself; elected councils, committees, secretaries, treasurers, offices and all the rest, are only means and not ends. The machinery has to be used to provide the services people want, and there are two requirements before very much can be done about services. The first is that the need for skilled men goes beyond secretaries and treasurers and extends to all manner of technicians, engineers, teachers and others. The second is that it needs money and that means more taxation. Even if there is a sufficient supply of technical people to staff the schools, health centres, and so on, their salaries must be paid and much building must be done to house their activities. There is a limit to the amount of money that any community can produce even if everyone is anxious to get the best possible services. There is no escaping these things, but it is so easy to overlook them. It would be a great tragedy if people should believe that the new elected councils can quickly provide services when, in fact, the resources of trained men and of money are insufficient, and so lose interest when they find nothing changes overnight. It is perhaps inevitable that in the enthusiasm of constitutional changes the main emphasis should be placed upon the structure and machinery of government.

I think I can say, having spent a happy time as a colleague of Mr Harris, that those who have the good fortune to listen to him talking about local government will not be allowed to forget that a machine does not exist for its own sake, but to secure that services should be established and extended and be run in a way that is in accordance with the wishes of the people for whom all these things exist.

R. M. JACKSON

St John's College
   Cambridge
5 July 1956

PREFACE

To the student and teacher of public administration it sometimes appears that legislation is regarded in Nigeria as a basis for discussion rather than as a firm statement of policy. Laws and regulations are amended with a bewildering frequency. The text which now goes to press has been revised not once but several times, in an effort to ensure that it shall be an accurate picture of current law and procedure. Indeed, if the need for a workbook for officials, a text-book for students and a detailed study for the citizen interested in the subject of local government, were not desperate in Nigeria at this time, it would be tempting to delay publication until the form and practice of local government had hardened. However, the need is desperate, and further delay would be most undesirable.

I am indebted to many friends for help with this book. First I am in debt to Dr R. M. Jackson not only for his encouragement and advice, but also for his generous Foreword. Mr R. E. Brown, Permanent Secretary to the Ministry of Local Government in the Western Region has given great help. Many of my hard worked friends in that Ministry have given of their patience and experience. Among these friends I must mention Mr I. D. Cameron, Mr P. S. G. Flint, Mr A. Bower, Mr P. Dyson and Mr C. J. M. Ross. I am also much in debt to Lt.-Col. E. C. Alderton, Permanent Secretary to the Ministry of Internal Affairs in the Eastern Region, who has read the text and made several valuable suggestions. To Mr I. R. Duncan and Mr L. M. D. Ogolo of that Ministry I am also indebted. Mr Duncan gave valuable help in the reading of the proofs.

If, in spite of so much help generously and patiently given, errors or omissions remain within this work, then they are my own. So too are any expressions of opinion that the book may contain. This is the first manual to be published on local government in Nigeria and I hope that it will be of use.

Philip J. Harris

IBADAN
8 August 1956

CONTENTS

Part IV

PART I

THE LOCAL GOVERNMENT
SYSTEM

CHAPTER I

ORIGINS OF LOCAL GOVERNMENT

1. *Local Government precedes Central Government.* In Nigeria, as in England, a form of local government preceded any form of central government. Long before Nigeria, or the Northern, Eastern and Western Regions of Nigeria, became accepted as geographical or political entities, government at the level of the village or extended family was, throughout Nigeria, a reality. Effective government extends only so far as there are means of communication. Where land communication was restricted to paths and tracks the unit of government normally covered a very small area. Kingdoms, such as the larger Fulani emirates, at times emerged. However, until the twentieth century, government in Nigeria seldom extended beyond the limits of local government.

When, in the second half of the last century, the territory now known as Nigeria came gradually and haphazardly under British rule, the newcomers discovered that in some areas the social and political life of its peoples was already efficiently and elaborately organised. The Fulani emirates and the kingdoms of the Yorubas and Binis were relatively well-developed local government organisations. In the East the highest functioning unit was seldom greater than the family or extended family, but even these small groups catered successfully for the basic needs of their communities. These indigenous institutions, owing nothing to European political concepts, were the foundations upon which local government in Nigeria has been built.

2. *Indirect Rule.* The early British administrators on their arrival were at pains not to disturb the existing political institutions. In so doing they took note of the fact that it would have been quite impossible for a handful of political and army officers to replace these institutions with an alien system. On 1 January 1914, the Colony and Protectorate of Nigeria was formally inaugurated

under the authority of Royal Letters Patent and Orders in Council. Sir Frederick Lugard was appointed the first Governor with the personal title of Governor-General. The policy of government which Lord Lugard (he was created a peer on 1 January 1928) evolved may be studied in his work *The Dual Mandate in British Tropical Africa* and in his *Political Memoranda*. Briefly, Lord Lugard's policy was that political officers should discover who were the traditional chiefs, the natural rulers, of the people in the area under their control, and proceed to rule through these chiefs. Where the traditional leaders could not easily be discovered, as in many areas in Eastern Nigeria, Government created 'warrant chiefs', many of whom had no traditional status in the community over which they were given authority. These traditional and warrant chiefs received official and legal recognition under the Native Authority Ordinance.[1] The native authority system in Nigeria was thus evolved from the practice and theory of indirect rule. The story of its evolution can best be studied in the standard works on the subject, such as those by Miss Margery Perham, Lord Hailey and Sir Alan Burns.[2]

Without detracting from the administrative brilliance of Lord Lugard it may be pointed out that indirect rule should be regarded less as a system of government invented by Europeans for the purpose of administering African territories, than as an ancient and obvious device to promote the easy and effective government of an occupied territory. Thus, for example, when the Allied armies occupied Germany in 1945 they governed the country by indirect rule. The first problem facing an occupying power is that of finding accommodation for its troops. One method of finding billets is to select certain properties at random and forcibly to eject the occupants. Another method is to call the local council chairman or burgomaster, to tell him what is required, and to ask him to make the necessary arrangements. The latter method tends to make less difficulties for the occupying army and less difficulties for the occupied people. The burgomaster can summon his council or advisers and with them

---

[1] The first Native Authority Ordinance to apply to the whole of Nigeria was Ordinance No. 14 of 1916.

[2] Margery Perham, *Native Administration in Nigeria*; Lord Hailey, *Native Administration in the British African Territories*; Sir Alan Burns, *History of Nigeria*.

work out how the housing requirements of the occupying troops can best be met. The local knowledge of the burgomaster will enable him to meet these demands with a minimum of hardship and suffering for the local people.

3. *The Native Authority System.* There was inherent in the system of indirect rule as worked out in Nigeria a certain dangerous lack of flexibility. Lugard had instructed his political officers to discover what were the traditional political authorities in the area under their command, then to issue their orders through these authorities. This system made little allowance for the fact that in a fast-developing territory, an institution that was acceptable in 1910 might not be generally accepted in 1930. This fact was appreciated during the governorship of Sir Donald Cameron (1931-35). Sir Donald emphasised that the native authority system needed fresh study and restatement. It had to be established whether or not the traditional institutions, so far as they had ever been apprehended by the early British administrators, continued to be acceptable to the people.

By the time of Sir Donald Cameron's governorship a considerable number of students and traders from Nigeria had visited the United Kingdom and had observed how deep a suspicion the British people had of despotism, and how great a respect they had for their own representative, democratic system of government. There followed, in a greatly varying degree of intensity in different parts of Nigeria, a certain resentment at the apparent attempt of the British to perpetuate the sometimes despotic rule of an Emir or Oba or other native authority. Appreciating this growing desire for representative government, confined though this desire was as yet to the educated minority, Sir Donald Cameron, in a speech delivered to Legislative Council on 6 March 1933, declared himself not unmindful 'of the difficulties which are presented where the native administration which we have created and recognised is based on a system of medieval polity dependent on the relation of vassal and superior'. However, something had to be done to ensure that native authorities kept pace with the times. 'I doubt sometimes whether we have done a great deal to impress on the minds of the native authorities concerned that the amelioration

5

of the social and economic conditions of a people is one of the primary duties of an administration and that the inspiration to improvement must come from within, from the native administration itself.'

4. *Modifications to the Native Authority System.* There followed a period of restatement and fresh examination of the native authority system and the enactment of a new Native Authority Ordinance (No.43 of 1933). This is readily available for study as an appendix to Miss Margery Perham's *Native Administration in Nigeria.* The Governor described this Ordinance as a modernised form of the previous Native Authority Ordinance. A further modernisation occurred in 1943 when yet another Native Authority Ordinance was enacted. It would not appear from a study of the text of the 1933 or 1943 Native Authority Ordinance that Sir Donald Cameron's policy of modifying and democratising native authorities had proceeded very far or fast. In section 3 (1) of the 1933 Ordinance and section 3 of the 1943 Ordinance it is still the Governor who decides what native authorities there shall be. By section 3 (1) of the 1933 Ordinance and section 5 (1) of the 1943 Ordinance it continues to be the Governor who decides who shall be appointed to these native authorities.

Changes in the native authority system there had been, but they came about less by legal enactment than by administrative policy and practice. Before the introduction of the first local government legislation in Nigeria some native authorities could claim to be operating as efficient and representative institutions. In many native authority councils decisions were already controlled by the majority vote of councillors, whose general acceptability had been confirmed by a form of election in the wards or villages from which they came. Many native authorities were already providing a substantial number of services for the people of their areas. Other native authorities had met exhortations towards social change and betterment only with inertia or suspicion. In some authorities personal emoluments consumed an unreasonable proportion of the revenue, leaving only a small contribution for social services. Whether efficient or inefficient, representative or unrepresentative, all native authorities were grounded in the assumption that they possessed an inherent authority which had in addition received the recognition and support of Government. This view of the constitutional position of local government was held to be out of place in a modern state moving towards self-determination.

5. *Local Government Legislation.* The Eastern Region Local Government Ordinance received the Royal Assent on 22 May 1950, and the Western Region Local Government Law received the Royal Assent on 25 February 1953. 1 July 1955 was the date of the commencement of the Eastern Region Local Government Law which replaced the Eastern Region Local Government Ordinance. The new Eastern Law was designed to meet the Constitutional requirement of Ministerial responsibility and to give a closer control of the actions of local government councils in the interest of efficiency and probity. The new law also offered greater elasticity of local government structure, making provision for all-purpose authorities in the large towns which had no affinities with the surrounding countryside.

The term 'local government' was not adopted in the Northern Region, but in 1954 the Legislature of this Region drew up the Northern Region Native Authority Law. This law indicates the lines by which it is proposed that local administration in the Northern Region should develop.

6. *Townships.* Before attempting to explain what in fact was new in these enactments some reference must be made to the peculiar position of townships. Early in the history of the British occupation of Nigeria it was felt that certain areas in which Europeans and native strangers predominated should be excluded from the control of native authorities. In 1900 Sir Frederick Lugard issued a Cantonments Proclamation by which an area of five square miles outside the area of Kano was excluded from the jurisdiction of the Emir. It was placed under the general control of a Station Magistrate, subordinate to the High Court, and employing Protectorate police. In this way special jurisdiction was provided for Europeans and others whose customs and way of life differed from that of the local people. A series of Townships Ordinances followed the 1900

Proclamation, and the Governor was by them empowered to declare any area or place to be a township. The inference to be drawn is that native authorities were at that time judged incapable of responding to the peculiar strains and influences which resulted when alien communities were established in their midst. It may be taken as evidence of the progress which has been made since the beginning of the century that wherever the Eastern and Western Region Local Government Laws are applied the Townships Ordinance as well as the Native Authority Ordinance ceases to have effect.[3]

7. *Influence of United Kingdom System.* Any consideration of the origins of local government in Nigeria must take note of the United Kingdom system of local government. In a country where a large proportion of the political and intellectual leaders received part of their education in the United Kingdom and were convinced of the merits of the system practised there, it was inherently probable that United Kingdom local government should be accepted as a model. It was natural that British officials when drafting local government legislation for Nigeria should frequently refer to the Local Government Act, 1933, for England and Wales. Indeed, this point leads to the first important respect in which the Nigerian local government legislation differed from the Native Authority Ordinance; the new legislation was specifically designed to set up a pattern of local authorities suited to a modern and sovereign state. Linked with this innovation was the disappearance of the very name 'Native Authority' which was for many associated with a position of political dependence and alien occupation. The new terms of County/Divisional, District and Local Councils carried associations with local government as practised in the United Kingdom.

8. *Innovation of Local Government Legislation.* Another important innovation is that whereas native authorities owed their existence and power to the Governor, local government councils are in the Eastern Region the creatures of the Minister, subject in some respects to the prior approval of the Governor-in-Council,

---

[3] E.R.L.G. Law, section 226; W.R.L.G. Law, section 227.

while in the Western Region they are the creatures of the Regional Authority. Section 3 of the Native Authority Ordinance empowered the Governor to constitute the office of Native Authority for any specified area. It is the Regional Authority upon whom section 3 of the Western Region Local Government Law confers a similar power in respect of local government councils. It is the Minister, with the prior approval of the Governor-in-Council, upon whom the power is conferred by section 3 of the Eastern Region Local Government Law.

A further innovation is the provision in the Eastern and Western Region Local Government Laws for the election of the majority or all of the council members.[4] While it is true that in many native authorities decisions were consistently taken by councillors elected by their respective wards and villages, in law it is the Governor who appoints all members of a native authority council. Elections under the native authority system may be regarded primarily as expressions of public opinion by which the Governor might be guided in the exercise of the power of appointment conferred on him by section 5 of the Native Authority Ordinance. From 1950 onwards it became the practice in the Western Region to make an Instrument of Appointment of Members in respect of native authority councils. Exercising the powers conferred on the Governor by section 5 (2) of the Native Authority Ordinance, and delegated to him, the Chief Commissioner of the Western Provinces directed that a native authority should be composed of a number of chiefs and a number of elected councillors. Under such an Instrument the election of councillors received legal recognition and validity. Not even this development of the native authority system can, however, obscure the significance of the requirement in the new local government legislation that the Instrument establishing a local government council should provide for the constitution of the council, for the number of councillors and for the date for the first election.

It is also significant that under the local government legislation the Minister in the Eastern Region and the Regional Authority in the Western Region are required to exercise the power to create or modify councils only after the wishes of the

---

[4] E.R.L.G. Law, section 5 (2) (d); W.R.L.G. Law, section 5 (1) (h).

inhabitants of the area concerned have been ascertained.[5] These wishes are ascertained by the appointment of an inquiring officer in the Eastern Region and by an inquiring committee wherever possible in the Western Region. While the Minister or Regional Authority is not bound to accept the recommendations of such a committee its report will invariably receive careful study. It was of the essence of the native authority system that administrations should be established in conformity with the political traditions of the people; it was invariably the practice in the latter days of the native authority system to conduct reforms and reorganisations only after widespread inquiry and discussion with the inhabitants of the area. This policy was, however, never written into the Native Authority Ordinance. The statutory requirement of the Eastern and Western Region Local Government Laws that the wishes of the inhabitants of the area concerned be ascertained before a council is established or modified must be regarded as an important innovation.

In both the Eastern and Western Regions local government councils derive their powers from the Legislature or from the Instrument establishing them. Unlike the native authority system one council is never made subordinate to another. No local government council is dependent in the exercise of its functions on the consent of another council.

For the most part the innovations of the Eastern and Western Region Local Government Laws are legal innovations giving legislative recognition to the development of the native authority system which had been taking place as a result of administrative action. Of one innovation this cannot be said. Native Authority and Townships legislation had been introduced and modified by British officials in accordance with their assessment of the needs and possibilities of the political situation. The Eastern Region Local Government Ordinance may be said to have been concerted between the administration and the unofficial representatives in the Eastern House of Assembly on the basis of the report prepared by Brigadier Gibbons.[6]

[5] E.R.L.G. Law, section 3 (1) and section 7 (1); W.R.L.G. Law, section 3 (4) and section 7 (1).

[6] Brigadier E. J. Gibbons, C.B.E., *African Local Government Reform: Kenya, Uganda, and Eastern Nigeria.*

The Western Region Local Government Law was introduced primarily at the instigation of, and in accordance with the policy of, the elected representatives of the people. When the Eastern Region Local Government Law replaced the Ordinance that had been drafted at an earlier stage of constitutional development, the change was made because the elected representatives of the people judged that the earlier legislation had been proved in some respects deficient. The local government law of both Regions is being applied in accordance with the policy of Regional Ministers of State. In both Regions local government has been made to conform to the present constitutional position.

CHAPTER II

THE CONSTITUTIONAL SETTING OF LOCAL GOVERNMENT COUNCILS

1. *Sovereignty*. The question of where sovereignty, the supreme power in a state, resides, has fascinated many political philosophers. In the person of the monarch who rules of divine right? In the community as a whole? In both king and people who must come together in a contract which will be of advantage to both? The question has never been satisfactorily answered.

For John Locke, writing to justify the English Revolution of 1688, sovereignty was vested in the community, but the people divested themselves of it in the act of setting up a government. Once a government had been set up it was the duty of the people to obey it. 'Every man, by consenting with others to make one body politic under one government, puts himself under an obligation to every one of that society to submit to the determination of the majority and to be concluded by it.'[1] For Locke, the supreme power was thus only to be exercised by the people on election days.

This theory accords closely with Dicey's principle of parliamentary sovereignty. Dicey describes the Monarch in Parliament, that is, the Queen, the House of Lords and the House of Commons, as the legal sovereign in the United Kingdom.[2] Constitutional arrangements in the United Kingdom are such that the will of the electors by regular constitutional means always in the end asserts itself. In practice, the supreme power is exercised by the people when casting a vote for a candidate for membership of the House of Commons.

2. *Federal Constitution of Nigeria*. Any attempt to apply the principle of parliamentary sovereignty to the federal constitution of Nigeria raises many legal and constitutional problems.

---

[1] John Locke, *Of Civil Government*, Bk. II, ch. 8.
[2] A. V. Dicey, *Law of the Constitution*.

It is the written constitution which must be supreme in any federal state. If the federation is to be preserved, neither the legislature of the federal unit nor the legislatures of the constituent Regions must be empowered to destroy the delicate balance of power involved in the desire for a measure of union compatible with a measure of independence of action. However, it would be possible to defend the proposition that in Nigeria sovereignty is vested in the Governor General (representing the Queen) and the House of Representatives in respect of those matters which have been assigned to the Federal Government; in the Governor (representing the Queen) and the Regional Legislative Houses (House of Assembly in the Eastern Region; House of Assembly and House of Chiefs in both the Northern and Western Regions) in respect of those matters which have been assigned to the Regional Governments.

3. *Nigeria (Constitution) Order in Council.* In the First Schedule to the Nigeria (Constitution) Order in Council 1954, which came into operation on 1 October 1954, appears the Exclusive Legislative List and the Concurrent Legislative List.[3] The former is a list of subjects exclusively assigned to the Federal Legislature and the latter is a list of subjects for which the Federal and the Regional Legislatures are jointly responsible. Local Government appears in neither of these lists. Subsection 3 of section 51 of the Nigeria (Constitution) Order in Council 1954 provides as follows:

Subject to the provisions of this Order, the Governor of a Region may, with the advice and consent of the Legislative Houses of that Region, make laws for the peace, order and good government of that Region or any part thereof with respect to any matter other than a matter that is included in the Exclusive Legislative List.

Local Government is not included in the Exclusive Legislative List nor even in the Concurrent Legislative List and may therefore be described as a 'residual' or exclusively Regional subject. Responsibility for local government matters is vested in the Regional Legislatures.

Returning to the attempt to apply John Locke's political

[3] L.N. 102 of 1954 Supplement to *Nigeria Gazette Extraordinary*, No. 43, Vol. 41, of 3 September 1954.

theory to the actualities of the present constitution of Nigeria it may be argued that when electing their respective Houses of Assembly the people of Nigeria divested themselves of the supreme power over local government matters and vested it in their Regional Legislatures. Sovereignty in respect of local government matters is vested in the Regional Legislatures, and local government councils can only be created by those Legislatures. Local authorities are the creatures of statute.

4. *Derivation of Powers.* The most obvious and most direct means by which local government councils derive their powers is by laws made by the Regional Legislatures. Examples are the Western Region Local Government Law of 1952, the Western Region Appointment and Recognition of Chiefs Law of 1954, the Western Region Education Law of 1954, and the Eastern Region Local Government Law of 1955. The legal position is somewhat complicated by the fact that local authorities derive some power from ordinances, such as the Direct Taxation Ordinance or the Labour Code Ordinance, which were enacted before constitutional changes brought about the present legal position. Moreover, the Southern Cameroons and the Federal Territory of Lagos do not fit into the Regional pattern.

In order to avoid crowding the time of a House of Assembly, the Regional Legislature confers a number of its powers upon the appropriate Regional Authority (i.e. to the Governor in Executive Council) or to the appropriate Minister. This delegation does not conflict with the fundamental principle that powers of local government councils must be derived from the Regional Legislatures; the process merely involves two steps in their derivation instead of one. For example, the power to establish local government councils has been conferred upon the Western Regional Authority by section 3 of the Western Region Local Government Law and upon the appropriate Minister by section 3 of the Eastern Region Local Government Law. Ultimately, however, it is always the Regional Legislature upon which a local government council is dependent for statutory authority, both for its existence and for its powers.

CHAPTER III

ESTABLISHMENT OF LOCAL GOVERNMENT COUNCILS

The Regional Authority is empowered by section 3 of the Western Region Local Government Law to establish by Instrument such local government councils as he thinks fit, subject only to the condition that the wishes of the inhabitants of the area concerned must first be consulted. Section 3 of the Eastern Region Local Government Law confers similar powers upon the Minister, who may act only after consulting the wishes of the inhabitants of the area concerned and after having obtained the prior approval of the Governor-in-Council. In the Instrument establishing a council the Regional Authority or Minister specifies that the council *shall* perform certain functions and *may* perform others.[1] In this way each council derives its existence and draws its powers direct from the Instrument establishing it. No provision is made for the subordination of one council to another. Every local government council is empowered to exercise the functions conferred upon it, free from interference from any other council, subject only to the controls imposed by law.

Every local government council when established is a body corporate, having perpetual succession and a common seal, having power to hold land and to sue and to be sued.[2] A comparable power was conferred on Native Authorities only in 1951.[3]

1. *Procedure prior to Establishment.* The Regional Authority is required before establishing a local government council to take steps to find out the wishes of the inhabitants of the area. In the Eastern Region, consultation has usually taken place through

[1] E.R.L.G. Law, section 5 (4); W.R.L.G. Law, section 5 (1) (e).
[2] E.R.L.G. Law, section 6; W.R.L.G. Law, section 6.
[3] Ordinance No. 34 of 1951.

an officer appointed to this special duty. The inquiring officer tours the area concerned, holds frequent meetings with the people, and finally submits a report to the Regional Authority setting out a pattern of local government councils acceptable to the people of the area. In the Western Region the practice has been for a small committee to be appointed locally to make the necessary inquiry. Such committees have normally been made responsible for conducting an inquiry throughout one administrative division. They have consisted of such persons as the local member of the Regional Legislature, the District Officer, representatives of the existing native authorities, together with a representative of native authority employees and one prominent local citizen, or more than one. The inquiry committee has usually toured extensively throughout the division, in accordance with an advertised programme, and by frequent public meetings has discovered the wishes of the people. In addition to holding open meetings the committee has usually received memoranda on the subject of local government reform from interested parties. When the wishes of the local community have been fully studied by its members the committee reports to the Minister responsible, informing him of the views of the local people and making recommendations as to the types of councils which should be established in the area.

The Minister is aware that the report should record the views of those who will be most closely concerned with the councils when they are set up, of those who have an intimate and detailed knowledge of the problems, traditions and prejudices of the area affected. The Minister must, however, assess these important local factors in the light of his knowledge of the Region as a whole. The Minister's final approval will extend beyond these local considerations, and will take into account the good government of the Region and the necessity of establishing a local government organisation which is financially sound and administratively efficient. It is only when the Minister is satisfied that the above conditions have been fulfilled that he will place before the Governor-in-Council a memorandum which sets out his own views on the local government organisation best suited to the needs of the community in question. This memorandum will then be considered by the Governor-in-Council, whose final decision will be followed by the publication in the *Regional Gazette* of Instruments establishing councils.[4]

2. *The Instrument.* The contents of an Instrument establishing a council are substantially the same in both Eastern and Western Regions of Nigeria. In both Regions it is provided that an Instrument *must* do certain things and *may* do others. All such Instruments must specify the name and type of council and the date on which it shall be established; must describe the device of the seal of the council; must define the limits of the area of the authority of the council; must provide for the constitution of the council, the number of councillors and the date for the first election.[5] An Instrument establishing a council in the Western Region must, in addition, provide for the appointment of a president of the council or for the election or appointment of a chairman, or both, and must specify the method of election or appointment. The Eastern Region Local Government Law makes no mention of a president,[6] but provides that an Instrument may specify the method of the election or the system of the appointment of a chairman of a council. Section 5 of the Western Region Local Government Law differs from section 5 of the Eastern Local Government Law in that it makes a number of provisions mandatory, which, in the Eastern Law, are permissive. Nevertheless, the contents of an Instrument are substantially the same in both Regions.

3. *Assignment of Property.* Section 221 of the Eastern Region Local Government Law provides that upon the establishment of a local council all sums of money and property belonging to a local authority, or native authority formerly constituted in the area, shall be transferred to and vested in the Minister. Such property must then be allocated by way of free grant to any newly-established local government council, upon such terms and conditions as the Minister may determine. The provisions of section 221 of the Western Region Local Government Law

[4] E.R.L.G. Law, section 4 (2); W.R.L.G. Law, section 4 (2).
[5] E.R.L.G. Law, section 5 (1) (a)-(d); W.R.L.G. Law, section 5 (1) (a)-(d).
[6] But see now section 9 of the E.R.L.G. (Amendment) Law, 1956 which provides that 'The Minister may by Instrument appoint a person by name, by title or by office to the President of a Council'.

are somewhat different. Upon the establishment of a local government council all money and property belonging to any local authority, or native authority formerly constituted in the area, shall be transferred direct to such new local government council as the Regional Authority may direct, subject to the Regional Authority's terms and conditions. The financial arrangements involved are dealt with in greater detail in a subsequent chapter.

4. *Subsisting Contracts.* Section 222 of the Western Law provides that upon the establishment of a council and upon a direction to that effect being given by the Regional Authority, the rights, obligations and liabilities of the outgoing native authorities and townships shall pass to the new local government council specified by the Regional Authority. Section 222 of the Eastern Law makes similar provisions except that the Minister is substituted for the Regional Authority. Any court actions involving an outgoing authority are immediately taken up by or against the new local government council. The term 'rights and liabilities' specifically includes the payment of any retiring allowance due to any person who was formerly employed by an outgoing native authority or township.

5. *Power to Amend Instrument.* Section 7 of the Western Region Local Government Law empowers the Regional Authority to amend an Instrument establishing a council. The wishes of the inhabitants of the area concerned must be consulted before this is done, although the Regional Authority is under no statutory obligation to implement these wishes. Section 7 of the Eastern Region Local Government Law makes similar provisions, but confers the power upon the appropriate Minister. The Regional Authority or Minister must also have published in the area concerned not less than thirty clear days' notice of his intention to amend the Instrument establishing a council, and must give an opportunity to the council concerned to make representations to him in writing.[7] This power would be exercised if the Regional Authority or Minister were convinced that a change was desirable in respect of the boundaries of the area of the

[7] E.R.L.G. Law, section 7 (2); W.R.L.G. Law, section 7 (2).

authority of a council, in respect of the status of a council, or in respect of the functions exercisable by a council. Section 10 of the Eastern Region Local Government Law and section 11 of the Western Region Local Government Law provide that unless the contrary intention appears, amendments to the Instruments establishing councils shall not affect the validity of any decision taken, or act done, before such amendment.

6. *Power to Dissolve a Council.* If any council in the Eastern Region fails on three consecutive occasions to meet with the minimum frequency the Minister must have an inquiry held at which the council concerned is to be given an opportunity of being heard. After considering the inquiry's report, and with the prior approval of the Governor-in-Council, the Minister may order a fresh election or may issue an amending Instrument dissolving the council. The Instrument will either establish a new council or will appoint not less than three persons to form a new council. These provisions are made in section 9 of the Eastern Region Local Government Law. In section 9 of the Western Law the Regional Authority is permitted to take similar action if at any time a council fails to meet with the frequency required. Not less than five persons may be appointed to form a new council. In the Eastern Region the Minister, and in the Western Region the Regional Authority, is empowered to dissolve a council after holding an inquiry, if it appears that the revenues of a council are not being properly used in the best interests of the area as a whole, or if a council fails properly to levy rates or fails to conform to its statutory obligations.[8]

7. *Power to Revoke Instruments.* In the Western Region 'The Regional Authority may of his own motion or in his absolute discretion on the application of any persons concerned, if he shall think fit, revoke the Instrument establishing any council, if he considers it in the interests of the persons living within the area to do so.'[9]

In the Eastern Region the Minister is empowered, by section 12 of the Eastern Region Local Government Law, to revoke the

[8] E.R.L.G. Law, section 9 (2); W.R.L.G. Law, section 10.
[9] W.R.L.G. Law, section 13.

Instrument establishing a council. The Minister is required to act only on the application of any persons concerned and only with the prior approval of the Governor-in-Council.

In both Western and Eastern Regions no such revocation of an Instrument may be made unless the council concerned has been given an opportunity of making representations on the matter. The revocation of the Instrument establishing a council deprives that council of all the authority it has derived directly and indirectly from the Regional Legislature. Upon such revocation the council ceases to exist.

CHAPTER IV

LOCAL GOVERNMENT STRUCTURE

1. *Types of Councils.* In the Eastern and Western Regions of Nigeria, as in England, there are, basically, three tiers of local government councils. In England, the first tier consists of administrative counties and county boroughs; the second consists of urban districts, rural districts, and municipal boroughs; the third, which occurs in the rural districts only, consists of parish councils and parish meetings. In the Western Region of Nigeria the first tier of councils consists of divisional councils and all-purpose district councils, the second tier consists of district councils and the third tier consists of local councils. In the Eastern Region of Nigeria the first tier consists of county councils, the second tier of urban and rural district councils and the third tier of local councils. The Municipality corresponds approximately to the English county borough.

Local government structure is, in England and Wales, the subject of much discussion and of firmly held opinions. With the growth of towns in modern times many boroughs have spread beyond the limits of their ancient boundaries. The citizens living in the built-up area surrounding a borough may well look to the borough to provide them with schools, shopping and recreation facilities. Yet the borough cannot levy a rate upon them, for they live outside the borough area as defined in its charter. Any application for a revision of the borough boundaries is likely to be vigorously opposed by the neighbouring or surrounding authority, which may stand to lose much of its most valuable rateable value by such a change.

The structure of local government councils has been the subject of many inquiries in England and Wales, but, so far, no formula has yet been evolved which is satisfactory to all the interests concerned. The view is often expressed that, while many features of English local government are worth imitating – the integrity of officials and council members, the principle of free and voluntary service, the respect for minority interests – it is ill-advised to adopt in Southern Nigeria a structure of local government which is under constant criticism in the country of its origin. The fact is, however, that the English local government structure was not copied blindly, but was adopted only after the most careful consideration of possible alternative systems. Moreover, when the English structure was decided upon, it was not followed slavishly. In the question of assignment of functions, particularly, both the Western Region Local Government Law and the Eastern Regional Local Government Law show a flexibility which is quite foreign to local government legislation in England and Wales.

2. *Assignment of Functions.* The basic assumption behind the three-tier system of local government is that, just as some functions of government can more efficiently be administered by local units than by a remote central government, so, among the local government functions, some will be administered most efficiently by village councils and others by councils covering a much larger area. The optimum unit of administration for the provision of services for the improvement of agriculture and livestock is very much larger in area than the optimum unit for the control of village markets. The optimum unit for the control of bush fires might well be somewhere between the two. Where there are three levels of councils in existence the legislature can confer a function upon whichever type of council is best able to exercise it efficiently and economically.

In the United Kingdom the powers conferred on local government councils by the acts which established them were few. Most of the functions exercised by councils have been conferred by way of General Acts dealing comprehensively with one particular service. The function has then, through the General Act, been conferred upon the tier of largest councils, the tier of medium-sized councils, or the tier of smallest councils. There has been little attempt to consider the capabilities of individual councils one by one, nor has much attention been given to the variations of local circumstance and tradition. Few allowances have been made for the wide variations of size, resources and importance between different councils within any one tier.

In the Eastern and Western Regions of Nigeria great flexibility is practised in the assignment of functions to local government councils. The Eastern Region Local Government Law and the Western Region Local Government Law confer certain powers and impose certain obligations on all councils throughout the Region or on all councils of a certain type throughout the Region. Thus it is the duty of every council throughout both Regions to the best of their ability to prevent the commission of any offence within the area of their authority.[1] In the Eastern Region it is a duty laid exclusively and directly upon every Municipality and District Council to act as the rating authority for its area.[2] However, the great majority of local government functions are not directly assigned to one tier of councils by the law, but may be conferred on any council through the Instrument establishing it.[3] In some areas local history and circumstance will result in the district councils having a stronger sense of belonging to them, than the divisional or county council. In others the larger unit will be supported by the strongest traditions of unity and loyalty, and the district councils may be administrative units without any strong historical sense of corporation. Such local variations can be respected by conferring a greater number of functions upon the district councils in one area, and a greater number upon the divisional, or county, councils in another area.

3. *Composition of Councils*. The composition of a local government council will be regulated by the Instrument by which the council is established.[4] In the Eastern Region a County, District, or Local Council is composed of a chairman, a vice chairman, and such number of councillors as is laid down in the Instrument. A Municipality consists of a mayor, a deputy mayor, and such number of councillors as is laid down in the Instrument. Council members may be elected or appointed or, in certain circumstances, co-opted.[5] Unless it is provided otherwise in the

---

[1] E.R.L.G. Law, section 70 (1); W.R.L.G. Law, section 58 (1).
[2] E.R.L.G. Law, section 121.
[3] E.R.L.G. Law, section 80; W.R.L.G. Law, section 77.
[4] E.R.L.G. Law, section 18; W.R.L.G. Law, section 19.
[5] E.R.L.G. Law, section 35 (3)-(4).

Instrument, the chairman or mayor will be elected annually by majority vote of the council members.[6]

In the Western Region a council is composed of both elected and traditional members. The Instrument establishing a council regulates the number of elected, and the number of traditional, members, but the number of elected members must never be less than three times the number of traditional members.[7] The members of a Divisional Council are normally elected or appointed from among the members of the District or Local Councils within its area. In certain circumstances a District or Local Council may elect a person other than one of its own members to be a member of the Divisional Council.[8] Elected members of District and Local Councils are elected by the majority vote of the electors of the ward concerned. Every council in the Western Region has an elected chairman who is elected annually by the council from among its members.[9] The Instrument establishing a council may provide that in addition to an elected chairman the council shall also have a president as named in the Instrument.[10]

[6] E.R.L.G. Law, section 24.   [8] W.R.L.G. Law, section 22 (2).
[7] W.R.L.G. Law, section 19 (2). [9] W.R.L.G. Law, section 29.
[10] W.R.L.G. Law, section 28.

CHAPTER V

LOCAL GOVERNMENT FUNCTIONS

It is widely assumed to be inherently right that the people of a nation should govern their own affairs. It is widely assumed that within a federation the people of each region or state should be allowed a large measure of self-government. If these assumptions are valid it is difficult to resist the conclusion that so far as is practicable the inhabitants of a town, of a district, or of a division should also be allowed a measure of self-government. Such functions of government as are in fact controlled at the level of the division, district, or town are regarded as local government functions.

Some functions of government can be in the most efficient way administered centrally, and some can best be administered locally, by people with an intimate knowledge of the needs, conditions and difficulties of the area concerned. When considering what functions of government should be vested in local government councils the Legislature must be guided in part by the criterion of utility. The law-makers will ask themselves what tasks can most conveniently and usefully be entrusted to the care of local council members and officials. The Legislature may also be guided by the assumption that it is inherently proper that local people should be closely associated with the provision of services for, and with the general administration of, their own area.

1. *Protective Services.* The first duty of government is to provide a secure background against which individual citizens can pursue their personal happiness and private prosperity. Security against external aggression will invariably be the responsibility of the central government. However, the maintenance of internal security throughout the area of a state cannot be completely ensured from its administrative headquarters. Responsibility for maintaining security within their areas is vested in

local government councils. Section 69 (1) of the Eastern Region Local Government Law provides that

It shall be the duty of every council established under this Law to discharge the functions conferred by this or any other written law and generally to maintain order and good government within the area of its authority.

Section 57 (1) of the Western Region Local Government Law makes similar provision. In the Eastern and Western Regions of Nigeria it has been made the duty of every council, together with the individual members thereof, to prevent to the best of their ability the commission of any offence within the area of its authority. A member of a council if called upon by a superior officer or administrative officer (a justice of the peace in the Western Region) to do so, must take any action necessary for the prevention of the commission of any offence. Failure to take such action may result in the councillor being fined a maximum of one hundred pounds.[1]

Local government councils in the Western Region are empowered by the Western Region Local Government Police Law to establish by order, with the approval of the appropriate Minister, a police force.[2] With the approval of the Regional Authority, a council in the Western Region may constitute or take over a prison, and, with the approval of the Local Government Inspector, may constitute a lock-up.[3] Section 3 of the Eastern Regional Local Constabularies Law, 1956 empowers a council or two or more councils to establish, with the approval of the Minister, a local constabulary. No comparable provisions appear in respect of prisons for in the Eastern Region of Nigeria prisons are operated as a function of the Federal Government.

In both Eastern and Western Regions a council may, through the Instrument establishing it, be permitted or required to establish and maintain fire brigades and to provide fire-fighting equipment.[4]

Other functions concerned with public order, which a council may be permitted or required to perform, are set out in section

[1] E.R.L.G. Law, section 70; W.R.L.G. Law, section 58.
[2] W.R. Local Government Police Law, 1955, section 3.
[3] W.R.L.G. Law, section 168 and 171.
[4] E.R.L.G. Law, section 80 (48); W.R.L.G. Law, section 71 (49).

80 of the Eastern Region Local Government Law, subsections (46)–(58), and in section 71 of the Western Region Local Government Law, subsections (46)–(55). Protective services may also regulate the demolition of dangerous buildings, the use of any inflammable material in building construction, the control of offensive trades and industries, and the provision of lighting in public places.

2. *Social Services*. Provision for education is the most important social service provided by local government councils. In the Eastern Region the building and maintenance of schools, the granting of scholarships and the financial support of libraries and museums may be conferred upon any council, through the Instrument by which it is established.[5] In the Western Region the provision of education services is the function of such councils as the Minister of Education may, with the concurrence of the Minister of Local Government, appoint to be local education authorities.[6] Such a local education authority must maintain public primary schools and secondary modern schools, and may, with the consent of the Minister of Education and of the Minister of Local Government, maintain secondary schools, special schools for handicapped children, and trade centres.[7]

Medical and health facilities constitute another important social service provided by local government councils. Subsections (33)–(45) of section 80 of the Eastern Region Local Government Law and subsections (34)–(45) of section 71 of the Western Region Local Government Law list the functions concerning public health which may be conferred on a council through its Instrument. The provision of a public water supply, the extermination of vermin, the disposal of nightsoil, the regulation of slaughtering and the sale of meat, the control of cemeteries, the maintenance of maternity homes and dispensaries – these are some of the functions listed.

The management of recreation grounds and open spaces, the granting of sums of money towards associations existing for the

---

[5] E.R.L.G. Law, section 80 (22-27).
[6] W.R. Education Law, section 8.
[7] W.R. Education Law, section 8.

welfare of children, the protection of African antique works of art, are also numbered among the social services which may be provided by local government councils.

3. *Economic Development.* Many local government functions are concerned with economic development, and it may be that in Nigeria these are the functions which should be most actively exercised. Raising this important question Ronald Wraith asks: whether local government in West Africa ought not to have a more strictly economic function than elsewhere. It may be said that in England local authorities administer expensive social services that the community can afford to pay for, and does in fact pay for. There is a danger that in West Africa they may be charged with the task of spending money which does not exist, and providing luxuries for people who cannot afford necessities.[8]

Subsections (58)–(67) of section 71 of the Western Region Local Government Law and subsections (61)–(70) of section 80 of the Eastern Region Local Government Law set out those functions in respect of the maintenance of roads and streets and of transport services by land or water which may be conferred upon a council by the Instrument establishing it. A list of the roads for the maintenance of which a council has been made responsible usually appears as an appendix to the Instrument establishing a council.

It is not only by improving means of communication that a council can promote the economic development of its area. In Eastern and Western Regions councils may be empowered or required to provide services for the improvement of agriculture and to control methods of husbandry.[9] The functions of a council may include the provision of services for the improvement of livestock and prevention and control of the outbreak of any disease among animals.;[10] they may include the maintenance of forest plantations and the sale of the products thereof.[11] One of the most important functions among those relating to natural resources concerns the prevention and control of soil erosion.[12]

---

[8] Ronald E. Wraith, *Local Government* p. 57.
[9] E.R.L.G. Law, section 80 (1) and (2); W.R.L.G. Law, section 71 (1) and (2).
[10] E.R.L.G. Law section 80 (8) and (7); W.R.L.G. Law, section 71 (8) and (7).
[11] E.R.L.G. Law, section 80 (28); W.R.L.G. Law, section 71 (26).
[12] E.R.L.G. Law, section 81 (1) (c); W.R.L.G. Law, section, 71 (27).

A local government council in the Eastern and Western Region may be empowered or required to build, maintain and control markets.[13] A council may also have functions conferred upon it concerning the control of public weighing machines, and concerning the fixing of the maximum price which may be demanded for any article of food in any market.[14]

Local government councils in both Western and Eastern Regions of Nigeria may expect, therefore, to have conferred upon them considerable powers for the furtherance of economic development in their areas. Their responsibilities for promoting such development are proportionately great. Local government in Nigeria will fail unless councillors and officials squarely face the danger of preoccupation with demands for luxuries at a time when some, at least, can still not afford necessities.

[13] E.R.L.G. Law, section 80 (30)-(32); W.R.L.G. Law, section 71 (31)-(33). But now also see section 13 of the Eastern Region Local Government (Amendment) Law, 1956 which inserts section 80A in the Principal Law. Section 80A empowers the Minister himself to appoint a Board of Market Control for the area of the authority of any Municipality or Urban District Council. The Minister is also empowered to make regulations concerning Boards of Market Control and such regulations have now been made.

[14] E.R.L.G. Law, section 80 (73) and (74); W.R.L.G. Law, section 71 (71) and (70).

CHAPTER VI

ELECTIONS

1. *Electoral Regulations*. Section 39 of the Eastern Region Local Government Law provides that the Minister, with the prior approval of the Governor-in-Council, may make regulations governing the election of local government councillors. In particular, these electoral regulations may make provision for the following matters:
   (*a*) Registration of electors;
   (*b*) Holding and conduct of elections;
   (*c*) Division of a council area into wards;
   (*d*) Method of nominating candidates;
   (*e*) Procedure to be followed when two or more candidates have received an equal number of votes in an election.

Section 33 of the Western Region Local Government Law empowers the Governor-in-Council to make regulations governing similar matters.

In the Western Region regulations have been made by the Governor-in-Council, common both to parliamentary and to local government elections. These regulations are known as the Parliamentary and Local Government Electoral Regulations, 1955.[1] Parts of these Regulations came into force on 15 August 1955. Other parts came into force on 1 May 1956.

In the Eastern Region regulations have been made governing local government elections only. These Local Government (Electoral) Regulations, 1955, came into force on 26 August 1955.[2]

2. *Qualifications of Electors*. Regulation 4 of the Eastern Region Local Government (Elections) Regulations, 1955, requires that

---

[1] W.R.L.N. 266 of 1955; Supplement to Western Region Gazette, No. 37 of Vol. 4.

[2] E.R.L.N., No. 190 of 1955; Supplement to *Eastern Region Gazette*, No. 44 of Vol. 4. See also E.R.L.N. No. 98 of 1956 for The Local Government (Elections) (Amendment) Regulations, 1956.

an elector shall have three qualifications. The first is that the elector must be at least twenty-one years old. The second is that either the elector or his or her father must have been born in the ward in which the election is to take place, or the elector must have been resident in the area of the ward for a period of six months immediately preceding the qualifying date. The third requirement is that the elector must apply to be registered on the register of electors. It is also provided that no person may have his name registered to vote in respect of more than one ward.

Regulation 10 of the Western Region Parliamentary and Local Government Electoral Regulations, 1955, provides that an elector may be qualified in one of two ways. The first way is for an elector to have been resident in the Division in which the constituency is situated for a continuous period of two years immediately preceding the qualifying date, and also to have paid, unless exempted from such payment, tax or rate in respect of the two financial years preceding the qualifying date. The second way is for an elector or his or her father to have been born in the Division in which the constituency is situated and, in addition, to be at least twenty-one years old or to have paid tax or a rate in respect of the financial year preceding the qualifying date.

3. *Disqualifications of Electors.* Regulation 5 of the Eastern Region Local Government (Elections) Regulations, 1955, provides that no person is entitled to have his name registered as an elector who acknowledges allegiance to any foreign power, who has been sentenced to death or to imprisonment and not completed his sentence nor received a free pardon, or who has been adjudged a lunatic.

Regulation 11 of the Western Region Parliamentary and Local Government Electoral Regulations, 1955, makes similar provisions, and provides in addition that no person shall be registered as an elector who has been convicted of an electoral offence.

4. *Qualifications of Councillors.* Section 19 of the Eastern Region Local Government Law provides that a person shall be qualified to be elected as a councillor if he satisfies three conditions. The

first is that the candidate must be a British subject or a British protected person of the age of twenty-one years or more. The second requirement is that the candidate or his father must have been born in the area of the authority of the council or he must have resided in the area of the authority of the council for a period of twelve months immediately preceding the date of the election. The third condition is that the name of the candidate must appear in the register of electors for the council in question.

Section 23 of the Western Region Local Government Law provides that a person who is a British subject or a British protected person may be qualified to be elected as an elected member of a District or Local Council in one of two ways. The first way is for the candidate to have been resident in the area of the council for a continuous period of two years immediately preceding the date of election and to have paid tax or rate in respect of the two previous financial years, unless exempted from payment. The second way is for a candidate to be twenty-one years of age or upwards and for him or his father to have been born in the area of the council concerned.

5. *Disqualifications of Councillors.* Section 20 of the Eastern Region Local Government Law provides that a person is disqualified from being elected, appointed or co-opted as a member of a local government council if he suffers from any of the following disabilities:

(*a*) If he owes allegiance to any foreign power;

(*b*) If he is an undischarged bankrupt;

(*c*) If he has been sentenced by a court to death or imprisonment and has not either suffered his punishment or received a free pardon;

(*d*) If he holds any paid office or place of profit in the gift of the Crown;

(*e*) If he holds any paid office or place of profit (other than that of Mayor or chairman)[3] in the gift of the council;

(*f*) If he has been adjudged a lunatic;

(*g*) If he has been surcharged to an amount exceeding five hundred pounds;

[3] Section 5 of E.R.L.G. (Amendment) Law, 1956 adds the offices of President, rate-collector and tax-collector.

(*h*) If he is a police officer;

(*i*) If he has been convicted of an election offence;

(*j*) If he holds an appointment to be a member of a Native Court.

Section 21 of the Eastern Region Local Government Law further provides that a person is disqualified from election or appointment as a local government councillor if he is a party to any subsisting contract with the council concerned and has not disclosed his interest in the contract within one month of the day of election.

Section 7 of the Eastern Region Local Government (Amendment) Law, 1956, adds a new section 20B to the principal Law. This new section governs membership of more than one council. A person may not remain a member of more than one council except that he may remain a member of a District Council and of any one Local Council within the area of the authority of such District Council, and except that he may remain a member of a County Council and of any one District Council within the area of the authority of such County Council.

Section 24 of the Western Region Local Government Law provides that no person may be elected to, or remain a member of, a local government council who suffers from any of the following disabilities:

(*a*) If he has, within the previous five years, been sentenced to death, or been serving imprisonment for a term exceeding two years, or been convicted of any offence involving dishonesty and been sentenced to imprisonment therefor, and has not been granted a free pardon;

(*b*) If he has been adjudged a lunatic;

(*c*) If he has, within five years before the date of election, been surcharged to an amount exceeding one hundred pounds;

(*d*) If he is disqualified by reason of an election offence;

(*e*) If he holds any paid office or other place of profit (other than that of chairman) in the gift of the council;

(*f*) If he has not, at the date of election, paid all sums which were due from him three months previously in respect of rates levied by the council;

(*g*) If he has, within a period of ten years preceding the date of election, been an unsuccessful candidate for any office or title of Chief in the area of the council, unless he has the consent in writing of the Regional Authority.

Section 25 of the Western Region Local Government Law further provides that a person is disqualified from being elected as a member of the council if he is a party to any subsisting contract with the council and has not disclosed this fact within one month before the date of the election.

6. *Conduct of Elections in the Eastern Region.* The Eastern Region Local Government (Elections) Regulations, 1955, provide for three types of elections. Under the method of election, Type A, the Electoral Officer is required to give not less than twenty-one days' notice of the election. Any person wishing to stand as a candidate for election must be nominated by two other persons qualified to vote in the ward for which he is a candidate. Nomination must be made on the requisite form and must be accompanied by a deposit of ten pounds. One member may be elected in respect of each ward in the council area. In the event of a contested election, each candidate within one ward will be allotted a symbol by the Electoral Officer. During his campaign for election a candidate may seek to identify himself and his photograph with the symbol which has been allotted to him. On the day of the election, any elector wishing to vote must present himself at a polling station in the ward in which he is entitled to vote. There the elector will be given a ballot paper marked with an official mark. This mark obviates the possibility of forgery of ballot papers. Electors will be allowed to enter, one at a time, a screened compartment in the polling station. In this screened compartment the elector will be confronted with as many sealed ballot boxes as there are candidates standing for election. On the front of each box will be reproduced one of the symbols which have been allotted to the candidates standing for election. The elector will post his ballot paper in a slot in the top of the ballot box bearing the symbol of the candidate of his choice. Because of the use of symbols, it is a simple matter for an elector to vote as he wishes even if he is unable to read or write. Special arrangements are made for electors who are unable to distinguish symbols, due to blindness or other causes. At the close of the polling ballot boxes are unsealed in the presence of

witnesses. The votes cast in respect of each candidate are then counted and the result announced.

Method of election, Type B, is similar to Type A, except that it dispenses with the requirement of a deposit of ten pounds in respect of each candidate nominated.

Method of election, Type C, as set out in the Local Government (Elections) (Amendment) Regulations 1956, differs from Types A and B in that the Electoral Officer is required to appoint a Returning Officer to be responsible for the conduct of the election. The Returning Officer must give fourteen days notice of the date and place of the election. No deposit is required from the candidates nominated.

7. *Conduct of Elections in the Western Region.* The Western Region Parliamentary and Local Government Electoral Regulations, 1955, provide for a method of direct and a method of indirect elections to local government councils. Election to Local and District Councils is normally by the method of direct election; election to Divisional Councils is normally by indirect election.

Part VI of the Western Region Electoral Regulations is devoted to direct elections. Under Regulation 33 the Electoral Officer is required to give not less than twenty-one days' notice of the date of elections. Regulation 35 requires every candidate in a local government election to secure nomination in writing by two persons whose names appear in the current register of electors of the ward concerned. Regulation 36 requires that before nomination a candidate must make a deposit of five pounds in the treasury of the council for which the election is held.

Where there is more than one candidate standing for election the Electoral Officer will allot a symbol to each candidate. In his election campaign a candidate may seek to identify himself in the minds of the electors with the symbol allotted to him. On the day of the election, any elector wishing to vote must present himself to a polling officer at the polling station at which he is entitled to vote. He will then receive a ballot paper which has been marked in such a way that forgery is impossible. On receiving the ballot paper the voter will be shown into a screened compartment in the polling station. In this screened compartment he will secretly record his vote by posting his ballot paper through

35

a slot in the top of the ballot box bearing the symbol of the candidate of his choice. At the close of the poll the ballot boxes will be unsealed and opened in the presence of witnesses. The votes will be counted and the result announced.

Part VII of the Western Region Electoral Regulations provides for indirect elections to Divisional Councils. When a date has been appointed for the holding of an election of members of a Divisional Council by the members of a District or Local Council, the Electoral Officer is required to give not less than fourteen days' notice of the election. The notice will appoint a time and place at which the District or Local Council concerned will meet in the event of a contested election. The Electoral Officer will also give notice concerning the method of the nomination of candidates. Every candidate must be nominated in writing by two members of the District or Local Council concerned. Every candidate is also required to make a deposit of five pounds. Not later than five days before the date appointed for the election the Electoral Officer must post in a public place a statement setting out the names of the persons who have been nominated. On the date of the election each member of the council who is present at the meeting will receive a ballot paper punched with an official mark. The ballot paper will be printed with the names of the candidates for election. In a screened compartment the voter will record his vote on the ballot paper by placing a cross against the name of each candidate in respect of each vacancy in the Divisional Council for whom he desires to vote. He will then fold the ballot paper and place it in the ballot box. Provision is made for any voter who requires assistance with the marking of his ballot paper. After the close of the poll the ballot box or boxes will be opened in the presence of the candidates and results will be announced.

8. *Election Offences.* Election offences are the subject of Part V of the Eastern Region Local Government Law; legal proceedings in respect of qualification and elections form the subject of Part VI of that law. No comparable sections appear in the Western Region Local Government Law, but similar provisions are made in Parts VIII and IX of the Western Region Parliamentary and Local Government Elections Regulations, 1955.

In both Regions, the following practices are regarded as election offences:

(*a*) Personation;

(*b*) Treating;

(*c*) Undue influence;

(*d*) Bribery, aiding and abetting, counselling or procuring the commission of any of these offences.

An election offence is deemed to be committed by a candidate if it is committed with his knowledge and consent.

Within one month after the date of an election, an election petition may be submitted by a person claiming to be an elector or by a person who has been a candidate at the election. An election petition may question the qualifications of a candidate, may allege corrupt practices or may claim that the person whose election is questioned was not duly elected by a majority of lawful votes. In the Eastern Region an election petition may also question the Electoral Officer's decision that a candidate for election had not been validly nominated.

In the Western Region every election petition must be tried by the High Court, and in the Eastern Region by the Supreme Court. At the completion of the trial the Court will determine whether the person whose election or return is questioned has been duly returned or elected, or whether any other person has been duly returned or elected, or whether the election was void.

CHAPTER VII

THE BALANCE BETWEEN REGIONAL GOVERNMENT & LOCAL GOVERNMENT

1. *Justification of Regional Control.* Local government councils derive their existence and their powers from the Regional Legislature. It follows that they are subject to certain controls exercised by that Legislature. Any consideration of the powerful means available to a Regional Government for the control of local government councils must take note of the fact that the local government electorate, in the Eastern and Western Regions at least, is composed of substantially the same persons who make up the electorate of the Regional House of Assembly. An adult male citizen will normally be qualified to cast a vote for the candidate of his choice in elections to the council established in his area, and also to vote for a candidate for the House of Assembly.

The Regional Houses of Assembly are elected by the same people who elect local government councils. It does not follow from this that the Regional Legislatures will not at times offend one particular council or another, but it does follow that the Regional Legislatures will not normally pursue a general policy contrary to the wishes of local government councils.

Even in a family, the smallest unit of government, it is held to be right that the wishes of one member should sometimes be overridden by the interests of the other members. Even in a town council it is held to be right that the wishes of one ward should be subordinated to the wishes of other wards. This is not held to be necessarily undemocratic nor necessarily autocratic. In just the same way the Regional Government must exercise some sort of control over the plans and aspirations of particular local government councils.

The methods by which a Regional Government exercises control may be considered under three heads. The first head is legislative control, the second is judicial control and the third head is executive or administrative control.

2. *Legislative Control*. The most obvious of these controls is exercised through legislation itself. A body which can pass, amend or revoke a Local Government Law is manifestly in a position of great authority *vis-à-vis* local government councils. Many other Regional laws will also confer powers and impose obligations on councils. Section 3 of the Western Region Appointment and Recognition of Chiefs Law provides that a council, if required to do so, shall make a declaration concerning certain details of local custom guiding the filling of a vacant chieftaincy. The Instrument establishing a council is the most potent manifestation of legislative control. Not only does its Instrument define the area of authority of a council and the functions it may perform within that area, but the Regional Authority or Minister who made the Instrument may amend or revoke it should that ever be considered necessary.[1] The Financial Memoranda which have been made under section 117 of the Eastern Region Local Government Law and section 107 of the Western Region Local Government Law are written instructions controlling the details of the financial machinery and accounting systems of local government councils. Thus, by direct and delegated legislation, control is exercised over local government councils.

3. *Judicial Control* One of the most important and one of the most misunderstood aspects of Regional control is exercised through the Judiciary. Legislative control is nullified unless there is an effective machinery by which laws may be enforced and by which breaches of laws may be punished. The Law Courts, the Judiciary, provide this machinery. It is the duty of the Judiciary to enforce enactments made by the Legislature. Councils, no less than individuals, can be punished for failing to obey the laws in force in the Region. However, it is also the duty of the Judiciary to interpret legislation. While the intention of the law-makers may be relevant to the interpretation of any statute, a court will hold itself bound by the wording of an enactment. It is the published and foreknowable words of the

[1] E.R.L.G. Law, sections 7 and 12; W.R.L.G. Law, sections 7 and 13.

law that will be enforced by the courts even if this is highly inconvenient to the Premier or to the Governor. The Judiciary may therefore be described as an instrument of Regional control, only with reservations. The Judiciary stands as an independent arbiter to which a council, no less than the Regional Government, may appeal for the enforcement of its legal rights. Judges, magistrates and the benches of local courts are appointed by the Governor-General or Governor representing the Queen. They are not appointed by Regional Governments nor may they be dismissed by Regional Governments.[2]

4. *Financial Control.* He who pays the piper calls the tune: an important aspect of the administrative control exercised by a Regional Government is applied through financial sanctions. Local authorities are largely dependent on Regional grants of one sort or another and could not maintain the standard of service which the ratepayers have come to expect if government grants were withheld for any reason. The threat to withhold a specific Regional grant-in-aid may well be sufficient to coerce a council into conforming with Regional policy.

The Regional Authority in the Western Region and the Minister in the Eastern Region have also been empowered to control any applications from a local government council to raise a loan.[3] If he thinks it desirable the Regional Authority or Minister can well insist that certain modifications be made to a capital works project as a condition to granting the council permission to raise a loan for the proposed development. Thus the Regional Government, exercising its responsibility for promoting the welfare of the inhabitants of all local authority areas in the Region, might insist that a water supply scheme should serve the people of two local authorities before a loan would be granted. This might well be economically sound and might further the greatest happiness of the greatest number. Yet without direction from the Regional Government an individual council might have overlooked these considerations in its under-

[2] But see now Section 3 of the Eastern Region Customary Courts Law, 1956, which empowers the Minister to establish such District Courts or County Courts as he shall think fit. Section 4 of this law empowers the Minister to appoint the persons who are to be members of such courts.

[3] E.R.L.G. Law section 112; W.R.L.G. Law, section 101.

standable preoccupation with the welfare of the citizens of its own particular area.

Throughout Nigeria, though not paralleled in the United Kingdom, the annual estimates of local authorities are at present subject to control. Section 108 of the Western Region Local Government Law provides that:

... every council shall submit to the Regional Authority, at such time and in such a manner as the Regional Authority may direct, a detailed estimate of its revenue and expenditure for the next ensuing financial year.

Section 118 of the Eastern Region Local Government Law makes a similar provision. The estimates of local authorities operating under the Native Authority Ordinance were equally subject to approval.[4]

5. *Control through Inspectorates.* Linked with financial control is the control exercised through the various inspectorates staffed by officials in the pay of the Regional Governments. The obvious sanction which such an inspector may invoke is the threat to recommend to the Minister through his senior officers that the appropriate grant-in-aid be withheld if certain changes are not made by the council. An inspector from the Ministry of Public Health who considers that an individual employed by the council in its health department is corrupt may recommend that the Regional grant in respect of health services be withheld until he be dismissed. An inspector from the Ministry of Education may recommend that a local authority school should not qualify for a Regional grant until it be provided with an adequate playing field. The council is, of course, entitled to make its own representations to the appropriate Minister in such an event. Control exercised through inspectors should, however, not be only of the negative kind. It is the duty of the inspectors to co-ordinate the development plans of neighbouring councils in any way within their power. They should advise councils of Regional policy and explain to local government officials the implications of the latest research and publications in their particular field.

[4] Native Authority Ordinance, section 36 G.

6. *Local Government Commissioners.* In the Eastern Region, though not in the Western, the Minister may by notice in the *Regional Gazette* appoint Local Government Commissioners. Section 17 of the Eastern Region Local Government Law provides that these Commissioners shall be described as County Commissioners, Municipal Commissioners or District Commissioners. To these Commissioners the Minister may delegate such of his functions as he wishes, with a few exceptions which include his powers concerning the establishment of a council by Instrument. Powers delegated to Local Government Commissioners include the approval of the appointment and dismissal of certain junior staff and the approval of contracts up to a value of £500. Local Government Commissioners contribute to the effectiveness with which the powers conferred on the Minister are exercised, and must be regarded as a powerful instrument of Regional control.

7. *Local Government Inspectorate.* In the Western Region, though not in the Eastern, the Ministry of Local Government has its own inspectorate. Section 17 of the Western Region Local Government Law empowers the Regional Authority to appoint Local Government Inspectors and Assistant Local Government Inspectors and to delegate to these officials a number of supervisory functions. In the following section of the law it is made the duty of the Local Government Inspector to render an annual report on the activities of each council in his Province. Local Government Inspectors and their assistants are appointed by Legal Notice in the *Regional Gazette.*

8. *Civil Servants as Chief Officers.* The workings of the Regional Inspectorates are complicated by the fact that a civil servant serving in a Regional department is sometimes asked, at least in the Western and Northern Regions of Nigeria, to act as a chief officer of a local government council. In response to a request from a council a Provincial Agricultural Officer may agree to act as the chief officer of the council's agricultural department, controlling that department of the council, controlling the relevant head in the council's expenditure estimates and attending meetings of the council's agricultural committee as an

official. The Provincial Agricultural Officer will at the same time be serving primarily as an inspector for the Regional Minister of Agriculture. This situation may be presumed to be temporary only and should disappear as soon as councils are able to employ more highly qualified officials. The chief officers of a council in the United Kingdom are often graduates and trained technicians. Until a similar situation is achieved in Nigeria, until, for instance, the head of a council's education department is both paid by the council and is possessed of qualifications equal to those of a Provincial Education Officer, it is inevitable that control through inspectorates will be more powerful in Nigeria than in the United Kingdom.

9. *Control by Audit*. Similar to the inspectorates, though differing in that they are quasi-judicial in their function, are the auditors. Section 173 of the Eastern Region Local Government Law and section 140 of the Western Region Local Government Law require a council to supply an annual statement of accounts together with all supporting documents to an auditor appointed by the Regional Authority or Minister. In the Western Region the Director of Audit has been so appointed.[5] It is also expressly provided in section 140 of the Western Region Local Government Law that the Regional Authority may appoint a member of the Local Government Inspectorate to be an auditor. Normally the accounts of a council will be audited once a year, and they may also be subject to an extraordinary audit if that is thought desirable. The auditor is the judge of what payments are reasonable and fair and what are unreasonable and extravagant. He may surcharge the responsible official, the responsible committee, or the whole council with a proportion or with the full amount of any payment which he considers to have been an improper use of the ratepayers' money. The powers of an auditor as set out in section 142 of the Western Region Local Government Law and section 175 of the Eastern Region Local Government Law are identical. These powers correspond closely with the powers of a district auditor in the United Kingdom as set out in the Local Government Act of 1933 (section 228). It would not be accurate to describe an auditor as an

[5] W.R.P.N. No. 79 in *Gazette* No. 10, vol. 3, of 11/3/54.

43

inspector sent out by a Regional Ministry. The auditor acts in a quasi-judicial capacity, and appeal may lie from his decision either to the Minister or Regional Authority, or to the Supreme Court, where an order of surcharge may be either quashed or upheld.[6]

10. *Control by Examiners of the Accounts.* By section 120 of the Eastern Region Local Government Law, the Minister is empowered by notice in the *Regional Gazette* to appoint Examiners of the Accounts of local government councils. The area of authority of an Examiner of the Accounts is to be specified, and, within that area, he has a right of access to all council and committee meetings. Within office hours he has a right of access to the records and accounts of any council in his area. An Examiner of the Accounts is expected to conduct periodic inspection, and by his supervision and advice to act as an instrument of Regional control.

11. *Control in Default.* Where a local government council fails to perform any of the functions or obligations laid upon it, and such failure constitutes a grave menace, the Minister or Regional Authority is empowered, after giving the council due warning, himself to take the action held to be necessary and to levy all expenses incurred in so doing as a charge upon that council's revenues. This power to act in default itself constitutes an instrument of control. Section 11 of the Eastern Region Local Government Law and section 12 of the Western Region Law set out the procedure. A similar power is conferred upon the appropriate Minister in a number of United Kingdom enactments. The National Health Service Act of 1946 empowers the Minister of Health ultimately to transfer to himself such functions, as he thinks fit, of a local authority which has been declared to be in default, and to recover from the defaulting authority any expenses incurred by him in discharging the transferred function.

12. *Control of Senior Staff.* In both Eastern and Western Regions a measure of Regional control is exercised over local government

[6] Section 180 of E.R.L.G. Law; Section 147 of W.R.L.G. Law.

staff. A council in the Western Region may neither engage nor dismiss a secretary, clerk to the council, nor treasurer, nor any official on a salary of £350 per annum or above, without the approval in writing of the Regional Authority. In the Eastern Region a council may appoint staff only with the approval of the Minister, and no member of staff may be dismissed without the approval of the Minister in writing.[7] A measure of control is exercised by the central government over certain local government officers in the United Kingdom. Section 110 of the Local Government Act, 1933, provides, for example, that certain medical officers and sanitary inspectors of the county boroughs and county districts:

... shall not be appointed for a limited time only and shall not be dismissed except by the council of the borough or district with the consent of the Minister, or by the Minister.

13. *Control through Correspondence.* Of less significance is the administrative control that is exercised over councils by the issue of circulars, memoranda and reports from Regional Ministries. Policy papers, reports of conferences, circulars concerning the results of the latest research, flow in a never-ending stream from Ministries to councils and to the appropriate principal officers of councils. A conference of the Food and Agriculture Organisation of the United Nations may have advocated the prohibition of the cultivation of hillsides except in a system of terraces. The Minister of Agriculture in the Eastern Region might accept advice from his Permanent Secretary to the effect that immediate action should be taken on this recommendation in order to check the threat of soil erosion to the nutritional standards of the people of the Region. If it were not convenient to legislate on this matter a circular would soon issue from the Ministry of Agriculture, Eastern Region, to all councils who by their Instrument were empowered to perform the function of preventing and controlling soil erosion,[8] recommending that they take early action to implement the recommendation of the Conference. A model bye-law might accompany the circular. It is in this way that administrative control and guidance of councils is exercised by the Regional Ministries.

[7] E.R.L.G. Law, section 94 and 95; W.R.L.G. Law, section 84 (2) and (3).
[8] E.R.L.G. Law, section 81 (1) (c).

14. *Regional Control may be Excessive.* It does not follow from the proposition that sovereignty in respect of local government matters resides in the Regional Legislature that interference in the affairs of local government councils may in no case constitute an abuse of Regional power. In a qualified sense local government councils are autonomous bodies. They are not primarily the agents of the Regional Government; local government officials are the servants of their councils and not of the Regional Government. Through local government councils, people of a specified area govern their own affairs. Local self-government is, within reason, a possible and desirable objective. It may be argued that Regional Government is justified in interfering in a council's conduct of its affairs only in either of two circumstances. The first circumstance arises when the members of a council are held to be abusing the fiduciary position in which they have been placed by the electorate. The second circumstance arises when a council pursues a course of action which is detrimental to the over-all welfare of the people of the Region. By avoiding these circumstances a local government council may seek to pursue its own course towards the exercise of functions and the discharge of obligations assigned to it. Vigorous councils will constantly be on the watch lest Regional policy or Regional officials attempt to encroach on their freedom of action.

15. *Resistance to Excessive Control.* The methods by which the Regional Government may legitimately exercise its authority over local government councils have already been discussed. Councils for their part have their own means of contesting what they hold to be inconsiderate or excessive Regional control. The point has already been made that the citizens who elect a council are substantially the same people who contribute towards the election of one or more members of the House of Assembly. Through the member of the House of Assembly representing its area a council has direct access to that body. It is true that members of the House of Assembly do not directly represent councils. They represent constituencies. This is, however, primarily an academic distinction. The local member of the Legislature may well agree to act both as the mouthpiece of

the local government councils in his constituency and as the person to whom any of these councils can turn for explanation of Regional policy and of the purpose of new legislation. By interviews with Ministers of State and with permanent officials an active member can achieve much for his electors and can convey to the fountain of power any protests which a council may wish to make. By questions asked in the Legislature the grievances and aspirations of a local government council can receive nation-wide publicity.

16. *Associations of Councils*. The views of local government councils can be expressed more forcibly where there are flourishing associations of councils. Section 129 of the United Kingdom Local Government Act, 1948, gives all local authorities power to subscribe to associations of local authorities or of their officers formed for the purpose of consultation as to their common interests, and to the discussion of matters relating to local government. The Western Region Local Government Law and the Eastern Region Local Government Law make similar provision.[9] An association of all the Divisional, County or District Councils in a Region can address the Regional Government from a position of power, for it may well be speaking with the mandate of the majority of the electors of the Region. Such associations can constitute a valuable element in the preservation of the constitutional principle of the balance of powers.

[9] E.R.L.G. Law, section 79; W.R.L.G. Law, section 69.

PART II
LOCAL GOVERNMENT PRACTICE AND PROCEDURE

CHAPTER VIII

THE COMMITTEE SYSTEM

1. *An Essential Feature of Local Government.* The committee system is an integral part of local government practice in the United Kingdom. There is every prospect that it will emerge as an equally essential feature of local government in Nigeria. The committee system is primarily a device to ensure that the council should not take decisions after inadequate consideration or based on inaccurate data. It is a good rule that nothing except a matter of extreme urgency should come before the council until it has first been considered by a committee, for it is at the committee stage that the facts of a matter can be ascertained and weighed in a business-like and unemotional atmosphere. It is in the committee room that the advice of the specialist officials will be considered along with statements of relevant statistics and precedents, that will have been compiled for the guidance of committee members. It is inevitable and indeed right that meetings of the council, with the press and members of the public present, will to a greater or lesser degree act as a display, an advertisement, for the merits of the councillors or of their political parties. If the council chamber acts as a shop window for the council, then the committee room must be the workshop where the goods are produced and the hard work is done.

2. *Definition of Terms.* The working of the committee system in England is very adequately treated in most of the standard works.[1] All that is needed here, so far as English practice is concerned, is a reference to the many adjectives which are applied to committees, and which students sometimes find more confusing than enlightening. A committee may be a 'standing' committee, an 'ad hoc' committee, a 'service' committee, a

---

[1] E.g. Herman Finer, *English Local Government*, pp. 232-49; J. H. Warren, *The English Local Government System*, ch. 8; W. Eric Jackson, *The Secretarial Practice of Local Authorities*, chs. 7-12.

'spending' committee, a 'vertical' committee, a 'horizontal' committee or a 'statutory' committee. Nor is this by any means an exhaustive list. However, a comprehension of what these terms are intended to convey should be sufficient to make the textbooks intelligible. A 'standing' committee is a committee which is a permanent part of the council machinery. The members of such a committee may change, but the committee itself continues to stand. An 'ad hoc' committee is a committee appointed for a special purpose. After that purpose has been achieved the committee will automatically be dissolved. A 'service' committee is charged with responsibility for the super-vision of a service which the council provides for the inhabitants of its area. A 'spending' committee is a committee entrusted with a degree of responsibility for spending a head or heads in the council's expenditure estimates. The terms 'vertical' and 'horizontal' are employed in order to illustrate the fact that the activities of certain committees must cut across the activities of many other committees. If the 'service' committees are re-garded as vertical lines, then the finance committee may be regarded as a horizontal line cutting across them all. No 'service' committee can achieve very much without becoming involved with the activities of the finance committee. The staff com-mittee, if any, may also be regarded as a horizontal committee. A 'statutory' committee is any committee which a council is required to appoint by law. Some committees may, of course, be described with equal accuracy by several of these adjectives. A finance committee could be described as a standing com-mittee, a statutory committee as a horizontal committee, or even – if it is charged with the supervision of the treasury department of the council – as a spending committee.

3. *Statutory Committees.* Section 62 of the Eastern Region Local Government Law provides that every County Council, every Municipality and every District Council shall appoint a Finance Committee for regulating and controlling the finances of the council. Section 53 of the Western Law makes a similar pro-vision in respect of Divisional and District Councils. Section 63 of the Eastern Law states that unless otherwise provided in the Instrument every County Council and Municipality and every

District Council shall appoint a Medical and Health Committee. There is no corresponding provision in the Western Region Local Government Law. A council in the Western Region which is a local education authority is required to establish an education committee.[2] Through the Instrument by which it is established a council in the Western Region may be required to set up any other standing committee. A similar requirement may be included in the Instrument establishing a council in the Eastern Region, and the Instrument may specify the composition of such committee, including the number and qualifications of any members who are not members of the council.[3]

4. *Establishment of Committees.* Section 65 of the Eastern Region Local Government Law provides that a 'council may appoint a committee for any such general or specific purpose as in the opinion of the council would be better regulated and managed by means of a committee'. Section 52 of the Western Region Local Government Law makes a similar provision. Subject to the requirements concerning statutory committees it is for the council to decide what pattern of committees it wishes to operate and what the size of its committees should be.

At the inaugural meeting of the new local government council an *ad hoc* selection committee might well be set up to recommend to the council the number and size of committees that should be appointed, together with the names of councillors who should sit on each. The responsibility facing such a committee is considerable. It is the duty of such a committee to ascertain the pattern and size of committees which will work most efficiently and economically, having regard to the actual circumstances of the council concerned. The special problems which arise in this connection when the business of a council is conducted on party lines will be discussed elsewhere.

It is generally agreed that the fewer committees the better, provided that in no case should a committee's responsibilities be greater than its members can be expected to discharge with efficiency. A key to the number of committees which might be

[2] Western Region Education Law, section 11 (1).
[3] E.R.L.G. Law, section 5 (2) (i); W.R.L.G. Law, section 5 (2) (c).

necessary for any given council lies in the expenditure section of that council's estimates. Thus, a council which makes substantial provision for expenditure on agricultural improvement and advisory services will probably need an agricultural committee. The estimates of expenditure are a more accurate guide to the work which a council is actually performing than is the Instrument establishing the council. In the Instrument will be contained not only the function which a council is required to perform, but also many which it is permitted to perform if it so chooses. The council's estimates of expenditure will show at once what functions the council is in fact performing and what services it is in fact providing. It is usual to assign to one committee responsibility for considering all matters which have not been specifically assigned to another committee. To this committee, responsible for residual matters, is given the name of General Purposes Committee. In all except the largest councils it is quite possible to add general purposes to the duties of the service committee which has the least work to do. Thus, a council may choose to make one committee responsible for Works and General Purposes, or Agriculture and General Purposes.

5. *Membership of Committees.* The composition of committees is left largely to the discretion of the council. In the Western Region a council is empowered to appoint to a committee other than to the finance committee persons who are not members of the council, with the proviso that at least two-thirds of the members of a committee must be members of the council[4]. In the education committee of a council in the Western Region up to two-thirds of the members may be from outside the council. The Western Region Local Government Law makes no provision for a committee itself to co-opt persons from outside the council to serve on the committee. It is the council alone which is empowered to appoint persons other than councillors to serve as committee members. A committee which considered that it would be strengthened by the inclusion in its membership of a person who was not a councillor would have to make a recommendation to this effect to the council.

[4] W.R.L.G. Law, section 52 (3).

In the Eastern Region any committee may include persons who are not members of the council up to one-third of the committee's membership. As in the Western Region such members must be appointed to committee membership by the council itself. Having been appointed such persons become full and voting members of the committee. In addition to such persons a committee in the Eastern though not in the Western Region may co-opt persons who are not members of the council. Any such co-opted members of a committee are not entitled to a vote.

There is no necessity for the council to find a place on a committee for every councillor nor is there any objection to the appointment of a councillor to two or more committees, as in fact will frequently happen. The council may, however, start with the presumption that, except where councillors are considered to be of very unequal ability and education, it is desirable to distribute committee work as equally as possible between them all.

When the size of committees is considered it should be borne in mind that co-ordination between committees will be facilitated if the chairman of the council is made an ex-officio member of all committees. Ex-officio members of committees are full and voting members, and allowance for them must be made when deciding how many members shall constitute a committee. Because of the number of ex-officio members which it will contain finance committees will probably be larger than the other committees. The council will wish, so far as is possible, to meet the wish of councillors concerning the committee or committees on which they shall serve. A useful device is to invite all councillors to complete a form setting out their order of preference in this matter, and the resultant information can be made available to the selection committee charged with making recommendations to the council concerning committee membership. The law leaves it open for a council to fix the term of office of committee members.[5] It is, however, usual to appoint a committee for a term of one year and to consider the appointment of new members or the reappointment of the old ones at the annual general meeting of the council.

[5] E.R.L.G. Law, section 66 (1); W.R.L.G. Law, section 53 (1).

6. *Assignment of Functions to Committees.* The decision as to the pattern of committees through which a council shall operate together with the size of these committees are subjects which, though open to review at any time, are of peculiar urgency to a newly formed council. Another problem of this type is the distribution of work and responsibility between such committees as are decided upon. Each committee should have carefully defined terms of reference which must be made the subject of a formal resolution of the council The terms of reference will make it clear which functions and responsibilities have been delegated to each committee and which have only been assigned for consideration and recommendation to the council. Section 67 of the Eastern Region Local Government Law and section 52 of the Western Region Local Government Law empower a council to delegate to committees any of its functions, or all of them if it so chooses, with three important exceptions. These exceptions are the power of making bye-laws, the power of levying a rate or issuing a precept, and the power of borrowing money. These powers can be exercised only by the council itself, though the council will of course be acting, normally, even in these matters, in accordance with a recommendation from a committee. The object of delegating powers to a committee is to avoid crowding the time of the full meeting of the council and to ensure that the routine business of the council is dealt with expeditiously. The degree to which a council should be advised to resort to delegation will therefore depend on the volume of work with which it is faced. Subject to any contractual obligations to which it may have been committed a council which delegated power to a committee may overrule any resolution made by that committee under its delegated power. A council should, however, consider carefully before making an order of delegation and should not delegate any power to a committee unless it is prepared for that committee to make any resolutions involved and to act on them without the likelihood of their being countermanded by the council.

7. *Reports by Committees.* Section 66 (5) of the Eastern Region Local Government Law requires every committee to report its proceedings to the council which appointed it. Section 56 of the

Western Region Local Government Law contains a similar requirement. Not only must a committee report to the council the recommendations which it has to make on subjects which have been assigned to it for consideration, the committee must also report the resolutions it has made under powers delegated to it by the council. Before action can be taken on the recommendations of the committee the council's agreement is required. Action to implement the resolutions of the committee will probably be under way by the time that the council is informed of them. Reports by committees can either take the form of a specially written summary by the chairman of the committee, or they can consist of a copy of the minutes of the committee. Provided that the minutes are written in a brief form, there is much to recommend the latter system. The preparation of much written work is thereby avoided, and it is a relatively simple matter for sufficient copies of the minutes of each committee meeting to be prepared to enable a copy of each to be issued to every councillor along with the summons for the next council meeting.

8. *Sub-committees.* No mention of sub-committees is made in either the Eastern Region Local Government Law or in the Western Region Local Government Law, but no special power for their appointment is needed. Few local government councils in Nigeria have a volume of work sufficient to make the establishment of sub-committees desirable. Where the volume of a committee's work is excessive sub-committees can afford to their parent committees advantages similar to those afforded by the appointment of committees by a council. Except where a statute expressly provides to the contrary a committee cannot delegate to a sub-committee powers which it has itself received from the council. It is the council itself which must delegate direct to the sub-committee.

9. *Local Committees.* Sections 87–89 of the Local Government Act of 1933 empower Rural District Councils and Parish Councils in England and Wales to set up parochial committees charged with certain responsibilities in respect of a particular area within the area of the council. Section 54 of the Western

Region Local Government Law makes a similar provision. With the prior approval of the Regional Authority any council may appoint a town, village or area committee and may delegate to it the power to exercise certain of the council's functions in respect of that area for which it has been appointed. No comparable provision is made in the Eastern Region Local Government Law.

10. *Joint Committees.* Legislative provision has been made in both the Eastern and Western Regions for the establishment of joint committees along the lines set out by section 91–93 of the Local Government Act of 1933. Section 64 of the Eastern Region Local Government Law provides that:

... a council may concur with any one or more councils in appointing from among their respective members a joint committee of such councils for any purpose in which they are jointly interested.

Section 149 of the Western Region Local Government Law makes a similar provision but requires the approval of the Minister for such an arrangement. Subsection (2) of section 149 adds that the Regional Authority may require any two or more councils to establish a joint committee for the operation of a joint service if he considers it expedient so to do. No comparable provision is made in the Eastern Law. This section also requires that before a joint committee to operate a joint service is established the necessary financial provision shall previously have been made in joint estimates. Sections 150–156 of the Western Region Local Government Law deal with detailed arrangements for the regulation of joint committees.

Where a waterworks supplies water to the people of two Divisional County Councils, or where a maternity clinic cares for the mothers of two council areas, the shared service may be best regulated by a joint committee of the two councils. Each of the two councils will elect members to the joint committee, probably in proportion related to the financial contribution of each council to the joint service. The joint committee will then proceed to engage or take over staff and generally to exercise such powers as may have been delegated to them by the parent councils.

11. *Finance and Staff Committees.* While the control of the staff and finances of local government councils will be dealt with elsewhere mention must be made here of the special position in the committee structure occupied by the finance and staff committees. In any except the busiest councils there is very much to be said for allocating the supervision of staff matters to the finance committee, that is, for appointing one joint finance and staff committee. The grading of staff almost always has a financial implication, since provision for salaries is so closely linked with grades and establishments. If one committee is dealing with both of these aspects of the council's activities much delay and extra work can be avoided.

The functions of the finance committees of a council in the Western Region are clearly summarised in Memorandum A/3 of the Financial Memoranda made under section 107 of the Western Region Local Government Law. This Memorandum ends with the following sentence:

The Finance Committee is the watchdog of the Council, not the master of the committees, and although it may quite properly inquire into proposals made by the spending committees and call for reports if it suspects waste or overspending it must not assume the role of a tribunal.

It is of the greatest importance that the functions of a council's finance committee should be clearly defined in the standing orders of the council. It would be normal for standing orders to provide that any recommendation with a financial implication and any recommendation affecting the finances of the council should stand referred to the finance committee. When considering recommendations from other committees the finance committee should confine its attention to the economy of these proposals and should not interfere with the general policy of service committees.

The staff or establishments committee of a council should be equally restricted in its activities. It is staff matters general to the council's staff as a whole which should be referred to the staff committee. Rates of pay, approved establishments and general conditions of service are the stuff of the agenda of a staff committee. This committee is responsible for seeing, so far as it is possible to do so, that equal ability, experience and responsibility is equally rewarded throughout the departments of the council, and that departments with a comparable volume of work have a staff of comparable size to perform that work. The details of appointment, discipline and postings within the staff of a department should be assigned to the appropriate service committee. The service committee can hardly bear responsibility for the standard of service provided for the rate-payers if it has no control over the staff employed in the department which it supervises. A tradition has been established in Nigeria that a staff committee should be responsible for the appointment, discipline and posting of all the employees of a council. It would be difficult to overstate the undesirability of such a concentration of control over employees, whether on the grounds of theory or of experience.

CHAPTER IX

CO-ORDINATION OF COUNCIL BUSINESS

1. *Danger of Fragmentation.* Inherent in the committee system is a certain danger of fragmentation. The committee system might easily lead to the division of a busy council into a number of groups of councillors, each group specialising in one aspect of the council's activities and having only a superficial knowledge of the work of departments supervised by the other groups. Every council member shares responsibility for all aspects of the council's work. It is not desirable for a committee member to be preoccupied with the department of the council with which his committee is concerned, to the exclusion of any interest in other departments. Nor could a council efficiently discharge its functions if each committee were to act without knowledge or consideration of the activities of other committees.

2. *Co-ordination by Reports of Committees.* One factor by which co-ordination of the different committees is achieved is the statutory requirement that a committee must report its proceedings to the council which appointed it.[1] If this requirement is met, as we advocated in the previous chapter, by supplying each council member with a copy of the minutes of all committee meetings, there can be little excuse for any member remaining ignorant of some of the council's activities.

3. *Co-ordination by Chairman of the Council.* Co-ordination between committees will be facilitated if the standing orders of the council provide that the chairman of the council shall be an ex-officio member of all committees. It cannot be expected that a council chairman will find the time to sit through all the meetings of all the committees of a busy council. However, if he has the right to attend a committee meeting whenever he finds

[1] E.R.L.G. Law, section 66 (5); W.R.L.G. Law, section 56.

it possible to do so the chairman of the council can keep himself informed of what is going on in all departments of the council. The chairman can make this knowledge available to any committee which is considering a matter having a bearing on a course being pursued by another committee. This knowledge of the over-all situation will enable the chairman to ensure that when considering a recommendation from one committee on a matter which has also been referred to another committee, the full council can consider both recommendations at the same time. If the health committee has recommended that provision for a dispensary be inserted in next year's estimates, and the finance committee, to which such a recommendation would stand referred, has recommended that the project be deferred for a further year, the council should not make a resolution on the subject without considering the recommendations of both committees. The chairman of the council can ensure that this is done if he keeps himself informed of the activities of all the council's committees.

4. *Co-ordination by Secretary of the Council*. Co-ordination is also the responsibility of the secretary of the council. It is desirable that he, no less than the chairman of the council, should attend as many meetings of all committees as his other duties will allow. In all except the smaller councils the secretary will not himself take minutes of the proceedings of a committee. This duty will normally be allocated to a committee clerk from the secretary's office. The presence of the secretary himself is, however, desirable, both because he is the legal adviser of the council and of its committees and also because he is the chief co-ordinating officer. The secretary cannot perform this role unless he is aware of the details of the policy and activities of every committee. Moreover, the secretary will be expected to assist the chairman in ensuring at full meetings of the council that whenever a matter has been the subject of a recommendation from more than one committee the council does not make a resolution on the matter without considering at one time all the relevant recommendations.

It is the responsibility of the secretary to ensure that the resolutions of a committee acting under delegated powers, and all resolutions of the council, are communicated to whatever official or other person is concerned. The secretary is primarily responsible for seeing that every department of the council is kept informed of the policy which is evolved for it in the committees and in full meetings of the council. The secretary should see every important letter addressed to the council and every important letter issuing from the council. In the larger councils the committee clerks should draft the letters occasioned by the decisions of committees assigned to them. The secretary will, however, wish to see such letters. Unless he is exceptionally fortunate in the standard of his committee clerks he will be well advised to insist that all such letters are submitted to him for signature. In the larger councils it is usual for departments of the council to conduct their own routine correspondence without reference to the secretary. The secretary should, however, request the official in charge of a department to send him a copy of any letter issuing direct from the department which does not deal with a purely routine matter. From the peculiar position which he occupies as the chief executive officer the secretary will be the official best able to co-ordinate the work of all committees and departments of the council.

5. *Co-ordination by Finance Committee.* In any council where standing orders provide that the chairmen of all spending committees shall be ex-officio members of finance committee the finance committee will serve as a powerful co-ordinating agent. Finance committee will have referred to it many recommendations from spending committees. It will assist finance committee if the chairman of the appropriate spending committee is present to explain the circumstances which have led to any recommendation, and to argue the case for expenditure proposed by his committee. Moreover, if finance committee finds itself unable to support a recommendation from a spending committee, the members of that spending committee will more readily understand the reasons for such lack of support if their own chairman can explain to them the considerations which led finance committee to adopt a contrary view. If all chairmen of spending committees meet together in finance committee full co-ordination of the various committees of the council will be greatly facilitated.

6. *Co-ordination of Councillors and Officials.* Local government rests on twin pillars. One pillar consists of the elected element – the council members – and the other pillar consists of the body of permanent officials. These twin pillars must be linked together, as it were by a co-ordinating arch, if the edifice of effective local government is to be raised upon them. Co-ordination between these two elements in local government is no less important than co-ordination between the activities of one committee and another. A council cannot give good service to the ratepayers unless the members of the council are working together.

7. *Co-operation between Committee Chairmen and Chief Officers.* This co-ordination can be effected through close co-operation between the chairmen of committees and the chief officers at the head of the council's departments. The chairman of the agricultural committee (as the spokesman of that committee) and the official in charge of the council's agricultural department are jointly responsible to the council for ensuring that, so far as agricultural services are concerned, the ratepayers receive good value for their money. The chairman of the council's works committee (as the spokesman of that committee) and the official in charge of the works department must consider themselves jointly responsible for the condition of the council's roads.

In an effective and smoothly running council the chairman of a committee will normally have frequent consultations with the chief officer of the appropriate department, and with the council's secretary. He will not attend a committee meeting without first studying the agenda with one or both of these officials. He will ask for additional information on items appearing in the agenda where he thinks this necessary. Before attending the committee meeting he will work out, so far as may prove possible, a policy agreed on by himself and by the officials. In the committee meeting the chairman will hope to sit with his chief officer on one side of him, with the secretary of the council on the other. In the meeting of the full council chairmen of committees will wish to have their chief officers sitting behind them. By exchange of notes or by whispered consultations, the chairman of a committee may thus have the benefit of the official's professional training and experience in any crisis which arises in the council. Similarly, the chairman of the council will have frequent consultations with the secretary and will arrange for this official to sit beside him at all meetings of the full council.

It is pointless to speculate whether it is more important to have good council members or to have good permanent officials. Both are essential. Neither can achieve success without the other. They are twin pillars. If a crack appears in either pillar, or if – though each pillar remains firm – a fault develops in the arch of co-operation which binds them together, then the edifice of efficient and effective local government must surely fall.

CHAPTER X

COUNCIL AND COMMITTEE PROCEEDINGS

The provisions of the Eastern Region Local Government Law concerning meetings and proceedings of councils and their committees are set out as in the First Schedule to the Law. The corresponding provisions constitute Part V of the Western Region Local Government Law.

1. *Frequency of Meetings*. Councils in the Eastern Region are required to hold in every year an annual meeting in April, and at least three other meetings. Councils in the Western Region are required to hold in every year at least four ordinary meetings for the transaction of business.[1] It follows from this requirement that if at a meeting called to show courtesy to a Minister or to the Governor other routine business is not transacted, such a meeting would not reckon as one of the four statutory meetings. In the Eastern Region it is prescribed that the annual meeting shall be held in April every year and that the other three meetings shall be as near as may be at regular intervals. In the Western Region Local Government Law no such direction concerning the dates on which council meetings should be held are found, but the Instruments establishing a council may indicate that the first meeting of the council to be held after an election should take place in April or May.

There is no statutory provision governing the frequency of meetings of committees, but this will normally be regulated by the council's standing orders. If committees are to promote the prompt discharge of the council's business they should meet at least once a month, even though the council may meet only once a quarter. Section 13 (2) of the Western Region Education Law requires that fourteen days, at least, before any meeting of its education committee a council which has been appointed a

[1] E.R.L.G. Law, First Schedule, para. 1 (1); W.R.L.G. Law, section 34.

66

Local Education Authority shall inform the Minister of Education of such meetings, specifying the business to be transacted.

2. *Convening of Meetings.* A meeting of the council for the purpose of electing a chairman is, in the Western Region, called by the 'clerk to the council'.[2] This term may be taken to mean the secretary of the council. It is in the general meeting to be held in April every year that a chairman of a council in the Eastern Region is elected. The chairman of a council may call a meeting of the council at any time. In the Western Region the president of a council also has this power.[3] If the chairman of a council (or, in the Western Region, the chairman or president) refuses or fails to call a meeting of the council within ten days after a written requisition to do so signed by one-third of the members of the council has been delivered to him, the persons who signed the requisition may themselves call a meeting of the council.[4]

3. *Notice of Meetings.* Normally, a notice of a council meeting is published at the council offices at least ten clear days before a meeting of a council.[5] This notice will set out the time and place of the meeting and the business listed for consideration at it. There is no requirement that such a notice shall be signed, but it is usually signed by the chairman or secretary of the council. Where a council meeting is being called not by the chairman or the president but by requisition of one-third of the members of the council each of the members calling the meeting must sign the notice.

The mayor of a Municipality or the chairman of an Urban District Council in the Eastern Region, and the president or chairman of any council in the Western Region, may call an emergency meeting after giving forty-eight hours' notice.[6]

In addition to the requirements concerning the publication of the notice of a meeting a summons to attend the meeting of any council in the Western Region, and any council other than

---

[2] W.R.L.G. Law, section 35 (3).
[3] E.R.L.G. Law, First Schedule, para. 2 (1); W.R.L.G. Law, section 35 (1).
[4] E.R.L.G. Law, First Schedule, para. 2 (2); W.R.L.G. Law, section 35 (2).
[5] E.R.L.G. Law, First Schedule, para. 3 (1); W.R.L.G. Law, section 36 (1).
[6] E.R.L.G. Law, First Schedule, para. 3 (2); W.R.L.G. Law, section 36 (2).

a local council in the Eastern Region, specifying the business to be transacted at the meeting, must be delivered to the usual place of residence of every member of such council.[7] The want of service of the summons on any member does not affect the validity of the meeting.

4. *The Agenda.* The summons is normally combined with the agenda paper, since the summons must specify the business to be transacted. Indeed, in the Eastern Region no business, apart from statutory business required to be transacted at the annual meeting of a council, may be transacted at a meeting of the council other than that specified in the summons relating to it. In the Western Region the position is the same except that business not specified in the summons may be transacted if the person presiding, and at least three-quarters of the persons present, at the meeting so approve.[8] The item 'Any other Business' should therefore not appear on the agenda paper. The agenda paper for a council or committee meeting can be in one of three forms. First, there is the short agenda which simply lists the subjects for discussion. Secondly, there is the long agenda in which a few lines of explanation and background details are given beneath each item listed for discussion. Thirdly, there is the form of short agenda in which each item appearing on the agenda paper is supported by a memorandum prepared by the appropriate official. Such a memorandum should clearly set out all aspects of the problem in order that members may fully consider the points at issue before attending the meeting. The item 'Confirmation of the Minutes' would be supported by a copy of the unsigned minutes of the previous meeting. The item 'Report and Recommendations of the Works Committee' appearing in the agenda of a council meeting might well be supported by the minutes of the meeting or meetings of that committee held since the last council meeting. An item in the agenda of a Health Committee listed as 'Dispensary for Ode Ado Village' should be supported by a memorandum prepared by the principal officer of the council's health department, giving a summary of the claims of this and other villages in the

---

[7] E.R.L.G. Law, First Schedule, para. 4; W.R.L.G. Law, section 38.
[8] E.R.L.G. Law, First Schedule, para. 5; W.R.L.G. Law, section 39.

council's area, the staff available, the capital and recurrent costs of such a project and any other information needed for the formation of a sound judgement on the proposal.

Of the three forms of agenda considered in this paragraph, the third, although involving the council's officials in additional work, alone ensures that council and committee members are, at the outset of a discussion, fully informed of all aspects of the problem.

5. *Minutes*. In both Eastern and Western Regions it is required that minutes should be kept of every meeting of a council and of its committees.[9] Minutes are to be regularly entered in books kept for that purpose and are to be read and confirmed or amended and signed by the person presiding at the same or the next following meeting of the council or committee. Minutes purporting to be so signed shall be received in evidence without further proof, and a meeting of which minutes are kept and signed as directed shall be deemed to have been duly convened and held. It is seldom practicable for minutes to be available for signature at the close of the meeting whose proceedings they record. It is normal, therefore, for minutes to be put to the next meeting for approval as a correct record, and if so approved, to be signed then.

There are various ways of satisfying the provision that minutes must be 'entered in a book kept for the purpose'. One satisfactory practice is for a copy of the cyclostyled minutes to be pasted into a large book and for the person presiding to sign his name across each page of the book, endorsing the minutes in the same way as a stamp on a receipt is endorsed. Minutes of a council meeting, though not of a committee meeting, must be open to inspection, and a copy or extract therefrom may be obtained upon payment of a specified fee. In the Eastern Region these facilities are available to 'any inhabitant of the area for which the council is established', in the Western Region they are available to 'any person'.[10]

Minutes should at all times be as brief as possible, and minutes of a committee meeting may well record only the date of the

[9] E.R.L.G. Law, First Schedule, para. 12; W.R.L.G. Law, section 45.
[10] E.R.L.G. Law, First Schedule, para. 13; W.R.L.G. Law, section 46.

meeting, the name of the person occupying the chair, the names of the members present and absent, and a series of resolutions and recommendations. In minutes of a council meeting some introductory statement may be unavoidable before the resolution is recorded. An interesting discussion on the practice of minuting and reporting in the United Kingdom may be found in Chapter IX of Mr J. H. Warren's *Municipal Administration*.

6. *Report of Committees*. Reports of committees form the main part of the agenda of any council whose standing orders require that nothing except a matter of extreme urgency should come before the council until it has first been considered by a committee. These reports will deal with action taken by committees under powers delegated to them, in respect of which no approval by the council is required, and with action which the committees recommend the council to take and which awaits the council's decision. Where a committee reports to the council through the means of its minutes and not through a specially drafted report all its actions under delegated powers as well as its recommendations to the council will be subject to scrutiny by the council. The practice by which councils deal with reports from their committees varies. Where report is made by way of minutes, and where minutes are brief, the chairman of the council normally gives to each committee chairman an opportunity to explain and comment on controversial items before formally moving that the report be received and the recommendations be accepted. This motion will be seconded and put to the vote, sometimes after a debate.

7. *Quorum*. In the Eastern Region no business may be transacted at a meeting of a council other than a Local Council unless at least one-third of the whole number of the members of the council are present. At a meeting of a Local Council no business may be transacted unless at least one-half of the whole number of the members are present.[11] In the Western Region no business may be transacted at a meeting of any local government council unless there is present such quorum as is specified in the Instrument establishing the council.[12] The quorum specified in most

[11] E.R.L.G. Law, First Schedule, para 7.
[12] W.R.L.G. Law, section 41.

70

Instruments is one-third of the whole number of the members. The quorum must be maintained throughout the meeting, and if at any point the number of members present falls below the required minimum the meeting must be adjourned once attention is drawn to the fact.

8. *Meetings to be Public.* In the Eastern and Western Regions every meeting of a council must be open to the public.[13] This requirement does not apply to a committee appointed by a council; indeed, the standing orders of a council may provide that meetings of its committees shall not be open to the public without special authority from the council. Neither does the requirement apply to a committee of the whole council. The motion that the council resolve into committee must therefore be moved if the council proposes to discuss an issue which it prefers to consider without the presence of the public.

In the Western Region only, the president or chairman of a council may invite any person to attend and to speak upon any matter at a meeting of a council, but such a person may not vote upon any matter. Further, the Minister may empower any person to attend any meeting or meetings of a council or committee, and such a person may address the meeting and require his advice on any matter to be recorded in the minutes.[14] The Director of Education for the Western Region or his representative has the right to attend any meeting of a local education authority or of its education committee and to take part in the proceedings. He may insist on his advice being recorded in the minutes of the meeting, but he may not vote on any matter.[15]

9. *Voting at Meetings.* The Western Region Local Government Law provides that all acts of a local government council and all questions coming or arising before such a council 'shall be done and decided by a majority of the members present and voting thereon at a meeting of the council'.[16] The Eastern Region Local Government Law makes an identical provision in respect of

[13] E.R.L.G. Law, First Schedule, para. 8; W.R.L.G. Law, section 42.
[14] W.R.L.G. Law, section 51.
[15] W.R. Education Law, section 13 (1)
[16] W.R.L.G. Law, section 43.

councils other than Local Councils.[17] Subject to the provisions of the Instrument establishing it all acts of a local council in the Eastern Region 'shall be done and decided by a majority of three-fourths of the councillors present and voting thereon at a meeting of the Local Council'. It follows that in both Eastern and Western Regions no effective decision for a council can be made at an informal meeting of councillors. A decision is effective only if taken at a duly convened meeting of the council. A member must be present in order to vote. A sick councillor may not send his vote on an issue by way of letter; a councillor who has to leave the meeting before the vote is taken on an issue may not record his vote before he goes. Moreover, although a member may be present at a meeting, he is not obliged to vote. He may abstain. Thus if at a council meeting with thirty councillors present four councillors abstain from voting a motion would be carried if fourteen councillors voted in favour of it. In the Eastern and Western Regions the person presiding at a council meeting has an original vote, and in the event of an equality of votes, he has a second or casting vote.[18]

In neither Region is the method of voting at council meetings prescribed by law. The normal procedure after the chairman has put a motion to the meeting is for councillors supporting the motion to raise one hand. The hands raised are then counted by the person presiding and by the secretary. The person presiding then announces the decision of the council. The method of voting in committees is usually laid down in the standing orders of the council and will normally be by show of hands by a majority of the members of the committee present and voting. In practice, a committee chairman frequently dispenses with a formal vote, as the majority view of the committee on an issue is quite apparent without it. The formal vote should, however, never be dispensed with at a full meeting of the council. Normally the minutes of a council or committee meeting will show only the decision of the meeting, not the number of votes cast for and against the motion, and not the names of those who voted. It is, however, a good practice for the chairman of a council or committee to accede to a request of any member that

[17] E.R.L.G. Law, First Schedule, para 9.
[18] E.R.L.G. Law, First Schedule, para. 9 (3); W.R.L.G. Law, Section 43 (2).

votes may be recorded on a particular issue. This request might be made by any member who considered that an improper decision had been taken from which he wished quite clearly to dissociate himself. A council or committee member whose name was recorded as having voted against a decision which resulted in expenditure which the auditor regarded as contrary to law would not himself receive an order of surcharge. When a request that votes be recorded has been made the secretary may call out the names of all members one by one. As his name is called out a member will answer 'For' or 'Against' or 'Not voting' and the secretary will record the way he votes. The name of those members who voted for and against the motion will then be recorded in the minutes of that meeting. The names of those members who abstained from voting should also be recorded.

Section 38 of the Eastern Region Local Government Law provides that

If a chairman, vice-chairman, person presiding or other member of a council or any committee thereof has any pecuniary or other interest, direct or indirect, in any contract or proposed contract or other matter, and is present at a meeting of the council or the committee at which the contract or other matter is the subject of consideration, he shall at the meeting disclose the fact and shall not take part in the consideration or discussion of or vote on any question with respect to the contract or other matter.

Section 50 of the Western Region Local Government Law makes a similar provision, and adds that if the person presiding so directs, the person concerned shall withdraw from the meeting during such consideration or discussion. No penalty is prescribed for a councillor who ignores these provisions. However, a councillor who wishes to keep a reputation for honest and unselfish service should invariably disclose his interest if he is liable to receive any sort of personal gain as the result of a council or committee decision.

10. *Chairman and President.* At a meeting of a council in the Eastern Region the chairman of the council, if present, must preside. In the absence of the chairman the vice-chairman will preside. If both chairman and vice-chairman are absent from a meeting the members of the council must elect a councillor to

preside on that occasion.[19] At a meeting of a council in the Western Region the chairman will preside whenever the president does not preside. If the chairman is absent from a meeting at which he is entitled to preside the members of the council present must elect one of their number to the chair.[20] The relationship of the president and chairman of a council in the Western Region is one of some delicacy. Section 28 of the Western Region Local Government Law provides that the president 'may preside, and may avail himself of the advice and assistance of the chairman, at any meeting of the council'. The normal practice is for the president to take the chair at the annual meeting when the chairman is elected, and on ceremonial occasions, such as the visit of the Governor or of a Minister. Otherwise he leaves the meeting and the chairman therefore takes over.

The chairman of a committee will normally be elected by simple majority vote at the first meeting of the newly appointed committee.

The most important duty of the person presiding at a council or committee meeting is the control of debate, and his powers will be contained in the standing orders of the council. The duties and powers of the person presiding with respect to breaches of order at a meeting are, however, prescribed by law.[21] If a councillor or other member of a committee shows disregard for the authority of the chairman or of the standing orders of the council, the person presiding is required to direct the attention of the meeting to the incident, mentioning the offender by name. The person presiding is empowered to suspend the offender from the exercise of his functions as a councillor or committee member. In the Eastern Region such an order of suspension must be in writing and is limited to a maximum of thirty days. In the case of grave disorder the person presiding is empowered to adjourn the meeting without moving any motion to that effect.

[19] E.R.L.G. Law, First Schedule, para. 6. See also section 9 of the E.R.L.G. (Amendment) Law, 1956 which empowers the Minister to appoint a person to be the President of a council. This section also sets out the powers and duties of such a President.
[20] W.R.L.G. Law, section 41.
[21] E.R.L.G. Law, First Schedule, para. 10; W.R.L.G. Law, section 44.

11. *Standing Orders.* Local government councils in the Eastern and Western Regions are empowered to make standing orders for the regulation of their proceedings and business.[22] Such standing orders must conform to the statutory requirements governing the convening and conduct of meetings. In the Western Region the Minister may make a standing order for a council if he considers this expedient and may declare invalid any standing order made by a council. A council wishing to make standing orders can obtain a copy of model standing orders from the appropriate Ministry and adapt the model to its own requirements. Standing orders made by different local authorities may vary greatly in their detail and complexity. At the present stage in Nigeria there is much to be said for making standing orders as brief and simple as possible. It should suffice to cover the dates and times of ordinary meetings, the order of business, the rules of debate, rules governing the inviting of tenders and the making of contracts, the custody and use of the council's seal, and the composition, terms of reference and procedure of committees.

12. *Committees of the Whole Council.* The standing orders of a council will normally contain a provision that no member, other than the mover of a motion, may speak more than once on the same motion. This is a most desirable provision if the council is to conduct its business expeditiously and is prepared to leave detailed discussion of complex issues to its committees. In a committee meeting no such standing order applies, and a member can speak on the same motion as often as the chairman allows. It sometimes happens that a motion under discussion by the full council does require unrestricted debate. In such a situation a member who has not yet participated in the discussion may move that the council resolve into committee. If this resolution is carried, the chairman may allow any member to speak more than once, and the press and public may be excluded from the council chamber.

A committee of the whole council is indeed a committee and is bound by those rules of procedure which the council has prescribed for its committees. It must report its proceedings to the

[22] E.R.L.G. Law, section 37; W.R.L.G. Law, section 48.

council. When the committttee of the whole council has concluded business a motion may be put that the meeting of the council be resumed. When this motion has been carried the provisions of the standing orders relating to the conduct of council meetings will again apply, the public being readmitted. The council may then proceed to consider the recommendations made by them while sitting as a committee. If these recommendations are accepted a formal resolution to that effect should be entered in the council's minutes.

It should be a rare occurrence for the council to go into committee. If the council's committee structure is functioning well the council itself will seldom find it necessary to do more than make decisions on matters of policy. Detailed discussion on a complex issue should be left for one of the standing committees, who will then invite the council to accept their carefully considered recommendations.

CHAPTER XI

RULES OF DEBATE

Conventions concerning the conduct of debate have been evolved in order to enable public meetings to be conducted in an orderly and predictable manner. These conventions are known as 'rules of debate' and may be compared to other rules of conduct by which an individual is expected to guide his life in society. Like other rules of conduct the rules of debate have themselves no legal force. They are, however, generally accepted. The rules of debate may be found in a number of handbooks on the conduct of public meetings in the same way as other rules of conduct may be found in books on etiquette. It is when an association or council embodies a number of rules of debate in its own standing orders that such rules become binding on that association. They then become more than accepted conventions. The standing orders or rules of a local government council should contain at least one rule devoted to the conventions of debate. Rule number twenty-seven of the Model Standing Rules issued by the Eastern Region Ministry of Internal Affairs constitutes a very valuable guide in this respect.

1. *Motions*. Debate is initiated by the moving of a motion to the effect that the council take certain action or refrain from taking certain action. Any member of a council may make such a motion, though standing rules will normally provide that, with certain exceptions, no motion shall be proposed at a meeting of the council unless notice has been given in writing to the secretary, seven, ten or more days before the next meeting of the council. This is to enable the secretary to refer the matter to the appropriate committee before the motion comes before the full council. This rule is normally taken not to apply to a variety of formal motions which are not outside the scope of the agenda or the notice convening the meeting. Such exceptions include the following:

77

(*a*) Appointment of a chairman of the meeting at which the motion is made;

(*b*) Closure of the debate (generally moved in the form 'That the question be now put');

(*c*) Adjournment of the debate (before this motion is put to the vote the mover of the original motion should be allowed the right of reply);

(*d*) Adjournment of the meeting;

(*e*) That a matter be referred back to a committee;

(*f*) That the council resolve into committee;

(*g*) Amendments to motions;

(*h*) Authority for the sealing of documents;

(*i*) A motion to carry out a statutory duty of the council which is, in the opinion of the chairman, of an urgent nature.

2. *Debate*. When a motion has been duly moved – and seconded if standing orders so require – debate on the issue may proceed. Every member who so desires should, where practicable, have an opportunity of speaking upon each motion. Standing rules normally provide that no member shall speak more than once on a motion, except that the mover of the original motion should have the right to wind up the debate before the vote is taken. Except in committee members should stand while speaking. Speeches should be addressed to the person presiding. Reference to persons by name should be avoided. Every member who speaks should direct his speech strictly to the motion under debate. The order in which members speak is determined by the chairman, but it is usually accepted that the first member who rises to speak, and who is observed by the chairman, is entitled to address the meeting. So far as is compatible with this principle the advocates and the opponents of the motion should be allowed to speak alternately. It is for the chairman to call to order any speaker for repetition, irrelevance or any other breach of order.

A speech may not be interrupted other than by the person presiding, in the proper exercise of his duty, except on a point of order or a point of explanation. While the enforcement of standing orders is properly the duty of the person presiding it is the right of any councillor to rise and direct the attention of the chair to any breach of these orders. This is known as a 'point of order'. Moreover, when a councillor feels that he has been misunderstood or misrepresented by a subsequent speaker he may expect that the person presiding will allow him to rise and interrupt with a brief explanation of his true position. This is known as a 'point of explanation'. Points of order and points of explanation should on no account be allowed to take the form of a speech. They must be as brief as possible. Apart from interruptions of this kind, which in a well-conducted council will be infrequent occurrences, a speaker may intervene in the debate on the motion, though he may not interrupt another speaker, by moving any one of the following fresh motions:

(a) To amend the motion;
(b) To move the closure;
(c) To postpone further discussion of the motion;
(d) To adjourn the meeting of the council;
(e) To refer the matter back to the appropriate committee;
(f) To resolve into a committee of the whole council.

Such interruptive motions should, if seconded, be put to the vote without discussion. The mover of such a motion is taken to have spoken once upon the motion before the council and he may not speak again during that debate.

3. *Amendments.* Amendments are generally of three kinds:
(a) To omit certain words;
(b) To omit certain words and insert or add others;
(c) To insert or add certain words.

An amendment must not be a mere negation of the motion. A councillor wishing to oppose a motion can invite the council to vote against it. He should not seek this end through a negative amendment. An amendment should be relevant to the original motion and should not have the effect of introducing a new proposal into it. No amendment may be moved after the taking of the vote upon the original motion. If the chairman so requires an amendment must be reduced to writing, and signed by the mover, before being put to the vote. No member can move more than one amendment to the same motion, for the moving of an amendment is taken as a speech on the original motion before the council. If an amendment is rejected another speaker may move a fresh amendment upon the original motion. If an amendment is carried the motion as amended takes the place of the original motion and becomes the motion upon which any further amendment may be moved.

Where an amendment to an admendment is allowed the procedure and the reasoning involved become somewhat complex. It is therefore a good rule not to allow any amendment of an amendment. It may be provided in the standing rules that a further amendment may not be moved until the council has disposed of the amendment previously moved. Where such a rule is in force it is usual to allow a member to announce his intention to move a different amendment if only the council will reject the amendment at present under discussion. When an amendment has been put to the meeting and carried, all that has been decided is that the original motion shall be modified in some way. The carrying of an amendment is not the same as the carrying of an amended motion. After the carrying of the amendment the amended motion must itself be voted upon by the council, after further debate if this is so desired.

4. *Control by Person Presiding.* The duties and power of the person presiding, with respect to the maintenance of order at a meeting, have been discussed in the previous chapter. His duties with respect to the guidance of debate are primarily to ensure that the proceedings are conducted in accordance with the law, and with the standing orders of the council, and also to ensure that the 'sense of the meeting', the wish of the council or committee, is properly ascertained with regard to any question which is properly before the meeting. More fully, the duties of the person presiding may be set out as follows:

(*a*) To ensure that the meeting is properly convened;

(*b*) To ensure that those who wish to speak on a motion are, so far as is possible, given an opportunity to express their views;

(*c*) To allow no discussion unless there is a motion before the meeting;

(*d*) To prevent irrelevance or verbosity in speeches;

(*e*) To arrive at the sense of the meeting by putting the motions and amendments in proper form;

(*f*) To ensure, so far as is possible, that the meeting attends to all the business that is listed in the agenda.

The person presiding has no right to prevent discussion upon a matter which is included in the notice convening a meeting. Apart from the powers conferred upon him by statute and by standing rules the person presiding may be said to derive his authority from the consent of the meeting. It is essential for him to seek a reputation for fairness and for impartiality in steering debate if he is to continue to rest securely upon the consent of the council or committee members. The ideal chairman is calm, dignified, quiet, and not given himself to making speeches. His first duty is to acquire a thorough knowledge of the standing orders of the council, and in this, as in other matters, he should be in frequent consultation with the secretary of the council.

CHAPTER XII

OFFICE ORGANISATION

The system of office organisation to be followed in the offices of a local government council is, within any directives which the council may choose to issue on the subject, primarily the responsibility of the secretary or chief executive officer. What is desirable in respect of office organisation will vary greatly in relation to the complexity of the council's business. What is possible will vary greatly in relation to the quality of the council's officials and employees. Zeal for office organisation and method must never be allowed to obscure the fact that efficiency is a means to facilitate the service which both officials and councillors can provide for the citizens of their area. Whatever system promotes that end is right, and any system that obstructs that end is wrong. It is not within the compass of this work to canvass a large variety of alternative systems of office organisation. Attention will be concentrated on one possible system that is frequently employed in Nigeria.

1. *Unified Office, or Departmental Offices.* The first question to be faced is whether the business of a council can best be conducted from one central office or whether each department of the council should be allowed to operate its own office. The answer to this question will depend partly on the actual office accommodation available, but mainly on the volume of work which the officials of the council are called upon to perform. Broadly speaking, in the largest and busiest councils, the public will be better served where departments maintain independent offices. In the smaller councils, where there may be a strictly limited number of trained clerks, efficiency will be promoted by the establishment of one central office. It is of course possible and convenient to maintain a number of independent offices within one secretariat building. It is also possible, though not convenient, to organise a unified office system where the council's

officials are divided between a number of separate office buildings. The answer to the question turns less on office accommodation than on the system by which records are filed.

Where records are issued from, and are received and stored in, one series of files, the office may be described as unified. Where a number of independent sets of files are employed the council may be said to operate a number of offices even though they may be contained in one office block. If the unified office is adopted then members of the public should be encouraged to address all correspondence to the secretary or chief executive officer of the council. If the council operates through a number of offices then members of the public should be encouraged to address the chief officer of the appropriate department.

2. *In-coming Mail.* It is convenient first to consider what should happen to letters received at the council's office or offices. In each office the senior official should hope to have the help of an assistant whom he can designate as his chief clerk. The chief clerk will, among other duties, be responsible for handling the in-coming mail. Whether he does everything himself, or whether he can delegate some of his duties, will depend upon the size and calibre of the junior staff. Any money, postal orders or cheques which are received in the mail, should be recorded in a list which must be signed by the clerk or clerks present at the opening of the mail.

The chief clerk will open all letters addressed to his senior officer and will stamp each letter with the day's date. These letters will then be placed, loose, in a file jacket labelled TO-DAY's MAIL which will be laid without delay on the chief officer's desk. The chief officer will initial each letter to show that he has seen it, and will pass the file jacket containing that day's letters back to the chief clerk. The chief clerk will then proceed to enter each letter in the 'In-coming Mail Register'.

This register should record the date and reference appearing on the letter, the name of the sender, the subject, and the number of the office file in which he proposes to file the letter. The chief clerk will then find from his store of files that file which is appropriate to the letter in question and will place the letter in the file. Papers are filed in order of receipt in the office and will consist of in-coming letters, and copies of out-going letters and instructions or 'minutes' from one official to another. The chief clerk will ensure that the papers within the file are numbered as pages, and that cross-references are inserted. If a member of the public begins his letter by referring to 'your letter of the 13th March', then the page in the file where the duplicate copy of this letter can be found should be recorded in the margin. When a reply to a letter is received a reference to this reply should be recorded on the file copy of that letter. A brief entry such as 'See page 98' is appropriate. When the in-coming mail has been filed all the files in which the letters have been placed will be returned to the desk of the chief officer who is responsible for taking action.

3. *Executive action.* On opening a file submitted to him for action, the chief officer will turn to the last page and should be able there to discover what is required of him. The last page in the file may consist of a letter sent in by a member of the public, a letter from a councillor, or a memorandum from an official. If the chief officer is able himself to deal with the matter he will draft the reply he wishes to send, place his draft in the file, and return the file to his chief clerk for the draft to be typed. If the inquiry should, in the opinion of the chief officer, be referred to one of the committees of the council, he will probably write in the file an instruction to the appropriate committee clerk to include consideration of the letter in the agenda of the next meeting of that committee. The chief officer will have to use his discretion as to whether the writer of such an inquiry should be kept waiting for a reply until after the committee has met, or whether he should at once send an interim reply to the effect that 'the matter is receiving attention and a further communication will be sent in due course'.

Not all the files placed before the chief officer for his attention will contain letters awaiting reply. A committee clerk may submit, in a file, draft minutes of a meeting of the council or of one of its committees. The committee clerk may be seeking his senior officer's approval before having the draft duplicated and despatched to the council or committee members concerned. A chief officer of another department may be seeking the opinion of the secretary as to whether or not certain action which he proposes to take has been authorised by the council or by a committee under powers delegated to it by the council. In such cases the secretary will record in the file his instructions or his opinion. He will sign or initial the entry that he has made, record the date, and pass the file out to his chief clerk to be forwarded to the official concerned.

Other files placed on the desk of a chief officer will contain out-going letters which have been typed on his instructions and which now await his signature. Before returning such files for signature of these letters the chief clerk will have placed the duplicate copy of the out-going letters in the files and will have inserted the page numbers and cross-references. In a busy office a chief officer is well advised to have on his desk a separate tray for files containing letters awaiting his signature. On occasion it may take him a day or two to work through the files awaiting attention in his 'IN' tray. To sign a typed letter requires only a few moments, and if files containing such letters are placed in a special tray, instead of at the bottom of the 'IN' tray, the chief officer can eliminate unnecessary delay in the despatch of correspondence.

4. *Out-going Mail*. When he receives back a file containing an out-going letter which his chief officer has signed, the chief clerk must arrange for the despatch of that letter without delay. First, however, the letter must be recorded in an out-going mail register. This register will record the date of the letter, the number of the file and the number of the page within that file where the duplicate of the letter can be found, the name of the official who signed the letter, the subject of the letter, and the name of the person to whom the letter was addressed. When the original of the letter has been sealed in an addressed envelope and delivered to the Post Office the chief clerk will record the word 'Issued' on the duplicate in the file and will add his initials and the date. The file will then be returned to the chief officer for his further instructions.

5. *Opening of New Files*. In order to facilitate the recording and tracing of the mass of papers accumulated in a large office it is

normal to divide them by subjects and to enclose them in different files. The question of how many files to open is not easy to answer, though an experienced official usually develops a certain instinct in the matter. If too many papers on a diversity of subjects are enclosed in one file it may take a long time to find a letter when it is urgently required. If a new file is opened every time the office receives a paper which is not obviously destined for one of the existing files, then many file jackets containing only one or two documents will soon be accumulated. Such a practice is extravagant, since file jackets are expensive, and will also complicate the work of the file registry. It is when it comes to the notice of the official responsible, that a subject is causing a considerable volume of correspondence, that a new file should be opened. The new file will have the subject in question written or stencilled on the front. Into this file will be removed or copied correspondence already received or sent out on this subject, and into it will be placed all subsequent correspondence on that particular subject.

6. *File Register*. Every file will be given a number as well as a subject, and a file register must be maintained. In this register the numbers of the files will be recorded serially, and the subject of the file in question will be shown against each number. Unless such a register is opened, and constantly referred to, it is woefully easy in a large office to open a new file on a subject for which a file is already in existence. When this occurs a chief officer who is preparing a memorandum for a committee will not have all the relevant information available. Similarly he is in danger of issuing letters which he would have realised were unnecessary or inaccurate had all the relevant papers been available to him.

7. *Tracing of files*. In addition to a file register a card index of all files should be maintained. Whenever a new file is opened a card should be made out recording the number and subject of the file. When a file is in the file store this card may be fixed inside the file. As soon as the file is called for by an official and it leaves the file store, the name of the official who has received the file, and the date on which it was passed out to him, should be

recorded on the card. The card should then be placed in its correct numerical position among the other cards in the card index. Files should be stored in numerical order, perhaps in groups of ten or more, in 'pigeon-holes'. When a chief officer suddenly calls for a file the chief clerk should look first in the file store. If the file cannot be found there he should know that the card in respect of that file will be found in the card index, which will show where that file has been sent and on what date.

8. *The 'B.U.' Diary*. When action on a certain matter has come to an end the chief officer may instruct his clerk that the file should be put away. This instruction may be given by writing the letters 'P.A.' on the last page in the file. Such an instruction should be initialled by the official making it, and the date should be recorded. When such an instruction is given the file should be placed in its right place in the file store. If there is a temporary lull in correspondence being conducted in a certain file the chief officer may ask for it to be brought up to him on a certain date. He may do this if he has written a letter to which a reply must be awaited. The chief officer may make this instruction by writing on the last page in the file the letters 'B.U.' and the date on which he wishes that file to be placed on his table. Such an entry should be initialled and dated.

The chief clerk should maintain a diary for files which he is required to bring up in this way. If the chief officer instructs that 'File Number 128, Subject, Waterworks' should be brought up to him on '13 July' an entry should be made in that page of the diary devoted to 13 July, recording the number and subject of that file and the name of the official who requires to see it. When such an entry has been made the file may be safely returned to the file store. One of the first duties of a chief clerk each morning is to refer to his 'B.U.' Diary to see what files must be brought up on that day. These files must then be placed on the desk of the chief officer who called for them, so that he may continue action.

PART III
LOCAL GOVERNMENT FINANCE

CHAPTER XIII

ESTABLISHMENT OF TREASURIES

Councils established under the Western Region Local Government Law and the Eastern Region Local Government Law are, in the discharge of their functions, responsible for the collection of various kinds of revenue and for the spending of such revenue for the maintenance of the public services for which they are responsible. Both enactments contain general provisions as to the financial powers and duties of councils.[1] In the Eastern Region the Minister, and in the Western Region the Regional Authority, is empowered to issue Financial Memoranda[2] 'for the better control and management of the financial business of councils'. The Financial Memoranda already issued in both Regions contain detailed accounting instructions for the guidance of councils and their treasury staff.

1. *Rating and Precepting Authorities.* In Eastern and Western Regions some councils are empowered to impose and collect rates and are therefore referred to as rating authorities. Councils which are not made rating authorities may issue demands for money, known as precepts, on the appropriate rating authority. In the Eastern Region the rating authorities are the District Councils and Municipalities[3] on which the appropriate County and Local Councils may precept; in the Western Region the rating authorities may be either the Divisional or District Councils[4] depending upon the particular circumstances pertaining to any area to which the Local Government Law is applied.

2. *The Eastern Region.* When established a local government council takes over the assets and liabilities of the out-going Townships or Native Authorities. Apart from the difference

[1] E.R.L.G. Law, Part XI; W.R.L.G. Law, Part X.
[2] E.R.L.G. Law, section 117; W.R.L.G. Law, section 107.
[3] E.R.L.G. Law, section 121.
[4] W.R.L.G. Law, section 109.

discussed under the heading 'Assignment of Property' in Chapter III, the procedure by which the necessary financial arrangements are made is, in practice, similar in both Regions. The system followed in the Eastern Region is set out in Memorandum No. 4 of the Financial Memoranda issued by the Minister. Whatever the pattern of the out-going authorities or of the newly established councils the first step is normally to allocate all the surplus funds to the District Councils and Municipalities in the proper proportions. The second step is then for the District Councils to contribute to the County Council a working balance in the proper proportions. Municipalities, as single-tier, all-purpose authorities, have no such contribution to make.

Where the area of the new County Council corresponds to the area of an out-going Divisional Native Authority each District Council receives the same proportions of the total surplus funds as the tax collected in the area of the District Council in the preceding financial year bears to the total amount of tax collected in the area of all the District Councils. County Councils should start operating with a working balance equal to twenty-five per cent of the total revenue shown in their approved estimates. District Councils in a County Council area contribute towards this amount in the proportion in which they received their own share of the native authority's surplus.

Where the areas of the newly established councils do not correspond to the areas of the old Native Authorities and Townships the transactions involved are somewhat complicated although the principles to be followed remain the same. This system of allocating surplus funds has not been followed as a hard and fast rule. Careful consideration is always given to the particular needs of the locality concerned, to the pattern of former Native Authority organisation and to the pattern of the new local government system. Assets have, on occasion, been allocated direct to form the working balance of a County Council as well as those of District Councils.

3. *The Western Region.* In the Western Region the method of transfer of the assets and liabilities of an out-going Native Authority or Township to a new local government council is

governed by Directions made by the Regional Authority as set out in Local Government Circular No. 10 of 1955. The initial step taken is to transfer the surplus of the out-going authority or authorities to the in-coming council which has been appointed as the Rating Authority, whether it be a Divisional or District Council. The Rating Authority is then charged with the responsibility of allocating working balances to the remaining councils other than the local councils. These initial working balances should be equal to twenty-five per cent. of the estimated annual revenue of the council concerned. There are instances in which it is not possible for the initial working balances to be established at twenty-five per cent of revenue without unduly depleting the funds of the contributing council or councils. In such instances the proportion of twenty-five per cent may be reduced as necessary. The detailed arrangements for dealing with the complications which thereby arise are dealt with in the Financial Memorandum No. A. 1.

4. *Advance and Deposit Accounts.* In the Eastern and Western Regions the advance and deposit accounts of the out-going Native Authorities and Townships are assigned to the councils to whom the advances are to be repaid or by whom the deposits are to be repaid in exercise of the functions conferred on them in their Instruments. Thus, an account in respect of a personal advance to a Native Authority employee is assigned to the council which is to employ him in the future. Sums of money deposited by litigants in the native courts are assigned to the council which is to be responsible for the future operation of those courts.

5. *Local Government Treasuries.* Municipalities, County and District Councils in the Eastern Region, and Divisional and District Councils in the Western Region, are required to provide themselves with treasury buildings and to employ whatever treasury staff is necessary. Local Councils are not expected to maintain an elaborate system of accounts and need not maintain a treasury.

In law, all tax collected by local government councils in the Eastern Region under the Finance Law and all tax collected by councils in the Western Region under Direct Taxation Ordinance is government tax. In practice, the Eastern Regional Government pays out of the Income Tax collected, block grants to the councils which assisted in its collection. In the Western Region, the Government takes only a fixed amount per taxpayer out of the Direct Tax collected. The Regional Government's share of Direct Tax is sometimes known as capitation tax. The balance of the tax is handed over to the local government council which originally collected it.

A student of local government practice in the United Kingdom might have expected that as the native authorities gave place to local government councils in the Eastern and Western Regions of Nigeria, Direct Tax as a source of revenue for local authorities would have been completely replaced by a system of rating. This has not happened. In the Eastern Region only, Direct Tax has been replaced, and there only by another form of government tax. Newly established councils have in fact derived a considerable degree of financial stability from the fact that their largest single source of revenue has been a share of government tax whose collection is ultimately assured by the powerful machinery of the Regional Governments. However, it cannot be regarded as permanently satisfactory that local authorities should have so little control over their principal source of revenue.

2. *Rates and Precepts.* In the United Kingdom, while government grants of one sort and another are rapidly assuming the first importance, the greatest single source of revenue of a local government council is the rates it levies or the precepts it issues. It is probable that rates and precepts will soon assume the same importance for councils in the Eastern and Western Regions of Nigeria. Under the native authority system rating was regarded primarily as a means of financing public utilities such as a water supply, or as an emergency measure to raise funds urgently required for the construction of a school, for the tarring of town roads, or of some similar project. Under the local government system rating is likely to become the principal source of general revenue for councils.

The systems of precepting and rating which apply in the two Regions are dealt with in Part XII of the Eastern Region Local Government Law, and Part XI of the Western Region Local Government Law. The systems are discussed in Memorandum No. 6 of the Financial Memoranda issued by the Minister in the Eastern Region and in Memoranda Nos. E. 2 and E. 3, in the Financial Memoranda issued by the Western Regional Authority. The alternative systems of rating may be considered as follows:

(a) Property rating;

(b) Capitation or flat rating;

(c) Income rating.

It is normally assumed to be right that an individual citizen should contribute to the cost of services provided by a local authority in proportion to his financial position and in proportion to the use which he makes of such services. In Nigeria a wealthy citizen does in practice tend to make greater claims on these services than a poor person. A man who owns motor lorries, and whose house contains valuable possessions, is evidently making greater use of roads maintained by the local authority and is more dependent upon the police and other protective services provided by the local authority than is a peasant who lives in a bare hut and who seldom leaves his village. This observation would, of course, not apply in the United Kingdom, where the poorer a man is the more dependent he becomes upon the housing and welfare services provided by his local authorities. Yet even in the United Kingdom an effort is made to ensure that a citizen should pay rates in proportion to his means.

The Instrument establishing a council will, in the case of a Municipality or District Council in the Eastern Region, and in the case of any council which is appointed as a rating authority in the Western Region, state the method or methods of rating to be employed by that particular council.

There are certain advantages and disadvantages associated with each system of rating. Property rating assumes that a citizen's ability to contribute to his council's revenue will normally be reflected in the type of house in which he lives. A poor man does not normally live in a two-story house with a pan roof, and a rich man is not normally content to live in a thatched hut. Moreover, it is not easy to evade the payment of dues which are based on the ownership or occupancy of property. Cattle tax may be avoided by driving the herd away to another area; head tax may be evaded by moving oneself and family away when payment becomes due; but real estate cannot be moved away, and if the owner absconds the council is able ultimately to sell up the property in question. The main difficulty in the way of wider application of property rating in Nigeria is that it necessitates a number of officials, competent to value property on a uniform and equitable basis. It is also argued that property rating encourages low building standards, as a man will be slow to improve his dwelling if this action is liable to involve him in the payment of increased rates. It is further argued that property rating reacts badly on a man with a large family. Such a person may have to live in a large house in order to accommodate all his family, and yet, because of the expense which such a family involves, he may be much less well off financially than a citizen who is able to accommodate a small family in a small property. It may, however, be anticipated that, as surveyors trained in house valuation become available, there will in Nigeria be a general move towards property rating, which is the system of rating employed throughout the United Kingdom.

Capitation or flat rating exacts a uniform contribution to the revenue of the council from all persons upon whom it is levied. If capitation rating is levied upon all adult males living in the council area, then all such persons, whether rich or poor, are required to pay a standard or flat rate. No system of rating could be more simple to administer. No expert officials are necessary, no assessment of individual incomes is called for. Accounting is extremely straightforward. Yet because capitation rating bears as heavily on the poor man as on the rich the system is generally regarded as suitable only for the less developed communities.

Rating on incomes is the system at present generally employed in Southern Nigeria. By section 126 of the Eastern Region Local Government Law a Municipality or District Council, if it is so stated by the Instrument by which it is established, may make and levy an annual rate upon any person or class of person over the age of sixteen years ordinarily resident within the area of its authority. The same power may be conferred upon rating authorities under section 112 (3) of the Western Region Local Government Law. In both Regions this power is conferred only in areas to which the Assessment Ordinance does not apply. While under a system of income rating a council is not able to rate their buildings, or their profits from commercial undertakings, it may be able to impose a rate on the income of all persons whether Africans or non-Africans. A particular advantage of the system of income rating is that it does not involve local government bodies in the establishment of their own assessment committees. The law provides that where such a system is adopted assessment of income shall be taken to be the same as that made under the Direct Taxation Ordinance.[2]

3. *Government Grants-in-Aid.* The only source of local government revenue which necessitates particular mention is that of Government grants-in-aid. It has already been pointed out that grants made by Government towards the cost of a particular local government service which it is desired to encourage constitute an important means by which the Regional Government can control the activities of councils. The present system is for the Region to reimburse a council a fixed percentage of expenditure on approved projects such as the provision of maternity centres and the maintenance of roads. This payment of a fixed percentage of expenditure is designed to encourage councils to devote a larger proportion of their resources to desirable projects. This result is generally achieved, but the system inevitably assists those councils which can afford to incur expenditure, and this gives to prosperous areas a higher share per unit of population than is offered to the poorer areas. The solution to this problem may well lie in the development of weighting Government grants in favour of those areas which are most in need of help.

[2] E.R.L.G. Law, section 125 (3); W.R.L.G. Law, section 112 (2) (iii). But in the Eastern Region the Eastern Region Finance Law, 1956, now replaces the Direct Taxation Ordinance (See Section 15 of the Eastern Region Local Government (Amendment) Law, 1956).

CHAPTER XV

BORROWING POWERS OF LOCAL GOVERNMENT COUNCILS

The power to 'raise loans within Nigeria of such amounts, from such sources, in such manner, upon such conditions' as the Regional Authority may approve is conferred upon local government councils by section 101 of the Western Region Local Government Law. Section 112 of the Eastern Region Local Government Law empowers councils 'to raise loans within the Eastern Region of such amounts, from such sources, in such manner and upon such conditions as the Minister may approve'. The power to raise loans, like the other powers of local authorities, can be derived, directly or indirectly, only from the Legislature. The granting of this power by the Legislature represents one of the most important financial innovations of the new local government legislation. It reflects a major change in the general financial policy envisaged for the future.

Native authorities have no legal powers to raise loans (although in fact some of them have been permitted to do so, usually in connection with water or electricity undertakings) and are required to finance all their services, including capital works projects, from their general revenue and accumulated surplus. In other words, they have first to raise and save revenue before they may incur expenditure. While such a policy has the advantage of enforcing caution on local government bodies with but little experience and with little executive or financial potential, its inevitable result is to restrict the volume of capital expenditure to an unnecessary degree and virtually to prohibit large-scale projects. Also the system of financing works projects from the saving of previous years means that the taxpayer is not in fact getting full value for his money. A part of his annual contribution to the native authority is not being spent on services for his benefit but is being saved for future expenditure on services he might not live to enjoy.

The procedure now envisaged is for councils to finance capital works projects from loans, although of course they may, if they wish, continue to finance such works from revenue or from previously accumulated surplus balances. In effect the credit of a council will be used to obtain money to provide amenities which will be paid for by instalments by those ratepayers who are to derive benefit from them. A system of financing a capital work, such as the building of a town hall, by a loan which is repaid by annual contributions spread over the estimated life of the town hall has two main advantages. The first is that the building is not delayed while the cost of the town hall is being accumulated as savings. The second advantage is that financing the project from a loan ensures that all the ratepayers who enjoy the town hall contribute to the cost of building it. It is not financed by ratepayers who accept very high rating for one or two years and who then present this valuable asset to future generations of ratepayers to enjoy without further payment. While this change in policy can be expected to speed up the provision of much needed amenities councils will need to exercise restraint in the use of their powers to raise loans. As in the past, everything will have to be paid for, even though the payment will be spread over a longer period of time; further, where works are financed from loans, the overall cost is in fact greater, as the authority lending the money expects to receive interest on it.

The sections of the Eastern Regional Local Government Law and the Western Region Local Government Law dealing with the powers of councils to raise loans are almost identical. They are more simply worded than the corresponding sections of the Local Government Act of 1933. However, it may be expected that the respective Ministries will issue more detailed information to councils, stating the types of expenditure which may be financed from loans, the maximum repayment periods, and the limits to loan indebtedness which will be permitted.

1. *Sources of Loans*. In practice it is almost certain that a council's powers to raise loans will be restricted largely by the lack of capital available for borrowing. In both Regions councils are permitted to borrow money only within Nigeria, so that they

will in the main have to seek loans from their respective Governments. In the Western Region the Production Development Board, and in the Eastern Region the Development Corporation, may also be a source of loan capital. The new Eastern Region Finance Corporation is specifically empowered to grant loans to local government bodies.[1]

From the local government viewpoint it is unfortunate that both Regional Governments are themselves engaged in large development programmes and are hardly likely to be in a position to make large sums available for loan purposes. The powers of the Western Region Production Development Board, the Eastern Region Development Corporation and of the Eastern Region Finance Corporation to lend money are restricted, by the legislation establishing them, to projects of direct economic importance, so that they cannot be expected to provide money for the usual types of capital expenditure made by a local government authority. These Corporations have only limited funds at their disposal and the sums not already committed are small. In theory, councils may be able to borrow money from banks or private persons, but whether funds will be available from these sources at moderate rates of interest over long repayment periods remains to be seen.

2. *Approval for Loans.* In both Regions a council is required to obtain approval before raising a loan, in the West from the Regional Authority, and in the East from the Minister. In both Regions a council is required by Financial Memoranda[2] to submit to the appropriate authority detailed information on the purposes of the loan, the repayment period, the effect on the annual rates of the repayment charges and so on.

3. *Estimates Procedure.* Expenditure on a works project financed from a loan is not shown in the main body of the annual estimates of a council but in an appendix to them. It would clearly be impracticable to include such expenditure in the estimates themselves, as it would then become a charge against the rates.

[1] Eastern Region Finance Corporation Law, 1954, section 3 (4).
[2] E.R.F.M. No. 5, para. 12; W.R. Financial Memorandum No. C5, para. 2.

Provision for the annual repayment of loan capital and interest is included in the annual expenditure estimates, thereby becoming a charge against the ratepayers for the year.

4. *Accounting Procedure.* When a loan is received from an external source the actual amount received is paid into a separate account, which is in fact a special type of deposit account and represents a financial liability. The cost of the project financed by the loan is then charged against the account as the work proceeds, so that by the time the project is completed the balance of the account will, in theory, be nil. Thus the liability to repay the loan to the authority which lent the money disappears from the accounts although the liability still exists. To overcome this difficulty councils are required to maintain separate records showing, in respect of each loan, the actual amount owing at any particular time. Further, a statement of loan indebtedness is to be included with the Annual Financial Statement.[3]

5. *Internal Loans.* In the Western Region councils are expressly permitted to raise internal loans.[4] Under this system a council borrows money from the previously accumulated surplus balance, on the understanding that the ratepayers will refund to the surplus balance, over a period of years, the amount borrowed. Under such a system the surplus balance is constantly replenished and continues to serve as a loan fund. Internal loans may be raised only with the approval of the Regional Authority. When an internal loan is raised the cost of the project financed by the loan is charged to an advance account in the treasury. This advance account is cleared over a period of years by the credit of the annual instalments of the loan repayment.

The balances of internal loan accounts are not shown in the annual accounts along with other advance account balances, for, if this were done, false assets (in the sense that buildings, etc., they represent are unrealisable) would be taken into consideration. Instead, such balances are shown on the liabilities side of the Statement of Assets and Liabilities as deductions from the general revenue balance.

[3] E.R.F.M. No. 10, para. 56; W.R. Financial Memorandum No. C5, para. 9.
[4] W.R. Financial Memorandum No. C5, paras. 10-14.

CHAPTER XVI

BUDGETARY CONTROL

Subject to the provisions of the Local Government Law a council in either the Eastern or Western Region may incur all expenditure 'necessary for, and incidental to,' the carrying out of its functions.[1] The council may delegate to a committee the power to approve expenditure, but such delegation does not relieve the council of its collective responsibility. All expenditure must be authorised by resolution whether of the full council or of a committee exercising delegated powers. The fact that provision is made in the estimates for an item of expenditure does not, in itself, give authority for the expenditure to be incurred. The council is quite free at any time during the financial year to decide not to authorise certain expenditure for which provision has been made in the estimates.

1. *Preparation of Estimates.* The estimates of a council form the basis of the council's annual accounts. The estimates should give a clear picture of the council's financial position and should set out the council's financial plans for the year to which they refer.

Under section 108 of the Western Region Local Government Law all councils in the Western Region are required to submit to the Regional Authority detailed estimates of revenue and expenditure for the next ensuing financial year. The Regional Authority is empowered to approve or disapprove such estimates as a whole or it may disapprove any particular item or items.[2] Where the Regional Authority so directs a council may control its own finances, in which case it forwards a copy of its estimates to the Regional Authority for information only.[3]

Under section 118 of the Eastern Region Local Government Law every County Council, every Municipality, and every

---

[1] E.R.L.G. Law, section 111; W.R.L.G. Law, section 100.
[2] W.R.L.G. Law, section 108 (2).
[3] W.R.L.G. Law, section 108 (9).

District Council is required to prepare estimates and to approve them by resolution. A copy of these estimates and a copy of this resolution must be submitted to the Minister on or before 31 December in each year.[4] The Minister may at any time require a Local Council to submit a detailed estimate of its revenue and expenditure.[5] The Minister is empowered to approve or disapprove such estimates as a whole, or he may disapprove any particular item or items.[6]

Estimates consist of the financial statement or summary, the estimates of revenue, and the estimates of expenditure. Detailed instructions concerning the form and lay-out of the estimates are given in the Financial Memoranda obtaining in each of the two Regions.

Estimates of revenue are prepared in the first instance by the treasurer. The treasurer will use the current year's estimates as a guide, and will be able to calculate the approximate increase or decrease in revenue which may be expected to follow from resolutions of the council, increasing or decreasing fees, and from sources of income other than rates or precepts. At this stage, the treasurer should assume that rates or precepts will remain unchanged.

Estimates of expenditure are prepared in the first instance by the appropriate spending committee, with the treasurer sitting as adviser. With the current year's estimates acting as a basis for discussion, the committee can calculate what increases and decreases in expenditure may be expected during the coming year. Since estimates are required to be submitted in December of each year this preliminary work should begin in the preceding June.

When preliminary estimates have been drawn up by the treasurer and by the spending committees, they are laid before finance committee. The treasurer must be able to inform finance committee of the amount of rates or precepts to be levied if the estimates as at present proposed are approved. If the level of rates or precepts is unacceptable to finance committee the spending committees may be urged to reconsider their proposals

[4] E.R.L.G. Law, section 118 (1).
[5] E.R.L.G. Law, section 118 (2).
[6] E.R.L.G. Law, section 118 (3).

with a view to effecting a reduction by a given percentage. The treasurer may also be invited to suggest possible sources of increased revenue other than by rates or precepts. When fresh proposals which appear acceptable to finance committee have been received that committee will make a recommendation to the full council. Before such a recommendation is made all aspects of the estimates will have been exhaustively discussed in the committees of the council. There should be no need to re-open such discussions before full council. All that is required is a resolution adopting the estimates as recommended by finance committee, and a special resolution making the rate or issuing the precept. Action must then be taken to publish the rate in the proper manner and to forward the whole of the estimates to the appropriate authority for approval or for information.

2. *Certificate of Urgency.* The council cannot itself exercise day-to-day control over all expenditure. Committees normally meet only once a month and will not always be available to authorise expenditure which is urgently required. The standing orders of a council may therefore provide that the treasurer may make payment on receipt of a certificate of urgency signed by certain specified persons. Standing orders may specify that the chairman of the council or the chairman of finance committee must sign certificates of urgency and that the secretary of the council must sign all such certificates. Payments made by the treasurer on certificates of urgency should be authorised by the appropriate committee, or by the council, at the next following meeting.

3. *Budgetary Control by Committees.* Whether or not a council delegates some or all of its powers in respect of the control of expenditure every head of expenditure in the council's estimates should be assigned to a committee for supervision. If the council does not delegate any of its powers in respect of the control of expenditure it will be for the appropriate committee to recommend expenditure to the council and not to authorise payment by way of resolution.

4. *Officer Controlling Vote.* For every head of expenditure a chief officer of the council should be appointed as 'officer controlling

the vote'. It will be the duty of this officer to advise the council or committee on the state of the votes he controls. If it comes to the notice of the officer controlling the vote that at the current rate of expenditure provision for a certain head in the approved estimates appears inadequate, he must at once report the matter to the council, or to the appropriate committee if powers have been delegated. The council or committee may empower the officer controlling the vote himself to authorise expenditure under the 'other charges' sub-head up to a certain limited amount.

The officer controlling the vote might well be empowered to authorise payment of their salaries, and of allowances claimed in accordance with Staff Regulations, to the established staff in his department. The officer might also authorise payment of daily paid staff employed by the department which he controls. The committee would probably require the officer controlling the vote to make a report to the next meeting of the committee of the sums which he had himself directly authorised. Where this system is followed the letter of appointment issued to a chief officer of the council should state the votes that he is to control and the limits to which he may authorise expenditure without previous reference to the committee. Where a chief officer is not competent to control a vote, and where a vote does not fall within the control of a departmental official, the treasurer should be appointed as 'officer controlling the vote'. It is most desirable to keep to a minimum the number of votes which the treasurer himself controls.

CHAPTER XVII

AUDIT

The accounts of all local government councils are subject to audit. It is considered that the normal processes of law and the power of the electorate periodically to change the membership of councils may not be sufficient to ensure that the funds of the council will invariably be properly safeguarded and properly spent. Moreover, the Regional Government wishes to ensure that grants made to councils from Regional funds are being properly spent in accordance with the prescribed conditions.

1. *Appointment of Auditors.* Auditors are appointed by the Regional Authority in the Western Region and by the Minister in the Eastern Region.[1] By W.R.P.N. No. 79 of 1954, and E.R.L.N. No. 256 of 1954, the Directors of Audit of the Western and Eastern Regions have been so appointed. An auditor should not, however, be regarded simply as the agent of the Regional Government nor of the Minister responsible for local government matters. An auditor acts in some respects as a judge. Having regard to the evidence before him, it is for the auditor to rule what expenditure is reasonable and justified and what payments are contrary to the law and improper. Neville Chamberlain, then United Kingdom Minister of Health, with responsibility for local government matters, is quoted as saying in 1927:

It has been said that the Auditors are my Auditors. They are not my Auditors. They are entirely independent of me. I have never attempted to give a District Auditor instructions as to what he should do; I have never sought to influence a District Auditor in carrying out his duties. It would never have been any use if I had. As a matter of fact the action of the District Auditor has often been the cause of some embarrassment.

The auditor acts in a quasi-judicial capacity and not simply as the agent of the Regional Authority.

[1] E.R.L.G. Law, section 172; W.R.L.G. Law, section 140 (1).

The Regional Authority of the Western Region is specifically empowered to appoint any Local Government Inspector or Assistant Local Government Inspector as an auditor in respect of any council.[2]

2. *Powers and Duties of Auditor.* The powers and duties of an auditor are set out in section 175 of the Eastern Region Local Government Law and in section 142 of the Western Region Local Government Law. These sections, which are identical in wording, closely follow section 228 of the Local Government Act, 1933. The auditor is empowered to disallow any item of expenditure which is contrary to law and to surcharge it upon those he considers responsible for it. That is to say that if the auditor considers that any official, councillor, committee or council has disposed of local government funds extravagantly or improperly, he may order them to pay an equivalent sum back into the treasury of the council out of their personal resources. The auditor is also empowered to surcharge any sum which has not been duly brought to account, or the amount of any loss or deficiency, upon the person responsible.

One important limitation of the auditor's power of disallowance and surcharge is made. The Western Region Law provides 'that no item of expenditure incurred by a council shall be disallowed by the auditor if it has been sanctioned by the Regional Authority'.[3] The Eastern Region Law makes a similar provision in respect of expenditure approved by the Minister.[4] This provision does not give the Regional Authority or Minister the power to legalise any payment which otherwise would be illegal, and a ratepayer who considers that public money has been improperly spent may take action in the courts against the party responsible, even though the expenditure in question has been specifically approved. The provision does, however, enable local government councils in cases of doubt to obtain beforehand an authoritative ruling on the propriety of proposed expenditure. It follows that councils would be wise to seek the sanction of the Regional Authority or Minister before undertaking many forms of expenditure.

[2] W.R.L.G. Law, section 140 (3).
[3] W.R.L.G. Law, section 142.
[4] E.R.L.G. Law, section 175.

Section 177 of the Eastern Region Local Government Law and section 144 of the Western Region Local Government Law set out in almost identical terms the power of an auditor to take evidence if he so desires, and the power to order a person to appear before him as before a court and to produce all books and papers which the auditor considers it necessary to examine. Any person who neglects or refuses to answer such a summons, or who refuses to take an oath, or who refuses to answer questions put to him by an auditor, is guilty of an offence.[5] Such a person is liable on conviction, in the Eastern Region to a fine not exceeding twenty-five pounds or to imprisonment for a term not exceeding six months, and in the Western Region to a fine not exceeding twenty-five pounds or to imprisonment for up to three months.

Subsection (5) of section 173 of the Eastern Region Local Government Law requires a council to provide an auditor with any explanation or information that he may need with regard to the accounts, even without the formality of summons. No comparable provision is made by the Western Region Local Government Law.

3. *Appeal against the Auditor's Decision.* The procedure for appeal against a decision of the auditor is similar in the Eastern and Western Regions and is set out in section 180 of the Eastern Region Law and section 147 of the Western Region Law. Where the disallowance or surcharge or other decision relates to an amount not exceeding two hundred pounds, appeal lies to the Regional Authority in the Western Region and to the Minister in the Eastern Region. Where the amount involved is greater than two hundred pounds, appeal may be made either to the Regional Authority/Minister or to the Supreme Court. The Regional Authority/Minister or the Supreme Court has power to confirm, vary or quash the decision of the auditor and may direct the auditor to give effect to the decision on appeal. Where appeal is made to the Regional Authority/Minister he may state a case for the opinion of the Supreme Court on any question of law, but, apart from this, the decision of the Regional Authority/Minister is final.

[5] E.R.L.G. Law, section 177 (2); W.R.L.G. Law, section 144 (2).

4. *Interpretation of 'Contrary to Law'*. The auditor may say that expenditure is *ultra vires* or illegal in character because it has been incurred in pursuance of a function not vested in the council by the Legislature. The auditor may also say that it is contrary to law because, in his opinion, it is unreasonably excessive. If a local government council spends at an unreasonable level, its expenditure is 'contrary to law' within the meaning of that phrase as used in local government legislation. In England a considerable volume of case law can guide an auditor or a court hearing an appeal concerning what is unreasonable. The most important of such cases is the Poplar Wage Case which is conveniently summarised in Memorandum No. 1 of the Financial Memoranda issued by the Minister in the Eastern Region. The story of this case is more fully set out by Dr Herman Finer.[6] The House of Lords upheld the order of surcharge made by the auditor upon the councillors of Poplar Borough Council, and the result of this judgement and the judgements in other similar cases is that the opinion of the auditor as to what is reasonable in regard to expenditure is held to override the views of the elected councillors. The auditor is the judge of what is reasonable and therefore lawful. There is at present a dearth of case law in Nigeria concerning orders of surcharge made by auditors, and until such case law becomes available the position in England must serve as a guide.

5. *Officials and Surcharge*. Section 176 of the Eastern Region Local Government Law and section 143 of the Western Region Local Government Law provide that no liability to surcharge shall be incurred by an officer or servant of the council who can prove to the satisfaction of the auditor that he acted in pursuance of and in accordance with the terms of a resolution of the council or of a committee duly appointed by the council, or on the written instructions of any senior officer of the council. Where a local government official perceives that his council is proposing to take a line of action which may result in an order of surcharge he should ensure that the advice which he offers to the council or committee is given in writing. An official who strongly and in writing advises against such a line of action need

<hr />

[6] Herman Finer, *English Local Government*, pp. 333-5.

not fear to implement the council's decision if his advice is ultimately rejected. It will not be difficult for him to satisfy the auditor that he has done his duty as the council's adviser and has dissociated himself from the resolution of the council which it subsequently became his duty to implement.

6. *Disqualification by Surcharge.* Section 24 (*b*) of the Western Law provides that no person shall be entitled to be elected as, or to remain a member of, a local government council who has within five years before the day of election been surcharged to an amount exceeding one hundred pounds. Section 20 (*g*) of the Eastern Law makes a similar provision in respect of a person surcharged to an amount exceeding five hundred pounds 'within five years before the date of election or since his election'. Where, in the Eastern Region, such an order of surcharge has, on appeal, been reduced to two hundred pounds or less (one hundred pounds or less in the Western Region) this disqualification does not apply.[7]

7. *Annual Statement of Accounts.* All councils are required to produce a yearly statement of accounts.[8] Such a statement of accounts must be laid before an auditor, who will make investigations into the accuracy and propriety of the statement and of the relevant accounts. The auditor is required to sign a report on such accounts and on the statement and to send a copy of such report to the Regional Authority in the Western Region and to the Minister in the Eastern Region. A council is required to produce for any inhabitant of the area who is willing to pay the fee prescribed a copy of the annual statement of accounts and of the auditor's report upon it. In this way the auditor assures the ratepayers that the funds to which they contribute are being properly administered.

[7] E.R.L.G. Law, section 180 (3); W.R.L.G. Law, section 147 (2).
[8] E.R.L.G. Law, section 173; W.R.L.G. Law, section 140.

PART IV
MISCELLANEOUS

CHAPTER XVIII

CONTROL OF STAFF

Control of local government staff is exercised at four distinct levels. Control is exercised by:

(*a*) The Regional Government;
(*b*) The council;
(*c*) The committees of the council;
(*d*) The chief officers of the council.

1. *Control by the Regional Government.* Under the principle of parliamentary sovereignty all power in local government matters stems from the Regional Legislature. In both Eastern and Western Regions the Legislature has conferred upon the appropriate Minister very wide powers in respect of local government staff. In the Eastern Region a council may engage staff only with the approval of the Minister. No person appointed by a council in any capacity may be dismissed by a council without the approval of the Minister in writing.[1] In the Western Region a council may not employ or dismiss a secretary or treasurer or any person at a salary of three hundred and fifty pounds per annum or above without the approval, in writing, of the the Regional Authority.[2]

In the Eastern Region the Minister, and in the Western Region the Regional Authority, is empowered to make Staff Regulations concerning appointments, dismissals, discipline, salary scales, allowances and a variety of other matters. Such regulations have already been issued in the Western Region and appeared in the supplement to the *Western Region of Nigeria Gazette*. No. 9 of Vol. 4, dated 24 February 1955. Under these Western Region (Local Government) Staff Regulations the Minister may direct a council to reconsider any dismissal or termination and may order the reinstatement of any employee whom he considers to have been treated harshly. Conversely, the

[1] E.R.L.G. Law, sections 94 and 95.
[2] W.R.L.G. Law, section 84.

Minister is empowered to order a council to take disciplinary measures, including dismissal, against any employee whom the Minister considers to have been too leniently treated.[3]

2. *Control by the Council.* Subject to that measure of control which is vested in the Regional Authority and Minister it is, in both Eastern and Western Regions, for a council to employ such persons as it thinks necessary for the efficient discharge of its functions.[4] Local government employees are not a branch of the Regional Civil Service. They work for the council which employs them and not for the Regional Government. A council will wish to do all that is reasonably possible to foster a sense of loyalty to, and enthusiasm for, the good reputation of the council throughout all grades of its staff.

Day-to-day administration of staff matters should not appear in the agenda of a full council meeting. Responsibility for routine staff matters should be delegated, either to a committee or to the chief officer in charge of a department. Certain important aspects of the control of staff should, however, not be delegated but be reserved to the full council. In the Western Region recommendations to the Regional Authority concerning the appointment of a secretary, treasurer, or any chief officer on a salary with a maximum of £350 per annum, should normally be made by resolution passed in full council. In the same way in the Eastern Region recommendations to the Minister concerning the employment or dismissal of a chief officer of the council should be the subject of a formal resolution by the full council. Any recommendations for increased establishment or for the upgrading of certain posts would normally be initiated by the appropriate service committee, considered by the establishments committee, and finally come before the full council in the reports from the committees concerned.

3. *Control by Departmental Committees.* Every department of the council should have a standing committee responsible for its general oversight and control. This committee will expect to have a powerful voice in the appointment, discipline and

---

[3] W.R. (Local Government) Staff Regulations J2 and J3.
[4] E.R.L.G. Law, section 94; W.R.L.G. Law, section 84.

dismissal of the staff working in the department for which it is responsible. If the departmental committee thinks that the number of staff working the department is insufficient, or if it thinks that certain members of its staff are underpaid and should be up-graded, then it will have to make recommendations on the subject to the full council. All such recommendations will be considered by the finance and establishments committee before they come before the council. The council will wish to have the comments of the establishments committee on any such proposals, with particular reference to the output of work by the staff of the department asking for additional staff as compared with the productivity of the staff of other departments. The establishments committee may also comment on the grading of staff bearing comparable responsibilities in the various departments of the council. The place of the establishments or staff committee was further considered in Chapter VIII on p.59.

A departmental committee may expect to have delegated to it the council's responsibility in respect of the appointment and dismissal of all staff in the department other than the chief officer. Subject to the control exercised by the Minister the filling of junior posts within the establishment approved by the council may well be made the responsibility of the departmental committee. Any appointments or dismissals made by a committee under delegated powers must in the Eastern Region be authorised by the written approval of the Minister.[5]

4. *Control by Chief Officers*. The term 'Chief Officer' may be defined as that official who is declared by the council to be responsible for the direction and supervision of a department or branch of the council. Since neither a council nor any of its committees can be in continuous session most of the routine direction of staff within the departments of the council will be left to the chief officers. It may be noted that the Western Region (Local Government) Staff Regulations, 1955, use the term 'Head of Department' in place of the term 'Chief Officer'. These staff Regulations confer much power and responsibility in respect of staff upon the 'Head of Department'. Before final selection of candidates for permanent establishment is made by the council,

[5] E.R.L.G. Law, section 95.

or by a committee under delegated powers, the appropriate head of department is required to produce a list of all applicants, indicating those who are considered by him as qualified and suitable for appointment. From among the names of those applicants deemed to be suitable the council or committee will make its final selection.[6]

Appointments of unestablished staff of a council are to be made in such manner as may be resolved by the council after consultation with the 'head of department concerned'.[7]

It is normal for a chief officer to be empowered to suspend any of his junior officers for gross misconduct, pending consideration of his report on the incident by the appropriate committee. It is normal, too, for a chief officer to be empowered to employ and dismiss daily paid staff. Thus the Works Committee may well recommend to the council that control of daily paid road labour be delegated not to the committee but direct to that official responsible for the supervision of the Works Department. The official would, of course, be bound by the establishment and estimates which the council had approved.

5. *Establishments Officer.* In the largest councils it may be necessary to appoint an official to the office of 'Establishments Officer' with his own small department. The establishments officer acts as adviser to the Establishments Committee in the same way that the treasurer acts as adviser to the Finance Committee. Such an establishments officer must keep under continuous review the numbers, grading and service conditions of all employees, so as to ensure that the decisions of the council are being effectively applied and that as far as is possible uniform standards obtain throughout the council's service. The establishments officer is also responsible for maintaining the necessary staff records. In all except the largest councils the best arrangement is for the secretary of the council to act as establishments officer. If the council operates a joint finance and establishments committee, both secretary and treasurer will be present whenever it meets, in order to offer advice.

[6] The Western Region (Local Government) Staff Regulations, 1955; Part B, Regulation 4.
[7] The Western Region (Local Government) Staff Regulations, 1955; Part B, Regulation 11.

6. *Records of service.* A record of service should be maintained in respect of every employee on the permanent establishment of the council. This record should show the full history of each employee's service with the council and should be consulted, for instance, whenever the possibility of promotion for the employee is being considered. The form of Record of Service to be employed by councils in the Western Region appears as appendix I. 1 to the Western Region (Local Government) Staff Regulations.

7. *Negotiating Machinery.* The method by which salaries, wages and conditions of service for local government staff may be negotiated has not yet clearly emerged in the Eastern and Western Regions of Nigeria. In England and Wales such negotiations are conducted by a number of National Joint Councils, some working through a system of provincial councils. On the councils sit local authority, or employer, representatives appointed by the local authority associations, and also local government staff, or employee, representatives, appointed by the staff associations or trade unions. One such is the National Joint Council for Local Authorities' Administrative, Professional, Technical and Clerical Services.

8. *Staff Associations.* There is already evidence that trade unionism will become a feature of the Nigerian local government scene. While a start has already been made, there is as yet little evidence of the emergence of powerful professional associations. A Regional or National Association of Local Government Treasurers, for instance, might have a very great contribution to make to the development of local government in Nigeria. An association which would pay the costs of prosecuting any one of its members suspected of corruption, and which would pay the costs of defending any one of its members subjected to corrupt pressures, might quickly raise the standard of conduct and morale among its members. Such an association might stipulate that only those treasurers possessing certain recognised qualifications were eligible to join the association. Expulsion from the association could be the fate of inefficient or corrupt members. Before long membership of such an association

would be a matter of pride and would bring both social position and tangible benefits. Local Government councils or associations of councils might eventually recognise the association as a powerful negotiator and as the custodian of the high reputation of its members.

9. *Local Government Service Board.* Mention must be made of the existence in the Eastern Region of a Local Government Service Board. To this Board the Minister or any council may refer for advice any matter relating to the appointment, dismissal or disciplinary control of any member of a council's staff. The Minister or council is not obliged to act in accordance with the advice offered by the Board.[8]

[8] E.R.L.G. Law, section 109.

CHAPTER XIX
BYE-LAWS

Local government councils, themselves the creatures of statute, possess no inherent power of legislation. However, by section 86 of the Eastern Region Local Government Law the Regional Legislature has empowered any council in the Eastern Region to 'make bye-laws for the carrying into effect and the purposes of any function conferred upon it by this Law or any other Law or Ordinance'. A similar power has been conferred on all councils in the Western Region by section 77 of the Western Region Local Government Law. In practice bye-laws constitute an essential Instrument in the exercise of many local government functions.

The law makes it quite clear that a council may make bye-laws only in respect of those functions which have been specifically conferred upon it. The majority of these functions will have been conferred in the Instrument establishing the council. A study of section 80 of the Eastern Region Local Government Law and section 77 of the Western Region Local Government Law will reveal many functions which cannot effectively be exercised unless bye-laws are first made.

1. *Penalties*. The Regional Legislatures, in conferring on local government councils the power to make bye-laws, have laid down a number of limitations restricting the exercise of this power. The first is in respect of penalties which may be prescribed in such bye-laws. Section 86(1) of the Eastern Law specifies a fine not exceeding twenty-five pounds, or, in default of payment, imprisonment not exceeding six months for any breach of bye-laws. Section 77(1) of the Western Law specifies a maximum fine of fifty pounds with the alternative of six months' imprisonment. Both sections prescribe further penalties for continuing offences. It should be noted that imprisonment can be prescribed only in default of payment of whatever fine is

imposed. Bye-laws should always specify the particular bye-laws (sections) the breach of which will render the offender liable to penalties. It is not enough to prescribe a penalty for 'any breach of these bye-laws'. Such a provision is described as an 'omnibus penalty clause' and is not acceptable.

2. *Payment of Fees*. Section 86 (2) of the Eastern Region Local Government Law allows bye-laws to make provision for the payment of such fees or charges as the council may deem fit. Section 86 (3) empowers a council to authorise the remission of any such fee or charge. In the Western Region Local Government Law sections 77 (3) and 77 (4) make identical provisions.

3. *Exercise of Concurrent Functions*. Section 77 (6) of the Western Region Local Government Law provides that a bye-law made by a District or Local Council shall not be inconsistent with any bye-law made by a Divisional Council which is in force within the area of authority of such District or Local Council. A paragraph is generally inserted in the Instrument establishing Divisional Councils to the effect that in any matter in which the Divisional Council and a District or Local Council are empowered to exercise concurrent functions, the Divisional Council shall not make bye-laws inconsistent with any provision of a bye-law made by a District or Local Council, and to which such a council objects, without the approval of the Ministry of Local Government.

By sections 86 (5) and 86 (6) of the Eastern Region Local Government Law the responsibility for avoiding inconsistency is thrown upon the council responsible for the smaller area. A bye-law made by a District or Local Council must not be inconsistent with any bye-law made by a County Council which is in force in the area; a bye-law made by a Local Council must not be inconsistent with any bye-law made by a District Council which is in force in the area.

4. *Notice of Intention to make Bye-laws*. Section 78 (2) of the Western Region Local Government Law requires that 'no bye-law shall be made by a council unless reasonable notice, in such a manner as the Regional Authority may approve, of the

intention of the council to make such bye-laws has been given to the inhabitants of the area to be affected thereby'. The powers of the Regional Authority under this subsection have been delegated to the Local Government Inspector.[1] It is to this official, therefore, that the council should, by resolution, suggest a method of giving reasonable notice under this subsection.

A similar provision is made by section 87 (3) of the Eastern Region Local Government Law, but here it is the Minister who is empowered to determine the manner in which notice shall be given. A ruling on this matter should be sought by any council when forwarding the first draft of any proposed bye-laws.

Councils in the Western Region when suggesting a method of giving reasonable notice might propose:

(1) To post a copy of the bye-laws in a prominent place at the council offices;

(2) To display notices in every Native Court in the area of jurisdiction of the council, drawing attention to the copy of the bye-laws posted in accordance with (1) above, and announcing the intention of the council to make the bye-laws on a specified date;

(3) To send a copy of the bye-laws to every other local government council within the area of jurisdiction of the council, giving notice of the council's intention to make the bye-laws on the specified date.

5. *Signification.* The power to make bye-laws cannot be delegated by a council to any of its committees,[2] and bye-laws must be laid before the full council for formal approval and signification. Section 87 (1) of the Eastern Region Local Government Law expressly provides that 'Bye-laws shall be made under the common seal of the council or in the case of a Local Council under the hand of two members of the council'. A similar provision occurs in section 78 (1) of the Western Region Local Government Law.

6. *Approval.* Having been signified under the common seal of the council bye-laws require approval. Approval is given in the Eastern Region by the Minister, and in the Western Region by

[1] W.R.L.N. 14 of 1954.
[2] E.R.L.G. Law, section 67; W.R.L.G. Law, section 52 (1).

the Regional Authority.[3] Before approving bye-laws the Minister or Regional Authority may amend them. It may be assumed that this power will normally be exercised only to correct minor errors, and that no major amendment would be made without reference back to the council concerned. The Regional Authority in the Western Region and the Minister in the Eastern Region may approve or refuse any bye-law submitted and may, upon the date of approval, fix the date on which the bye-law is to come into operation.[4] In the Western Region these powers have been delegated by W.R.L.N. 14 of 1954 to the Permanent Secretary to the Ministry of Local Government in the case of bye-laws made by a Divisional or District Council; to Local Government Inspectors in the case of bye-laws made by Local Councils.

7. *Publication.* Section 87 (5) of the Eastern Region Local Government Law requires that 'All bye-laws shall be published in the *Regional Gazette* or in such manner as the Minister shall determine'. Section 79 of the Western Region Local Government Law requires that 'bye-laws shall be published in such manner as the Regional Authority may approve'. This power of approval has been delegated to Local Government Inspectors by W.R.L.N. 14 of 1954, and it is to this official that the council should recommend a method of publication when forwarding bye-laws for approval. In the Western Region, as in the Eastern Region, the normal method is to publish bye-laws in the *Regional Gazette.*

8. *Distribution to Council Offices.* Section 89 (1) of the Eastern Region Local Government Law and section 81 (1) of the Western Region Local Government Law make identical provisions concerning the action to be taken on bye-laws after they have been approved. A copy of every approved bye-law must be deposited at the offices of the council by whom it was made and must at all reasonable times be open to public inspection without payment. Furthermore, a copy of such bye-laws must on application be furnished to any person on payment of such sum as the council may determine. A County Council in the Eastern

---

[3] E.R.L.G. Law, section 87 (1); W.R.L.G. Law, section 78 (1).
[4] E.R.L.G. Law, section 87 (4); W.R.L.G. Law, section 78 (3).

Region must send a copy of every bye-law made by it to every District Council situate within the area of its authority. The District Council is required to send on a copy of every bye-law received in this way to every Local Council to which they apply. Where a District Council in the Eastern Region makes a bye-law it must send a copy to the County Council and to every Local Council to which it applies.[5] In the Western Region a Divisional Council must send a copy of every bye-law made by it to every other council to whose area the bye-law applies.[6] Any council receiving a copy of a bye-law under these provisions must deposit it at its offices and make it available for inspection by the public without payment.[7]

9. *Power of Regional Authority or Minister to make Bye-laws.* By section 80 of the Western Region Local Government Law the Regional Authority is empowered at any time after having given the council reasonable notice, and having considered the representations of the council thereon, to make any bye-laws which such council is empowered to make, or to amend or revoke any bye-law made by such council. Section 88 of the Eastern Region Local Government Law confers similar power upon the Minister.

10. *Enforcement by other Councils.* Section 83 of the Western Region Local Government Law empowers a District or Local Council which has been authorised in that behalf by any bye-law made by a Divisional Council to enforce such bye-laws within the area of its authority. By section 90 of the Eastern Region Local Government Law a District Council is empowered to enforce all bye-laws made by a County Council which are for the time being in force in the area of its authority. By section 91 the same power is conferred on Local Councils in respect of bye-laws made by a District or County Council.

11. *Evidence of Bye-laws.* Section 82 of the Western Region Local Government Law provides that any court may accept as evidence without further proof a copy of a bye-law upon which is endorsed a certificate signed by the chairman of the council

---

[5] E.R.L.G. Law, section 89 (2), (3) and (4).
[6] W.R.L.G. Law, section 81 (2).
[7] E.R.L.G. Law, section 89 (5) and (6); W.R.L.G. Law, section 81 (3) and (4).

or by any other duly authorised officer, to the following effect:

(*a*) That the bye-law was made and published by the council in the prescribed manner;

(*b*) That the copy is a true copy of the bye-law;

(*c*) That on a specified date the bye-law was confirmed by the Regional Authority and came into operation on a specified date.

It follows that any official in the Western Region whose duties include the conduct of prosecutions arising out of any breach of a council's bye-laws should obtain a copy of the relevant bye-laws bearing the chairman's certificate.

12. *Native Authority Bye-laws.* Finally, reference must be made to section 223 of the Eastern Region Local Government Law and to section 223 of the Western Region Local Government Law. These sections provide that any subsidiary legislation (rules, bye-laws or orders) made by a local or native authority remains in force until revoked or replaced by any local government council established in the area of such local or native authority. Such revocation or replacement would, of course, have to be made in accordance with the provision of the law, and would normally be made in the form of amending bye-laws. In other words, when a native or local authority has been replaced by a local government council the subsidiary legislation made by such local or native authority remains in force until revoked by bye-laws made by the new council.

13. *Adoptive Bye-laws.* Section 78 A of the Western Region Local Government Law empowers the Minister to make adoptive bye-laws in respect of any local government function. A council may, by resolution, adopt any bye-laws so made, provided that they relate to a function exercised by the council. Notice of the intention to adopt such bye-laws must be given in the same way as notice is to be given of the intention to make bye-laws. When a council has made a resolution to adopt bye-laws notice to this effect is published in the *Regional Gazette*. The adoption of the bye-laws takes effect from the date of the publication of this notice.

CHAPTER XX

ACQUISITION OF LAND

A local government council in the Western Region of Nigeria is empowered for the purpose of any of its lawful functions to acquire, by agreement, land within the area of the authority of the council.[1] In the Eastern Region this is extended to cover land within or without the area of the council.[2] Subject to certain conditions a council may let or lease any land vested in it. With the consent of the Minister in the Eastern Region, and with the consent of the Regional Authority in the Western Region, a council may sell or mortgage or exchange any land which it may possess.[3]

1. *Compulsory Acquisition of Land.* Part XVI of the Eastern Region Local Government Law and Part XVII of the Western Local Government Law deal with the acquisition and disposal of land. Most of the sections in each of these parts deal with the procedure for acquiring by compulsion land which is required for the purposes of the council, and which the owner or owners are unwilling to sell by normal agreement. Land is a frequent subject of litigation in Nigeria, and it is of the greatest importance that the secretary of a council should clearly understand the legal requirements which must be satisfied before the council may obtain possession under compulsory powers. It is also important that members of a council should understand these steps, and should realise that acquisition by compulsion can never be a speedy process.

The following conditions must be satisfied before the process of compulsory acquisition may be begun:

(*a*) The land must be required for local government purposes;

(*b*) The consent of the Minister in the Eastern Region, and of

---

[1] W.R.L.G. Law, section 181.
[2] E.R.L.G. Law, section 182.
[3] E.R.L.G. Law, sections 183 and 185; W.R.L.G. Law, sections 182 and 183.

the Regional Authority in the Western Region, must be first obtained;

(c) In the Western Region, only, the land in question must be within the area of the council's jurisdiction.[4]

2. *Stages in Compulsory Acquisition.* A council must proceed to compulsory acquisition by the following stages:

(a) Prepare a preliminary survey of the land. – For this purpose officials of the council who have been authorised by the council to do so may enter the land to take levels, or dig under the subsoil, or mark out boundaries. Any damage done must be paid for by the official concerned. A dwelling or domestic compound or garden may not be entered except with the consent of the occupier, unless at least seven days' notice has been given.[5]

(b) Publish a notice of the intention to acquire the land. – Such a notice must be published in a prominent position on the land to be acquired, and outside the offices of the council. In addition, it must be published 'in such manner as is customary' in the area. A copy of the notice must be served on the persons interested or claiming to be interested in the land, 'or to such of them as shall after reasonable inquiry be known to the council'.[6] The form of this notice is set out in the Third Schedule to the Eastern Region Local Government Law and in the First Schedule to the Western Region Local Government Law. In the Eastern Region the notice states the intention of the council to seek the authority of the Minister to acquire by compulsion. In the Western Region the notice states that the consent of the Regional Authority to compulsory acquisition has already been given. In both Regions the notice must describe the land to be acquired, give the local government purposes for which the land is to be acquired, state whether the land is to be acquired permanently or for a period of years only. Where, in the Western Region, the council decides to offer alternative land to the owners this fact is to be stated in the notice.[7]

(c) Await claims from interested persons. – In the Eastern Region any person claiming to have an interest in the land

---

[4] E.R.L.G. Law, section 187; W.R.L.G. Law, section 187.
[5] E.R.L.G. Law, section 188; W.R.L.G. Law, section 188.
[6] E.R.L.G. Law, section 189; W.R.L.G. Law, section 189.
[7] E.R.L.G. Law, section 190; W.R.L.G. Law, section 189.

described in the notice must, within sixty days of the publication of the notice, deliver to the council a written statement setting out the nature of his claim. No claims are to be entertained which are not received within this period. These claims, together with a copy of the notice, are then sent to the Minister, who may make an order authorising the compulsory acquisition.[8] In the Western Region the council may take possession of the land at the expiration of the period specified in the notice, which must not be less than six weeks. Claims in the Western Region must be made by interested persons within six months of the publication of the notice, and no claim made after the six months has elapsed will be considered.[9]

(d) Settlement of claims. – In the Eastern Region claims over which there is no dispute are to be paid to the persons concerned. Disputes over compensation are to be settled in the Magistrates' Court or Supreme Court.[10] In the Western Region claims by persons who have been served with notices of the council's intention to acquire the land may be paid at the expiry of a six-month period, provided that no other claims have been lodged, and provided there is no dispute as to the amount of compensation. Disputes over the amount of compensation payable and over the apportionment of the compensation are to be determined by a native court or by an arbitrator. Any claims made within the six-month period by persons not served with a notice of the council's intention to acquire may either be agreed upon, and paid by the council, or be referred to a native court or arbitrator.[11] Any claimant in the Western Region who prefers the dispute not to be settled by a native court can choose to have the matter referred to an arbitrator. If the claimant and the council cannot agree upon the appointment of an arbitrator, the council can apply to the Regional Authority who will appoint one.[12]

3. *Registration of title.* Section 195 of the Eastern Region Local Government Law makes it compulsory for a council which has

[8] E.R.L.G. Law, sections, 192, 193 and 194.
[9] W.R.L.G. Law, sections 190 and 192.
[10] E.R.L.G. Law, sections 198 and 199.
[11] W.R.L.G. Law, sections 192, 193 and 194.
[12] W.R.L.G. Law, section 195.

acquired land by compulsion to file in the appropriate office of the Land Registry a copy of the notice of the intention to acquire, a copy of the order of the Minister, and a plan of the land in question. This plan must be of sufficient accuracy to enable the boundaries of the land to be accurately described. Section 201 of the Western Region Local Government Law permits a council to file in the appropriate office of the Land Registry the following documents:

(*a*) A copy of the notice of the council's intention to acquire;

(*b*) A plan on which is delineated as accurately as is practicable the boundaries of the land in question;

(*c*) A certificate signed by the Commissioner of Lands, to the effect that the approval of the Regional Authority has been given, that notice of the intention to acquire was properly published, and that this notice was served upon the proper persons.

CHAPTER XXI

CONTRACTS AND TENDERS

Subject to the provisions of section 63 of the Western Region Local Government Law and of section 74 of the Eastern Region Local Government Law, a council may enter into any contract necessary for the discharge of any of its functions.

1. *Approval required for Certain Contracts.* No council in the Western Region may enter into a contract to the value of two thousand pounds or upwards without the prior approval of the Regional Authority.[1] No council in the Eastern Region may enter into a contract involving the expenditure of more than one hundred pounds without the approval of the Minister.[2] In the Eastern Region the Minister may make regulations giving effect to the provisions of section 74 of the Eastern Region Local Government Law. Such regulations may provide for the establishment of tender boards and the manner in which they shall perform their functions, and also for the payment by councils of allowances to the members of such boards.[3]

2. *Invitation to Tender.* For any contract made by a council in the Eastern Region involving the expenditure of more than fifty pounds, but not exceeding the limit of one hundred pounds, in which case the Minister's approval is necessary, it is required that notice of the intention of the council to enter into the contract should be published. For such contracts tenders are to be invited. These provisions are restricted to contracts for the supply of goods and materials or for the execution of works.[4] In the Western Region any contract made by a council must be made in accordance with the standing orders of the council. In the case of

---

[1] W.R.L.G. Law, section 63 (1).
[2] E.R.L.G. Law, section 74 (2).
[3] E.R.L.G. Law, section 74 (4). Such regulations have now been made and appeared as The Local Government Tenders Boards, Regulations, 1956 in E.R.L.N. No. 94 of 1956.
[4] E.R.L.G. Law, section 74 (3).

contracts for the supply of goods and materials, or for the execution of works to the value of two hundred and fifty pounds and upwards, the standing orders of a council must require that notice of the intention of the council to enter into the contract shall be published and tenders invited. Standing orders must also regulate the manner of the publication of the notice and the manner of the award of tenders.[5] Standing orders may well require that notice of the intention of the council to enter into a contract must be published within the area of the council by the exhibition of a notice on the notice board at the offices of the council.

3. *Receipt of Tenders.* The notice of the council's intention to enter into a contract should ask for tenders to be addressed to the secretary of the council, and that these should be enclosed in a sealed envelope, marked with some description of the contract for which the tender is submitted. A brief phrase such as 'Tender for supply of school meals', or 'Tender for whitewashing of dispensaries', written on the outside of the envelope, would be appropriate. The notice of the council's intention to enter into a contract should also state the latest time and day by which tenders may be received. The secretary should place unopened in his safe every envelope containing a tender which he receives before the closing time and date. Any envelope containing a tender which is received late should be opened by the secretary at once and returned to the sender with a note to the effect that the offer was received too late for consideration.

4. *Opening of Tenders.* A council is entitled to require that tenders should be opened in full council, but it is more normal for this duty to be assigned to a committee. A committee controlling expenditure might expect to be authorised to commit the council to contracts within the limits of the funds which it controls, and to open and examine the relevant tenders. Envelopes containing tenders are usually opened by the secretary of the council, while sitting by the side of the chairman of the appropriate committee, at the meeting of the committee following the last date for the receipt of tenders. As each tender is removed from its envelope the secretary should read out its contents. He should

[5] W.R.L.G. Law, section 63 (2).

mark each tender with a number. The secretary should have a sheet of paper at his side on which to record the number given to each tender, the amount of each tender and the name of the person submitting it. The secretary should request the chairman of the committee to initial each tender as having been announced to the committee.

5. *Acceptance of Tenders*. A council is not obliged to accept the lowest tender submitted, nor need it accept any of the tenders received. If all are thought to be unreasonable the council is fully entitled to reject them all and to make other arrangements for the work required. Standing orders may, however, require that a tender, other than the lowest tender if payment is to be made by the council, or other than the highest tender if payment is to be received by the council, must not be accepted unless the committee concerned has first considered a report on the matter from the appropriate chief officer. When the committee has decided which tender is to be accepted all persons who submitted tenders should be so informed. Where the approval of the Minister or Regional Authority is required for a tender a conditional acceptance may be sent at once to the maker of the offer which the council proposes to accept.

6. *Form of Contract*. Standing Orders may well require that every contract which exceeds fifty, or perhaps one hundred pounds in amount, must be in writing and must contain a Fair Wages Clause. The object of the Fair Wages Clause is to bind the contractor to offer pay and conditions of work to his employees which are in accordance with subsisting negotiated rates and conditions. A local government council should always seek to maintain a reputation for being a model employer. Even when its works are being carried out by contract, and not by direct labour, a council should ensure that proper working conditions are maintained. Suitable wording for such a Fair Wages Clause would be suggested by the appropriate Ministry. Contracts entered into by councils must normally be made under seal, though this formality may be waived in respect of contracts for, say, less than an amount of ten pounds. Having been sealed the formal contract and the successful tender should be kept in safe custody among the important documents of the council.

CHAPTER XXII

PARTY POLITICS IN LOCAL GOVERNMENT

The participation of national political parties in local government elections and the effects of this participation on local government practice need special consideration. The composition of many local government councils in the United Kingdom is partly or wholly political. Some or all of the elected council members have contested the elections on the basis of allegiance to one of the national political parties and have invited the electorate to vote for them primarily because of their political allegiance. It appears that in Nigeria elections to the majority of local government councils will, from their inception, be conducted on party lines.

1. *Advantages of the Party System.* The extent to which the council he serves is divided on the lines of allegiance to national political parties is no direct concern of a council official. He must take his council as he finds it. Yet even for the local government official a consideration of the advantages and disadvantages of the advent of party politics into local government is of more than purely academic interest. The party system can impose peculiar strains on the organisation of a council and on the tolerance of the council members. If an official has considered the advantages and disadvantages involved in the party system he may well be able to offer to the committees and leaders of the council advice which may assist them in meeting these strains, and indeed may enable them to direct the party system to the service of efficient administration and to the advantage of the ratepayers.

There is no doubt that the incursion of national party politics into the local government scene has in the United Kingdom been responsible for an increased interest in local government elections. The interest that has been aroused by many of the first elections to councils in Nigeria is similarly attributable in part to the rivalry of political parties. Not only are these parties interested in the outcome of local government elections as a demonstration of popular support for their policies; local government elections are also frequently regarded as a training and testing ground for the party machinery. It follows that all the administrative resources of a party may be made available to a candidate for election to a district council, who would otherwise have been content with a little canvassing among his friends and neighbours as the extent of his election campaign.

Party politics can lead to a greater consistency of policy in a local government council and can help to clarify the issue before the electorate. In the United Kingdom the primary difference between the domestic policy of the two main political parties may, somewhat crudely, be summarised as 'to tax or rate high and provide generous services' (Socialism), or 'to tax or rate low and be content with less generous services' (Conservatism). This is an issue which has been apprehended by the electorate. A person voting for the Conservative candidate at a local government election understands in general terms the policy which he is supporting. The candidate, if successful, will be committed by the political philosophy of his party to a consistent line of action. Where the electorate is invited to vote for an individual because of his personal integrity and intrinsic worth the alternatives facing the elector may be less easy to grasp. The results of choosing between one independent candidate or another may be less predictable than the results of choosing between the candidate of one political party or another.

Local government officials are presented with many problems by a council which conducts its business on party lines, but there are compensating advantages. Where discipline is effective and his majority support secure the chairman of a council run on party lines may with confidence predict a decision of the council or of one of its committees. This may on occasion make the work of the council's officials easier.

2. *Disadvantages of the Party System.* There are many potential candidates for council membership who have no wish to support the policy, or submit to the discipline, of one of the political

parties. Where elections to a local government council are being conducted on party lines, such a candidate stands less chance of election. It must be regarded as a disadvantage of the party system that, by it, independent candidates having ability and integrity to offer to the service of the community are frequently excluded from council membership.

It cannot be expected that a member of the National Legislature will be personally known to all the electors in his constituency. This can, however, be hoped for of a member of a local government council. Most of the electors in a ward may well be personally acquainted with all the candidates standing for election to a council, and may hold an opinion as to which candidate is the best person, and the person most deserving of election as a councillor. However, if the elections are being fought on party lines an elector may not feel able to vote for the best man, because this candidate happens to be contesting with the support of a political party to whose national policy the elector is opposed.

A further undesirable effect of the party system in local government councils is that a good and reasonable motion may be defeated merely because it was initiated by a member of the party in the minority on the council. It sometimes happens that a suggestion of obvious merit is turned down by majority vote of the council when one party sponsors it, and is introduced at a later date in a slightly varied form by the majority party, who ensure that this time it is accepted by the council. The party system may thus delay the introduction of an improvement because of the determination of one party that no beneficial measure should be associated in the mind of the electorate with their political rivals.

The irrelevance of national party policies to most local lgovernment decisions is often apparent. There can be no part ine on the selection of a site for a new Muslim cemetery. Party politics are not involved in a consideration of how best to combat soil erosion. A solution to such problems as these must be sought on the merits of the case by people having intimate knowledge of the locality. Such is the business of local government. Considerations of party politics must often appear as an extraneous complication.

3. *Party Politics in the Machinery of Local Government.* Where a local council is organised on party lines it is natural and right that the chairman of the council should be a member of the majority party. It is also natural that the majority party should ensure that a majority of its own supporters should be appointed to each committee of the council. It is most undesirable that a party should use its majority in the council to exclude from committee membership all councillors of other political persuasions. It is a good principle that seats on all committees should, by agreement, be allocated in the same proportions as political parties are represented in the council. Once one political party uses its majority to ensure that no member of another party shall serve as a committee member there is a danger that this action will be regarded as the standard practice for that council. Then, if at a subsequent election a different party secures the majority of seats in the council, none of the members of the committees of the previous council will stand a chance of re-appointment to a committee. There will be no continuity of committee policy, and the benefit of the experience gained by the previous set of committee members will be lost to the council. Efficient administration will suffer while completely fresh committee members acquire their experience. On the other hand, a majority party which agrees that some places on each committee shall be filled by supporters of rival parties can expect to receive similar treatment if changes in political fortunes subsequently leave it with a minority on the council. In local government tolerance is the best policy.

A committee is free to elect its own chairman by majority vote. Ideally a committee should select that member who is best suited to act as chairman. Such a person may have proved his ability in a profession or in commerce. The chairman of a committee has no legal powers which are not common to all the committee members, and the majority party has nothing to fear in seeing a supporter of another party elected to the chair of a committee. The majority party will justifiably wish to have a majority of their own supporters on the finance committee. Where chairmen of standing committees are ex-officio members of finance committee this point must be borne in mind. If in one or two committees the person best qualified to act as chairman happens to be a member of another party it would be commendable if the majority party agreed to support his election.

4. *Local Government Officials and Party Politics.* By Regulation 17 of Part F of the Western Region (Local Government) Staff Regulations, 1954,[1] all employees of local government councils are forbidden to engage in local, regional or national political activities. It is also the policy of the Eastern Region Government to ensure that any employee of a council who is elected to the Regional or Federal Legislature must relinquish his employment with the council. Wherever he is serving a local government official can hardly expect that his advice will be accepted as the impartial opinion of a specialist if he has closely identified himself with the fortunes of one political party or another. It would be only reasonable for a newly elected council to be uneasy about the loyalty of an official who had identified himself closely with a political party which commanded the majority in a previous council. Senior local government officials, no less than senior civil servants, should keep any political convictions which they may have entirely to themselves.

[1] Made by the Regional Authority under powers conferred by section 92 of the Western Region Local Government Law.

APPENDICES

The Western Region Local Government Law, 1952, is printed with all amendments made up to 1 October 1955 inserted in the text. This version has been taken from the Local Government Manual issued by the Government of the Western Region of Nigeria for the guidance of Local Government Councils.

WESTERN REGION LOCAL GOVERNMENT LAW, 1952

ARRANGEMENT OF SECTIONS

144

A LAW TO MAKE PROVISION FOR LOCAL GOVERNMENT IN THE WESTERN REGION AND FOR PURPOSES CONNECTED THEREWITH

Date of commencement: 26 February 1953

PART I. PRELIMINARY

Short title

1. This Law may be cited as the Western Region Local Government Law, 1952.

Definitions

2. Definitions:

'casual vacancy' means a vacancy in a council occurring otherwise than by reason of the retirement of members of the council in accordance with section 30 of this Law;

'chairman' means the chairman of a council elected or appointed under section 29 of this Law, and includes any person presiding at a meeting of a council in the absence of the chairman by virtue of the provisions of section 40 of this Law.

'chief' means any person recognised as a chief by the Governor.

'council' means any local government council established by Instrument under the provision of this Law.

'councillor' means a member of a council, whether traditional or elected;

'court' includes the Supreme Court, the High Court, a Magistrate's Court and a Native Court;

'functions' include duties and powers;

'High Court' means the High Court of the Western Region; provided that until that court shall have assumed its functions in accordance with the provisions of the Law by which it is established any reference to the High Court shall be construed as a reference to the Supreme Court of Nigeria;

'Instrument' means the Instrument by which a local government council is established under the provisions of this Law and shall include any Instrument varying or amending such Instrument;

'land' means all land other than Crown Lands and land which is the subject of a lease under the Crown Lands Ordinance;

'local government purposes' mean for exclusive local government use or for carrying out any of the duties imposed by this Law or for the purposes of Parts XV and XVI of this Law or for the provision of any public service (whether partly or wholly provided by the council) or for the preservation and development of natural resources and without derogation from the generality of the foregoing shall include provision for any of the following:

(a) water and electricity supplies;

(b) installations, structures or schemes in connection with sanitation or public health;

(c) schemes for laying out or planning existing or new towns or villages;

(d) community centres and places of public assembly under the control of the council;

(e) schools, colleges, laboratories and training institutions;

(f) public reading rooms, libraries, and museums;

(g) hospitals and dispensaries;

(h) markets and pounds;

(i) open spaces and recreation grounds;

(j) burial grounds;

(k) grazing grounds and cattle staging posts;

(l) offices and buildings for council departments;

(m) housing for council staff;

(n) experimental and demonstration farms or seed or stock multiplication centres;

(o) schemes for planned rural development or settlement; and

(p) native courts and lock-ups;

'member of a council' and 'member of a committee' include the chairman and a councillor of that council or committee whether elected, appointed or co-opted;

'the Minister' means the Minister to whom responsibility for local government is assigned in accordance with section 119 of the Nigeria (Constitution) Order in Council, 1954;

'native authority' means a native authority appointed under the Native Authority Ordinance (Cap. 140) and includes a subordinate native authority;

'officer' includes servant;

'Primary school' and 'Secondary school' have the meanings assigned to these terms in the Education Law, 1954;

'Regional Authority' means the Governor in Council;

'traditional member' means a chief appointed or elected by name or by reference to his title as a traditional member of a council as provided in the Instrument.

NOTE. The definition of 'casual vacancy' was inserted by Law No. 18 of 1955; the words 'or appointed' were inserted in the definition of 'chairman' by Law No. 13 of 1955; the definitions of 'councillor', 'High Court' and 'the Minister' were inserted by Law No. 13 of 1955; the words 'High Court' were inserted in the definition of 'court' by Law No. 13 of 1955; the definition of 'Primary School' and 'Secondary School' was amended by Law No. 6 of 1955.

Throughout the Law the references to 'Lieutenant-Governor' and 'Lieutenant-Governor in Council' were altered to 'Governor' and 'Governor-in-Council' by Legal Notice No. 131 of 1954.

PART II.   ESTABLISHMENT OF LOCAL GOVERNMENT COUNCILS

Establishment of councils [see pp.15-20]

3. (1) Subject to the provisions of subsections (3) and (4) of this section the Regional Authority may by Instrument establish such council or councils for the purposes of local government as he may deem necessary or expedient.

(2) (*a*) Such councils shall be Divisional Councils, District Councils, or Local Councils, as the Regional Authority may determine.

(*b*) A District Council may be designated by the Regional Authority, in the Instrument relating to the council, as an Urban District Council or a Rural District Council.

(4) Before any council is established under subsection (1) of this section the Regional Authority shall cause to be made such inquiries as he may deem desirable for the purpose of ascertaining the wishes of the inhabitants of the area concerned and may treat any inquiries in that behalf made before the commencement of this Law as inquiries made in pursuance of the provisions of this subsection.

NOTE. Subsection (2) was substituted by Law No. 13 of 1955; subsection (3) as originally enacted was deleted by Legal Notice 131 of 1954.

Publication and construction of Instrument

4. (1) Every Instrument shall be prepared in duplicate and shall be signed by the Regional Authority in such manner as the Regional Authority may determine; one copy shall be retained by the Regional Authority and one by the council concerned.

(2) Every Instrument shall be published in the *Regional Gazette.*

(3) Every Instrument shall be read and construed as one with this Law and shall be of the same force and effect as if it were enacted in this Law:

Provided that in the event of any conflict between the provisions of any Instrument and the provisions of this Law, the provisions of this Law shall prevail.

Contents of Instrument [see p.17]

5. (1) In addition to any other matter which is required by this Law to be inserted in an Instrument, every Instrument establishing a council shall:

(*a*) specify the name and type of council and the date it shall be established;

(*b*) describe the device of the seal of the council;

(*c*) define the limits of the area of the authority of the council;

(*d*) provide for the constitution of the council, the number of councillors and the date for the first election;

(*e*) define the functions of the council;

(*f*) provide for the appointment of a president of the council or for the election or appointment of a chairman, or both;

(*g*) specify the method of the election or the system of the appointment of a chairman of a council;

(*h*) provide for the election or appointment of councillors or the election of some and the appointment of other councillors of the same council;

(*i*) specify the method of election, or the system of appointment of traditional members of the council;

(*j*) specify the qualifications of the persons or bodies of persons entitled to elect or to appoint a chairman or traditional members as the case may be; and

(*k*) provide for the quorum of the council.

(2) An Instrument may:

(*a*) provide for the division of the area of the authority of the council into wards; and specify the number of councillors to represent each ward;

(*b*) subject to the provisions of this Law, specify the system of rating where a council is empowered to levy or collect rates;

(*c*) require a council to set up a standing committee other than a Finance Committee for any specified purpose;

(*d*) specify the date or dates for the election of councillors;

(*e*) provide for the use of a rubber stamp in lieu of a seal until such time as a seal be procured;

(*f*) require a council to engage and pay adequate staff (including clerks) for any Native Court which is established or situate within the area of its authority, and give directions regarding the disposal of the fees, fines, forfeitures, and penalties payable in respect of or as a result of proceedings in such Court; and

(g) generally make such other provision not inconsistent with this Law as is necessary or expedient for the establishment and conduct of the council and the proper performance of its functions.

NOTE. Law No. 18 of 1955 substituted paragraph (i) for that paragraph as originally enacted and amended paragraph (j) by substituting the words 'traditional members' for the word 'councillors'.

Incorporation of councils

6. Every council established under the provisions of this Law shall be a body corporate having perpetual succession and a common seal and power to hold land and to sue and and be sued.

PART III. POWERS OF THE REGIONAL AUTHORITY

Power to amend Instrument [see pp.18-19]

7. (1) Subject to the provisions of this section and of section 8 of this Law, the Regional Authority may of his own motion or in his absolute discretion on the application of any person concerned, if he shall think fit, amend the Instrument establishing any council.

(2) The Regional Authority shall not amend an Instrument in any of the following ways, unless he has complied with the provisions of subsection (3) of this section:

(a) change the name of the council;

(b) alter the status of the council;

(c) add to, take away from or impose any conditions upon the exercise of any of the functions of the council; or

(d) alter the constitution of the council, the method of election or appointment of the president or chairman, or the councillors, or the system of rating.

(3) Before making an amendment in any of the respects specified in subsection (2) of this section the Regional Authority shall:

(a) cause to be published in the area concerned not less than thirty clear days' notice of his intention to exercise his powers under this section;

(b) give an opportunity to the council concerned to make representations to him in writing; and

(c) cause such inquiries to be made as he may deem desirable for the purpose of ascertaining the wishes of the inhabitants of the area concerned.

(4) The Regional Authority shall not issue an amending Instrument dissolving a council except in accordance with the provisions of section 9 or 10 of this Law.

NOTE. This section was substituted for section 7 as originally enacted by the amendment contained in Law No. 13 of 1955.

Alteration of the area of the authority of a council

8. (1) Where the Regional Authority considers, either on the receipt of proposals from the council concerned, or otherwise, that a *prima facie* case exists for any of the following changes, namely:

(a) an alteration or definition of the boundaries of the area of the authority of a council;

(b) the division of the area of the authority of a council;

(c) the transfer of any part of the area of the authority of a council to another council;

(d) the union of the area of the authority of a council with the area of the authority of another council;

(e) the formation of a new council in the area of or part of the area of the authority of an existing council;

the Regional Authority shall cause an inquiry to be held under the provisions of section 14 in the locality concerned.

(2) If the Regional Authority is satisfied after holding such inquiry that any such change as aforesaid is desirable, he may by an amending Instrument give effect to such change.

(3) The Regional Authority may by Instrument make such incidental consequential or supplemental provisions with respect to administrative arrangements as may appear to be necessary or proper for the purposes of carrying out such change or for giving full effect thereto and without prejudice to the generality of the foregoing may by such Instrument:

(a) provide for the abolition or establishment, or the restriction or extension of the jurisdiction of any council in or over any part of the area affected by such Instrument;

(c) provide for the adjustment or alteration of the boundaries of any area affected by such change or of the area of the authority of any council wholly or in part situate within such affected area, or for the union of the area of the authority of any councils;

(d) transfer, extend or limit the functions of any council within the area affected;

(e) provide for the constitution and election of a council in any such area or for the amendment, alteration, extension or exclusion of any constitution or system of election of any existing council with respect to such altered area;

(*f*) provide for the transfer of any writs, process, records or documents relating to or to be executed in any part of the area affected by such change and for determining questions arising from such transfer; or

(*g*) provide for the adjustment of any property, debt, right or liability affected by such change.

Failure to hold meetings [see p.19]

9. (1) If any council shall at any time fail to meet with the minimum frequency required by the provisions of section 34 (1) of Part V of this Law the Regional Authority may cause an inquiry to be held under the provisions of section 14, at which inquiry the council concerned shall be given an opportunity of being heard.

(2) The Regional Authority upon considering the report of such inquiry may issue an amending Instrument dissolving the council and shall by the same Instrument establish a new council under the provisions of this Law or appoint other fit and proper persons, not being less than five in number, to form a new council for the purposes of this Law.

Failure properly to apply revenues, to levy rates, or to conform to statutory obligations

10. (1) If at any time it shall appear that the revenues of a council are not being properly used in the best interest of the area as a whole, or that the administration of the affairs of the council has failed, or that there has been substantial failure to carry out the provisions of this Law relating to the levy of rates or to act in conformity with the provisions of this Law, the Regional Authority shall cause an inquiry to be held under the provisions of section 14 at which inquiry the council concerned shall be given an opportunity of being heard.

(2) The Regional Authority upon considering the report of such inquiry, and if he shall consider it in the best interests of the area as a whole to do so may issue an amending Instrument dissolving the council and shall by the same Instrument establish a new council under the provisions of this Law or appoint other fit and proper persons, not being less than five in number, to form a new council for the purposes of this Law.

Effect of issue of amending Instrument

11. An Instrument issued under the provisions of sections 7, 8, 9

or 10 shall not unless the contrary intention appears affect the validity of any decision taken or act done by the council existing at the time of the issue of such Instrument and shall not affect any right, privilege, obligation or liability accrued or incurred or existing at the time of the issue of such Instrument.

Failure to carry out work or to make or to enforce bye-laws [see p. 44]

12. If any council shall fail to do or carry out any work or thing which it is or may be empowered under the provisions of this or any other Law or Ordinance to do or carry out, or shall fail to make, amend, revoke or enforce any bye-laws on any matters upon which it is empowered to make, amend, revoke or enforce bye-laws, and such failure on the part of the council constitutes, in the opinion of the Regional Authority, a grave danger and menace to the health safety or welfare of the public within or without the area, the Regional Authority may give notice to the council in default, requiring it to take measures within its powers under the provisions of this or any other Law to abate and remove such danger within such time as he may specify; and if the council shall fail to take and properly carry out the required measures, the Regional Authority, upon being satisfied that the council has so failed without reasonable cause, may, notwithstanding the provisions of section 80:

(*a*) make such bye-laws as may be necessary to abate and remove such danger, and such bye-laws shall, until revoked by the Regional Authority, have the force and effect of law within the area concerned;

(*b*) authorise any person or persons to do or carry out any works or things and to spend such moneys in so doing or carrying out works or things as to him may seem necessary and such person or persons shall be deemed to have vested in him or them all of the powers of the council in respect of the doing or carrying out of the particular work or thing; and any moneys so expended under the authority of the Regional Authority shall be a debt due to the Regional Authority charged on the revenues of the council concerned.

Revocation of Instruments [see pp. 19-20]

13. (1) Subject to the provisions of this section the Regional Authority may of his own motion or in his absolute discretion on the application of any persons concerned, if he shall think fit, revoke the Instrument relating to a Council.

(2) Before revoking an Instrument the Regional Authority shall give an opportunity to the council concerned to make representations to him in writing with respect to such revocation:

Provided that an Instrument may be revoked by the Regional Authority at any time before the date appointed for the first election to the council without the council being given an opportunity to make representations as aforesaid.

NOTE. Law No. 18 substituted this section for section 13 as originally enacted

Power to hold inquiries

14. (1) The Regional Authority may cause such inquiries to be held at such times and in such places as he may consider necessary or desirable for the purposes of this Law.

(2) The Regional Authority may appoint in writing any person to conduct any such inquiry.

(3) A person so appointed may sit with or without assessors and shall submit a report of such inquiry to the Regional Authority.

(4) The Regional Authority or persons appointed by him under this section shall cause a notice of the time and place of the inquiry to be given to the councils and persons appearing to him to be interested.

(5) Where the Regional Authority causes an inquiry to be held the costs of such inquiry shall be defrayed by such council or person as he may direct and the amount certified by him to be paid by such council or person shall be a debt due to the Regional Authority from that council or person.

Powers of Regional Authority or person appointed to hold inquiry

15. The Regional Authority and any person appointed by him in writing under section 14 shall have the following powers:

(*a*) to procure all such evidence, written or oral, and to examine all such persons as witnesses as the Regional Authority or person appointed by him may think necessary;

(*b*) to require the evidence of any witness to be made on oath or declaration, such oath or declaration to be that which could be required of the witness if he were giving evidence in a Magistrate's Court;

(*c*) to summon any person in the Region to attend any inquiry to give evidence or procure any document or other thing in his possession and examine him as a witness or require him to produce any document or other thing in his possession;

(*d*) to issue a warrant to compel the attendance of any person who, after having been summoned to attend, fails to do so, and does not excuse such failure to the satisfaction of the Regional Authority or person appointed by him, and to order him to pay all costs which may have been occasioned in compelling his attendance or by reason of his refusal to obey the summons, and also to fine such a person a sum not exceeding fifty pounds, such fine to be recoverable in the same manner as a fine imposed by a Magistrate's Court;

(*e*) to enter upon any land, including Crown land, for the purpose of obtaining information or evidence; and

(*f*) to admit any evidence whether written or oral which might be inadmissible in civil or criminal proceedings.

Obligation of witness at inquiry to answer

16. A person called as a witness in any inquiry held under section 14 shall not be excused from answering any question on the ground that the answer thereto may criminate or tend to criminate himself or on the ground of privilege:

Provided that an answer by a person to a question put by or before the person presiding at the inquiry shall not, except in the case of any criminal proceedings for perjury in respect of such evidence, be in any proceedings, civil or criminal, admissible in evidence.

Appointment of Local Government Inspectors and Assistant Local Government Inspectors [see p. 42]

17. (1) The Regional Authority may by notice in the *Regional Gazette* appoint in respect of any council or group of councils a Local Government Inspector and such Assistant Local Government Inspectors as may be deemed necessary and may delegate to them such of his functions as he may think fit, except the functions conferred by sections 3, 4, 33, 92, 94, 128 and 217 of this Law.

(2) Any delegation made under the provisions of subsection (1) shall be revocable at will, and no such delegation shall be deemed to prevent the exercise of any delegated function by the Regional Authority.

(3) In the exercise of any function delegated to him under subsection (1) of this section and of any other functions conferred upon him by or under this Law a Local Government Inspector or an Assistant Local Government Inspector shall act on behalf of the Regional Authority and in accordance with any general or particular instructions issued to him by the Regional Authority, but the

the consent, in writing, of the Regional Authority, who has, within a period of ten years immediately before the date of election or appointment, been an unsuccessful candidate for any office or title of chief in or associated with the area of such council.

(3) For the purpose of subsection (2), the term 'unsuccessful candidate' shall mean any candidate, claimant, pretender or contestant for any office or title of chief, other than the person expressly recognised as the holder of such office or title by the person or body entitled to accord such recognition, who has been a party in a dispute within the provisions of subsection (2) of section 2 of the Appointment and Deposition of Chiefs Ordinance or any Law or Ordinance (Cap. 12).

NOTE. Paragraph (aa) in subsection (1) was inserted by Law No. 13 of 1955; the proviso to paragraph (d) in subsection (1) was substituted by Law No. 13 of 1955; subsections (2) and (3) were inserted by Law No. 8 of 1953.

Disqualification for office by reason of non-disclosure of contract with council [see p. 34]

25. A person shall be disqualified for being elected or appointed to be a member of a council if he is a party to any subsisting contract with the council concerned for and on account of the public service, and has not published within one month before the day of election to the electors in the area concerned a notice setting out the nature of such contract and his interest therein or informed the person or body of persons by whom he is to be appointed as the case may be:

Provided that a person shall not be disqualified for being a councillor by reason only of his holding the office of returning officer for that council unless he has directly or indirectly by himself or his partner received any profit or remuneration in respect of that office.

Tenure of office of members of council

26. (1) Every member of a council shall, without prejudice to his re-election or re-appointment in accordance with the provisions of this Law, cease to be a member of the council at the expiration of his term of office under section 30 of this Law, or previously thereto if his seat becomes vacant under the provisions of this Law.

(2) The seat of a member of a council shall become vacant:

(a) upon his death; or

(aa) upon a dissolution of the council; or

(b) if he is absent from four consecutive ordinary meetings of the council without good cause or without having obtained from the chairman, before the termination of any such meeting, permission to be absent or to remain absent therefrom:

Provided that the provisions of this paragraph shall not apply to a traditional member of a council; or

(*c*) if, being a chief and a traditional member, he ceases to be a chief:

Provided that in such case he shall be eligible for re-appointment if he again becomes a chief; or

(*d*) if, not being authorised by the Regional Authority to retain his seat, he is appointed to, or to act in, any office or place of profit in the gift or disposal of the council;

(*e*) if by writing addressed to the chairman he resigns his seat; or

(*f*) if he becomes subject to any of the disqualifications specified in section 24 of this Law.

(3) Any person whose seat in a council has become vacant may, if qualified, again be elected or appointed as a member of a council from time to time.

NOTE. Law No. 13 of 1955 inserted paragraph (*aa*) and substituted paragraph (*b*) for that paragraph as originally enacted.

Decision of questions as to membership

27. All questions which may arise under section 26 of this Law as to the right of any person to remain a member of a council shall be referred to and determined by the Minister.

NOTE. Law No. 13 of 1955 substituted this section for section 27 as originally enacted.

President of council [see p. 74]

28. (1) A council may have a president to be named in the Instrument, who may preside, and may avail himself of the advice and assistance of the chairman, at any meeting of the council.

(2) The president shall be an *ex officio* member of the council.

(3) Notwithstanding that there is no president for the time being of a council, the council may perform and exercise all its duties, functions and powers sitting with a chairman as provided in section 29 of this Law.

Chairman of council [see p. 24]

29. (1) Every council shall have an elected chairman.

(2) The chairman of a council shall be elected annually by the council from among the elected and traditional members thereof and shall be eligible for re-election:

Provided that if a majority of the total membership of a council so desire the Regional Authority may appoint the president of the council to be the chairman of the council.

(3) Whenever a casual vacancy occurs in the office of chairman, an election to fill the vacancy shall be held at the next meeting of the council held after the date on which the vacancy occurs. A person elected to fill such casual vacancy shall hold office until the date upon which the person in whose place he is elected would regularly have retired and he shall then retire, but shall be eligible for re-election.

(4) No person shall be elected as chairman without his consent to be so elected.

(5) A chairman of a council, at any time during his term of office, may resign or may be removed from his office by resolution carried by three-fourths of the total membership of the council.

Term of office of the members of council

30. (1) Unless otherwise provided in the Instrument the term of office of the elected and traditional members shall be three years and the whole number of such members of the council shall retire:

(a) in the case of District and Local Councils on the 15th day of April; and

(b) in the case of Divisional Councils on the 30th day of April; in every third year, and their places shall be filled by newly elected or appointed members who shall come into office on that date:

Provided that the Instrument may specify that every year on the respective days of April one-third (or as near as may be) of the elected members shall retire, the names of those required to retire after each of the first two years being decided by lot.

(2) Any person about to retire under the provisions of this section may, if qualified, seek re-election or be re-appointed for a further term of office.

(3) No person shall be elected or appointed to be a member of a council without his consent.

Vacant seats to be reported

31. Whenever a casual vacancy occurs among the members of the council the chairman shall forthwith report the vacancy to the Minister in writing.

Filling of casual vacancies

32. (1) Where a casual vacancy has occurred among the members of a council, a new member to fill such vacancy shall, within sixty days from the date of the occurrence of the vacancy, be elected or

appointed, as the case may be, in the same manner as the person whose place he is to take was elected or appointed:

Provided that, in the case of a vacancy among the elected members of a District or Local Council, if the vacancy occurs within a period of less than six months before the next general local election, the vacancy shall not be filled.

(2) A person elected or appointed under this section to fill a casual vacancy shall hold office until the date upon which the person in whose place he is elected or appointed would ordinarily have retired, and he shall then retire.

(3) In this section 'general local election' means, in relation to a council, an election to fill the vacancies on the council caused by the retirement of members of the council in accordance with the provisions of section 30 of this Law.

NOTE: Subsection (3) was inserted by Law No. 13 of 1955.

Regulations as to elections [see p. 30]

33. (1) Subject to the provisions of this Law, the Governor-in-Council may by regulation make provision for the election of persons as elected members of Divisional, District or Local Councils including (without prejudice to the generality of the foregoing power) the following matters:

(*a*) the registration of electors;

(*aa*) the qualifications and disqualifications of electors;

(*b*) the ascertainment of the qualifications of persons who submit themselves for election;

(*c*) the holding of elections, direct or indirect;

(*d*) the division of the area of authority of any council for any purposes connected with election;

and any regulations made under this subsection may provide for different methods of election in respect of different kinds of council or in respect of different parts of the Region.

(2) The Governor-in-Council may by regulation make provision for:

(*a*) the disqualification of any person for membership of a council by reason of his holding or acting in any office the functions of which involve:

(i) any responsibility for, or in connection with, the conduct of any election; or

(ii) any responsibility for, or in connection with, the compilation or revision of any electoral register; and (*b*) the definition and trial of offences relating to elections and the imposition of penalties therefor, not exceeding a fine of two hundred pounds or imprisonment for two years, including disqualification for membership of a council, or for registration as an elector, or for voting at elections, of any person concerned in any such offence.

(3) (*a*) The Governor-in-Council may by regulation provide that:

(i) in any case in which an election of elected members of a council is carried out by a process of indirect election, a person shall not be qualified to be elected as a member of that council at such election unless he is a member of such electoral body as may be prescribed by such regulations;

(ii) in any case in which an election of elected members of a council is carried out by a process of direct election, a person shall not be qualified to be elected as a member of that council at such election unless he is registered as an elector for the purposes of that election.

(*b*) In this sub-section 'electoral body' means a body of persons constituted in accordance with regulations made under this section for the purpose of the election of members of a council.

(4) The Governor-in-Council may by regulation provide for determining whether any person has become an elected member of a council and for determining any question which may arise as to the right of any person to remain an elected member of a council other than questions required to be referred to and determined by the Minister in accordance with section 2 of this Law.

NOTE. Law No. 13 of 1955 substituted this section for the section originally enacted as section 33; paragraph (*aa*) was inserted by Law No. 18 of 1955. Subsidiary legislation made under this section and in force on 1 September 1955, is the Western Region (Local Government) (Elections) Regulations 1953 (Regulations 1 of 1953) as amended by Western Region Legal Notices 1 of 1954 and 101 of 1955; these regulations will cease to have effect upon the commencement of all parts of the Parliamentary and Local Government Electoral Regulations, 1955, which will then be, in so far as it provides for elections to local government councils, the subsidiary legislation in force under this section.

PART V. MEETINGS AND PROCEEDINGS OF COUNCILS

Number of meetings [see p. 66]

34. (1) A council shall in every year hold at least four (or such greater number as the Regional Authority may direct) ordinary meetings for the transaction of general business.

(2) Such meetings shall be held on such days as the council may by Standing Order determine.

Convening of meetings [see p. 67]

35. (1) The president or the chairman of a council may call a meeting of the council at any time either on his own motion or upon requisition of one-third of the members of the council.

(2) If the president or the chairman of a council refuses to call a meeting of the council after a written requisition so to do signed by one-third of the members of the council has been presented to him, or if, without so refusing, such president or chairman does not, within ten days after such requisition has been presented to him, cause to be published, in accordance with the provisions of section 36 of this Law, a notice calling a meeting not later than ten days after such publication, the persons presenting the requisition may forthwith, on such refusal or on expiration of ten days, as the case may be, call a meeting of the council.

(3) A meeting of the council for the purpose of electing a chairman shall be called by the clerk to the council within fourteen days of the date upon which, after a general local election, the newly elected members take office, and within fourteen days of the date when any vacancy in the chairmanship occurs.

(4) The date of the first meeting of a council after the commencement of this Law shall be prescribed by the Instrument.

Notice of meetings [see pp. 67-8]

36. (1) Except as provided in subsection (2) of this section a notice shall be published, at least ten clear days before a meeting of a council, other than the first meeting of such council after the commencement of this Law, at the offices or regular place of meeting of the council, stating the time and place of the meeting and the business proposed to be transacted thereat.

(2) The president or the chairman of a council may call an emergency meeting upon giving forty-eight hours notice thereof published in the manner specified in subsection (1) of this section.

(3) Every such notice shall be signed by the president or the chairman except when the meeting is called under subsection (2) or subsection (3) of section 35 of this Law, when the notice shall be signed by the members calling the meeting or by the clerk to the council, as the case may be.

Meetings to be within council area

37. All meetings of a council shall be held within the area of authority of such council unless the Instrument otherwise provides.

Summons to councillors to attend [see p. 68]

38. A summons to attend the meeting of any council specifying the business proposed to be transacted thereat shall be delivered to, or left at or sent by post to the usual place of residence of, every member of such council:

Provided that want of service of the summons on any member shall not affect the validity of a meeting.

Business to be transacted at meeting [see p. 68]

39. Except with the approval of the person presiding and at least three-quarters of the members present at the meeting, no business shall be transacted at a meeting of a council other than that specified in the summons relating thereto.

Chairman to preside at meetings [see p. 74]

40. (1) Except when the president of a council is presiding under the provisions of section 28 of this Law, the chairman of the council shall, if present, preside at meetings of the council.

(2) If the chairman is absent from a meeting of the council at which he is entitled to preside, such member as the members of the council present shall choose, shall preside.

Quorum [see pp. 70-1]

41. No business shall be transacted at a meeting of a council unless there is present such quorum as shall be specified in the Instrument.

Meetings to be public [see p. 71]

42. Every meeting of a council shall be open to the public:

Provided that this section shall not apply to any committee appointed by a council nor to a committee of the whole council.

Decision on question [see pp. 71-3]

43. (1) Subject to the provisions of this Law and of the Instrument, all acts of a council and all questions coming or arising before a council shall be done and decided by a majority of the members present and voting thereon at a meeting of the council.

(2) The person presiding shall have an original vote and, in the event of an equality of votes, shall have a second or casting vote.

Breaches of order at meetings [see p. 74]

44. (1) At any meeting of a council, if a member of the council shows disregard for the authority of the person presiding, or abuses the standing orders of the council by persistently and wilfully obstructing the business of the council or otherwise, the person presiding shall direct the attention of the meeting to the incident mentioning by name the person concerned, and may suspend such person from the exercise of his functions as a member of the council for the remainder of the meeting.

(2) In the case of grave disorder arising in any meeting of a council, the person presiding may, if he thinks it necessary so to do, adjourn the meeting without question put, or suspend any meeting for a time to be specified by him.

(3) The person presiding at any meeting of a committee of a council shall have, and may exercise in relation to such committee, the like powers as are conferred upon a person presiding in relation to a council by subsections (1) and (2) of this section.

Minutes [see pp. 69-70]

45. (1) Minutes of the proceedings of every meeting of a council or of a committee thereof shall be regularly entered in books kept for that purpose, and shall be read, and confirmed or amended, as the case may require, and signed by the person presiding at the same or next ensuing meeting of the council or committee, as the case may be, and any minute purporting to be so signed shall be received in evidence without further proof.

(2) The names of members of a council or of a committee thereof present at a meeting of the council or committee, as the case may be, shall be recorded in the minutes.

(3) Until the contrary be proved, a meeting of a council or of a committee thereof, in respect of the proceedings whereof a minute has been made and signed as provided in subsection (1) of this section, shall be deemed to have been duly convened and held and all members present at the meeting shall be deemed to have been qualified, and where the proceedings are proceedings of a committee, the committee shall be deemed to have been duly constituted and to have had power to deal with the matter referred to in the minutes.

Minutes to be open to inspection [see p. 69]

46. The minutes of the proceedings of a council shall at all reasonable times be open to inspection, and any person may obtain a copy thereof or an extract therefrom upon payment of such fee as may be specified by the council.

Vacancy, etc., not to invalidate proceedings

47. The proceedings of a council or committee thereof shall not be invalidated by any vacancy among its members, or the want of qualification of any member.

Standing Orders [see p. 75]

48. (1) Subject to the provisions of this Law, a council may make Standing Orders for the regulation of its proceedings and business and may amend or revoke such Standing Orders.

(2) If it appears to the Minister that it is expedient for the good administration of the business of a council that any Standing Order which the council has power to issue, should be made, he may, by notice in writing addressed to council, make such Standing Order.

(3) If it appears to the Minister that any Standing Order made by a council is invalid or that it is contrary to the interests of the public in the good administration of the council's business, he may, by notice in writing addressed to the council, amend or revoke such Standing Order.

(4) A Standing Order or any amendment to a Standing Order made by the Minister shall have the same effect as if it had been made by the council.

(5) A council shall send two copies of its Standing Orders and of any amendments thereto to the Local Government Inspector appointed in respect of the council, and shall send one copy of such Standing Orders and amendments to the Minister.

NOTE. This section was substituted for the section originally enacted as section 48 by Law No. 13 of 1955.

Councillors' expenses

49. A council may by resolution make provision for the payment of reasonable out-of-pocket expenses of the members of such council or of a committee thereof when engaged on the business of the council.

Disability of members for voting on account of interest [see p. 73]

50. If a member of a council or any committee thereof has any pecuniary interest, direct or indirect, in any contract or proposed contract or other matter, and is present at a meeting of the council or the committee at which the contract or other matter is the subject of consideration, he shall at the meeting disclose the fact and shall not take part in the consideration or discussion of or vote on any question with respect to the contract or other matter and, if the person presiding so directs, he shall withdraw from the meeting during such consideration or discussion:

Provided that this section shall not apply to an interest in a contract or other matter which a member of a council or committee may have as a ratepayer or an inhabitant of the area.

Rights of certain persons to attend and take part, but not to vote, at meetings

51. (1) The president or the chairman of a council may invite any person to attend, and to speak upon any matter, at any meeting of a council, but no such person shall vote upon any matter.

(2) The Minister may, by writing under his hand, empower any person to attend any meeting or meetings of a council or committee thereof, and any person so empowered may attend such meeting or meetings and may take part in the proceedings thereat, and, if he so requests, his advice on any matter shall be recorded in the minutes of the meeting, but he shall not vote upon any matter.

NOTE. In subsection (2) the word 'Minister' was substituted for the words 'Local Government Inspector' by Law No. 13 of 1955.

PART VI. COMMITTEES

Appointment of committees [see pp. 53-4]

52. (1) A council may appoint a committee for any such general or special purpose as in the opinion of the council would be better regulated and managed by means of a committee and may delegate to a committee so appointed with or without restrictions or conditions, as it thinks fit, any function exercisable by the council either with respect to the whole or any part of the area of the authority of the council, except the power of making bye-laws, levying a rate or issuing a precept or borrowing money.

(2) The number of the members of a committee appointed under this section, their term of office, and the area within which the committee is to exercise its authority shall be specified by the council.

(3) A committee appointed under this section may include persons who are not members of the council:

Provided that:

(*a*) at least two-thirds of every such committee shall be members of the council;

(*b*) no such person shall be appointed a member of a committee who was an unsuccessful candidate at the most recent general election to the council.

(4) No person other than a member of the council shall be appointed to be a member of a committee appointed under the provisions of subsection (3), except with his own consent.

(5) Nothing in this section shall authorise the appointment of an education committee by a council which is a local education authority for the purposes of the Education Law, 1954, or shall apply to an education committee appointed under that Law.

NOTE. Law No. 18 of 1955 substituted subsection (3) of this section; subsection (5) was inserted by Law No. 6 of 1955 (the Education Law, 1954).

For the appointment of education committees by local education authorities see Part IV of the Education Law, 1954.

Finance Committees [see p. 52]

53. (1) Every Divisional and District Council shall appoint a Finance Committee consisting of such number of members of the council as they think fit for regulating and controlling the finance of the council and shall fix the term of office of the members of the committee.

NOTE. Subsection (2) as originally enacted was deleted by Law No. 13 of 1955.

Town, village, or area committees [see pp. 57-8]

54. (1) Subject to the provisions of this Law and of the Instrument, and with the prior approval of the Regional Authority, a council may appoint such town, village, or area committees within the area of its authority as it may deem necessary or expedient, and may delegate to a town, village, or area committee so appointed, with or without restrictions or conditions as it thinks fit, any function exercisable by the council with respect to the area of authority of the town, village, or area committee, except the power of making bye-laws, approving annual estimates, levying a rate or issuing a precept, or borrowing money.

(2) The number of members of a town, village, or area committee appointed under this section, their term of office and method of selection, and the area within which the committee is to exercise its authority, shall be specified by the council.

Standing orders for committees

55. (1) Subject to the provisions of this Law and of the Instrument, a council appointing a committee (including any town, village, or area committee) and councils which concur in appointing a joint committee, as provided for in Part XIV of this Law, may make, vary and revoke standing orders respecting the quorum, proceedings and place of meeting of the committee or joint committee. Subject to any such standing orders the quorum, proceedings and place of meeting shall be such as the committee or joint committee may determine.

(2) Standing orders made under this section shall not be inconsistent with the standing orders of the council concerned made under section 48 of this Law.

Committees to report [see pp. 56-7]

56. Every committee appointed under the provisions of this part of this Law shall report its proceedings to the council or councils appointing such committee.

PART VII. FUNCTIONS OF COUNCILS

Duty to discharge functions [see p. 26]

57. (1) It shall be the duty of every council established under this Law to discharge the functions conferred by this Law or any other Law or Ordinance and generally to maintain order and good government within the area of its authority; and for these purposes, a council may, within the limits of the functions so conferred, either by its own officers or by duly appointed agents do all such things as are necessary or desirable for the discharge of such functions;

(2) Any function conferred upon the council shall be exercisable over all persons within the area of its authority save as is otherwise expressly provided in this Law or in the Instrument.

Prevention of crime [see p. 26]

58. (1) It shall be the duty of every council together with the individual members thereof to the best of their ability to prevent the commission of any offence within the area of its authority by any person.

(2) A council or town, village or area committee or any individual member thereof, knowing of the occurrence of any act which is likely to result in a serious breach of the peace within the area of the authority of the council shall report the matter to the nearest police officer, court officer, or justice of the peace immediately, and failure

to report such an act shall be an offence and shall render any individual member of the council, or town, village, or area committee concerned to a fine not exceeding one hundred pounds.

(3) Any member of a council or of a town, village, or area committee within the area in which he resides shall, if called upon by a superior police officer, or a justice of the peace to do so, take any action necessary for the prevention of the commission of any offence, and failure to take such action shall be an offence and shall render the individual liable to a fine not exceeding one hundred pounds.

NOTE. Law No. 13 of 1955 substituted references to justices of the peace for references to Local Government Inspectors and Assistant Local Government Inspectors which occurred in the section as originally enacted.

Powers of a council to order stranger to leave its area

59. (1) A council may order any person who is not a member of a native community living in the area of its authority, and who fails, when so required by the council to produce reasonable proof to the council that his means and legitimate labour are sufficient for the adequate support of himself and his dependents, to leave such area within such time after the order has been communicated to him, not being less than fourteen days, as the council may direct:

Provided that any person so ordered to leave such area may within fourteen days of the order being communicated to him appeal against the order to a magistrate's court, but the court shall not set aside the order unless such person satisfies the court that his means and legitimate labour are sufficient for the adequate support of himself and his dependents.

(2) Any person who fails to obey an order made under this section, or who, having left the area which he was directed by the order to leave, returns to such area without the consent of the council, shall be liable to a fine of twenty-five pounds or to imprisonment for six months, or to both such fine and imprisonment.

Declaration and modification of local customary law

60. (1) A council may, and where the Regional Authority so requires, shall, record in writing a declaration of what in the opinion of the council is the local customary law relating to any subject either as applying throughout the area of the authority of such council or in any specific part thereof or so affecting specified persons or classes of persons in such area or in any part thereof, and submit such declaration to the Regional Authority.

(2) A council may, if in the opinion of the council it is expedient for the good government and welfare of the inhabitants of the area of its authority, submit for the consideration of the Regional Authority a recommendation for the modification of any local customary law, whether or not a declaration has been recorded and an order made under the provisions of this section in respect of such local customary law, relating to any subject either as applying throughout the area of its authority or in any part thereof or as affecting certain specified persons or classes of persons or any part thereof.

(3) If the Regional Authority is satisfied that such declaration accurately records the local customary law with respect to the subject to which it relates, or that such modification is expedient and that such local customary law or modification is not repugnant to justice, equity or good conscience, nor incompatible either in its terms or by necessary implication with any Ordinance or Law, he may by order direct such declaration or such modification to be the local customary law in respect of the subject to which it relates and to be in force in the area concerned.

NOTE. This section as originally enacted contained references only to local customary law with respect to land tenure; it was amended by Law No. 8 of 1953 to refer to customary law with respect to any subject.

Power to accept gifts

61. A council may accept, hold and administer any gift of property for any public purpose, or for the benefit of the inhabitants of the area of its authority or any part thereof, and may execute any works (including works of maintenance and improvement) incidental to or consequential on the exercise of the powers conferred by this section.

Fees

62. (1) Subject to the prior approval of the Regional Authority, a council may charge fees for any service or facility provided by the council or for any licence or permit issued by such council under the provisions of this Law or of any regulations or bye-laws made thereunder.

(2) Subject to the prior approval of the Regional Authority, a council may for good cause authorise the remission of any fees or other charges imposed under the provisions of this Law or any regulations or bye-laws made thereunder.

Power to contract [see p.131]

63. (1) A council may enter into any contract necessary for the discharge of any of its functions under this or any other Law:

Provided that a council shall not enter into any contract to the value of two thousand pounds or upwards without the prior approval of the Regional Authority.

(2) Any contract made by a council shall be made in accordance with the standing orders of the council and, in the case of contracts for the supply of goods and materials or for the execution of works to the value of two hundred and fifty pounds and upwards, such standing orders shall:

(*a*) require that notice of the intention of the council to enter into the contract shall be published and tenders invited; and

(*b*) regulate the manner in which such notice shall be published and such tenders given.

(3) A person entering into a contract with a council shall not be bound to enquire whether the standing orders of the council which apply to the contract have been complied with or, in the case of a contract to the value of two thousand pounds or upwards, whether the prior approval of the Regional Authority has been obtained, and all contracts entered into by a council, if otherwise valid, shall have full force and effect notwithstanding that the standing orders applicable thereto have not been complied with or that the approval of the Regional Authority has not been obtained.

Insurance

64. A council may insure all or any of its property against risks of any type.

Writing-off of irrecoverable arrears of revenue

65. A council may, from time to time, by resolution authorise the writing off, as an irrecoverable debt in regard to which no further proceedings need be taken, of any sum due or payable to the council from or by any person, on the ground of the poverty of such person or for other sufficient cause:

Provided that no such sum shall be written off as an irrecoverable debt without the prior approval of the Regional Authority if it exceeds one hundred pounds in any one case, or if, by so writing it off, the total sum written off in any financial year will exceed the sum of two hundred and fifty pounds.

Writing-off of deficiencies of cash and stores

66. A council may from time to time by resolution authorise the writing off of deficiencies of cash or stores:

Provided that no such deficiency shall be written off without the prior approval of the Regional Authority if it exceeds one hundred pounds in value in any one case, or if, by so writing it off, the total value of such deficiencies written off in any financial year will exceed the value of two hundred and fifty pounds.

NOTE. The amounts specified in sections 65 and 66 in respect of which irrecoverable arears of revenue and deficiencies in cash and stores may be written off without the prior approval of the Regional Authority were altered by Law No. 13 of 1955.

Provision of offices, etc., by councils

67. (1) A council may:

(*a*) build, acquire, provide or hire and furnish buildings within the area of the authority of such council to be used for the purpose of transacting the business of the council and for public meetings and assemblies; or

(*b*) combine with any other council for the purpose of building, acquiring, providing or hiring and furnishing any such buildings; or

(*c*) contribute towards the expense incurred by any other council in building, acquiring, providing or hiring and furnishing any building within the area of the authority of such council suitable for use for any of the aforesaid purposes.

(2) A council may build, provide or hire and maintain quarters or houses for any officer or employee of the council.

Newspapers and publications

68. A council may publish newspapers or periodicals and may provide information services.

Local Government Associations [see p. 47]

69. A council may contribute to Local Government Associations and incur expenditure incidental to the holding of meetings thereof.

Power to make grants to other councils

69A. A council may make grants to any other council for the purposes of any of the functions of the last-named council.

NOTE. This section was inserted by Law No. 13 of 1955.

70. It shall be the duty of a District Council, or, where no District Council has been established, of a Local Council to cause to be made from time to time inspection of the area of its authority with a view to ascertaining what nuisances exist, calling for abatement under the provisions of the Public Health Ordinance, and to ensure that the provisions of that Ordinance to abate the same are enforced.

Functions [see pp. 22-3]

71. The Regional Authority may by Instrument declare that, subject to such limitations and conditions as he may impose, a council either shall perform or may perform all or any of the following functions in respect of the area for which it is established:

Agriculture

(1) provide services for the improvement of agriculture, and control diseases, pests or weeds, ordering if necessary the destruction of any tree, crop or plant.

(2) control methods of husbandry, including the clearing of land by burning;

Animals

(3) prohibit, restrict or regulate the movement in or through the area of the council of any livestock;

(4) establish, maintain and control pounds, seize and impound any stray animal, and provide for the payment of compensation for damage done by such animal;

(5) prohibit cruelty to animals, and any specified acts of cruelty to animals;

(6) prohibit, restrict and regulate the keeping of livestock of any description;

(7) prevent and control the outbreak or the prevalence of any disease among animals;

(8) provide services for the improvement of livestock;

Buildings

(9) prescribe the conditions subject to which the erection and construction, demolition, re-erection and construction, conversion and re-conversion, alteration, repair, sanitation and ventilation of public and private buildings and structures may be undertaken and carried out;

(10) provide for building lines and layout of buildings;

(11) make advances upon such conditions as shall be thought fit for the purpose of enabling ratepayers to build or to buy dwelling houses;

(12) prepare and undertake and otherwise control schemes for improved housing layout and settlement;

(13) prescribe the conditions to be satisfied by a site for any building or for any class of building;

(14) prohibit the construction of any new building unless and until the plans thereof have been submitted to, and approved by, the council;

(15) provide for the demolition of dangerous buildings if necessary at the expense of the owner, or occupier, and provide for the recovery of such expenses;

(16) prohibit or regulate the use in any defined area of any inflammable material in the construction or repair of any building;

(17) build, equip and maintain social centres, public libraries, communal feeding centres, restaurants, catering and other rest houses, or buildings designed and used for public purposes;

(18) build, equip, maintain and let shops;

(19) prohibit or regulate the making of borrow pits or other excavations;

(20) control and regulate the siting of advertisements and hoardings or other structures designed for the display of advertisements;

Education

(22) grant sums of money towards the establishment, equipment or maintenance of any Primary School, Secondary School, or other educational institution;

(23) grant and maintain scholarships or bursaries to suitable persons to attend any school or other educational institution in Nigeria or elsewhere;

(25) grant sums of money towards the establishment or maintenance of any public library, museum or to any association existing for the promotion of arts, and crafts, or recreation and sport;

Forestry

(26) establish and maintain tree nurseries, forest plantations and forest reserves and sell the produce thereof;

(27) prevent and control soil erosion;

Land

(28) provide for the fencing of land and for the maintenance and repair of such fences;

(29) require any person to cultivate land to such extent and with such crops as will secure an adequate supply of food for the support of such person and of those dependent upon him;

Liquor

(30) prohibit, restrict, regulate or license the manufacture, distillation, sale, transport, distribution, supply, possession, and consumption of palm wine and any kind or description of fermented liquor usually made by the natives of Nigeria or in the adjacent territories;

Markets

(31) build, equip, open, close and maintain markets and prohibit the erection of stalls in places other than markets;

(32) regulate and control markets including the fixing of and collection of stallages, rents and tolls;

(33) fix the days and hours during each day on which a market may be held and prevent the sale and purchase of goods in markets on any day or at any hours except those fixed;

Public Health

(34) safeguard and promote public health including the prevention of and the dealing with any outbreak or the prevalence of any disease;

(35) build, equip, and maintain, or grant sums of money towards the establishment, equipment or maintenance of any hospital, maternity home, dispensary, asylum for the aged, destitute or infirm or for orphans or asylums and settlements for lepers;

(36) exterminate and prevent the spread of tsetse fly, mosquitoes, rats, bugs and other vermin;

(37) establish and operate ambulance services;

(38) establish, install, build, maintain, and control drains, latrines, public lavatories and wash places and any sewage systems;

(39) establish, maintain, and carry out sanitary services for the removal and destruction of and otherwise dealing with nightsoil and all kind of refuse;

(40) provide, erect and maintain a public water supply, regulate or prohibit the sinking of wells and provide for the closing of wells;

(41) prevent the pollution of the water in any river, stream, watercourse, water hole or drain and prevent the obstruction of any river, stream or water-course;

(42) build, manage, license and control slaughter houses;

(43) regulate the slaughter of and provide for the inspection of animals intended for the food of man;

(44) regulate the preparation and sale of meat;

(45) establish, maintain and control cemeteries and burial grounds;

Public Order

(46) prohibit any act or conduct which in the opinion of the council is likely to cause a riot or any disturbance or a breach of the peace;

(47) prohibit, regulate or restrict the carrying and possession of weapons;

(47a) prohibit, restrict and regulate the migration of persons from or to the area of the council;

(48) prevent fires and control grass or bush fires;

(49) establish and maintain fire brigades and provide for the use and custody of any appliance for the extinguishing of fires;

(50) prohibit or regulate gambling;

(51) license and regulate guides, porters and carriers;

(52) control the movement of beggars in streets and public places;

(53) suppress brothels, disorderly houses, and take measures to prevent prostitution;

(54) prohibit, restrict or control the hawking of wares;

(55) regulate and control public collections in streets and public places;

(55a) regulate and control drumming and public musical entertainments (including licensing drummers or performers at public musical entertainments);

Registration of persons

(56) provide for the registration of persons residing within the area of the authority of the council or in any part thereof;

(57) require the marriage, birth or death of any person within the area of the authority of the council to be reported to or registered with the council and to appoint registration offices and registrars for such purposes;

Roads, streets, etc.

(58) make, alter, divert and maintain roads, streets, paths, culverts, bridges, street-drains and water-courses;

(59) provide or arrange for lighting in public places;

(60) regulate all traffic in the area;

(61) license bicycles and vehicles other than motor vehicles including motor bicycles;

(62) establish, provide and maintain parks for motor and other vehicles;

(63) require persons to carry lights during certain hours in certain areas;

(64) establish, acquire and maintain transport services by land or water including ferries;

(65) regulate or prohibit the planting, cutting, tapping or destruction of any trees or vegetation growing along any street, road or path or in any public place;

(66) provide that the owner or occupier of any land or tenements maintain clear and keep free from vegetation the roads, streets or paths adjoining their land or tenements;

(67) regulate the naming of roads and streets and the numbering of houses;

Trade and industry

(68) prescribe the conditions under which any offensive trade or industry may be carried on;

(69) engage in any form of trade or industry;

(70) fix the maximum price which may be demanded in the sale by retail for any article of food in any market;

(71) establish, erect, maintain and control public weighing machines and other instruments of measurement;

Various matters

(72) protect, preserve and prohibit the removal from any place of any African antique work of art;

(72a) regulate child betrothals;

(73) establish, control and manage recreation grounds, open spaces and parks;

(74) provide for the maintenance of any traditional office or customary title which is on the date of the commencement of this Law receiving such maintenance, or which is recognised by a vote of three-quarters of the total membership of the council in the area;

(75) provide for the licensing of any suitable building or other place for the performance of stage plays, cinematograph films or other public entertainment and to prescribe the conditions under which such plays, films or entertainments may be shown;

(76) prescribe the duties of any person employed by the council in connexion with any function of such council;

(77) prohibit, restrict or regulate the capture, killing or sale of fish or any specified kind of fish;

(78) erect, extend or alter any pier subject to the provisions of the Piers Ordinance;

(79) provide welfare services for children and young persons (including the establishment, equipment or maintenance of remand homes, approved schools and clubs) and grant sums of money to Associations existing for the benefit and welfare of children and young persons;

(80) provide for the preservation, development or exploitation of natural resources;

(81) provide for the establishment and administration of schemes of planned rural development or settlement;

(81a) regulate native marriages (including dowry) and the dissolution of such marriages;

(82) provide for the control of the movement, isolation and treatment of persons suffering from leprosy or any infectious or contagious disease;

(83) provide for the building, equipping or maintenance of rural postal agencies and rural postal services which have been approved by the Director of Posts and Telegraphs;

(84) clean and improve waterways.

Nothing in this section should be deemed to confer on any council authority to perform any act which would constitute a contravention of the terms of any law or ordinance.

NOTE. Paragraphs (21) and (24) as originally enacted were deleted by Law No. 6 of 1955; paragraph (47a) was inserted by Law No. 8 of 1953; paragraph (55a) was inserted by Law No. 13 of 1955; paragraph (72a) was inserted by Law No. 8 of 1953; paragraph (79) was substituted by Law No. 13 of 1955; paragraph (81a) was substituted by Law No. 2 of 1954; paragraph (83) was inserted by Law No. 2 of 1954; paragraph (84) was inserted by Law No. 13 of 1955.

For the functions of councils with respect to education see, in addition, Part IV of the Education Law, 1954.

Health Officer deemed to be officer of council for purposes of bye-laws
(Cap. 183)

72. Any person who fulfils the duties of Health Officer under the provisions of the Public Health Ordinance for any area in which a council is established shall be deemed to be an officer of such council for the purposes of giving effect to and enforcing any bye-laws relating to public health made by such council.

Delegation of functions by Divisional Councils to District Councils

73. (1) A Divisional Council may, with the concurrence of the council concerned and with the prior approval of the Regional Authority, delegate to any District Council within the area of its authority, with or without restrictions or conditions, any of its functions under this Law except any function excluded by the Instrument from the operation of this section.

(2) Where functions are delegated under this section to a District Council, the District Council in the discharge of those functions shall act as agent for the Divisional Council.

Report by Divisional Council in certain cases

74. If it appears to a Divisional Council that any other council within the area of its authority has made default in the performance of any function conferred upon it by an Instrument which specifies that it is the duty of such council to perform such function, the Divisional Council shall report such fact to the Minister.

Power to enforce functions of councils

75. (1) If the Regional Authority, on the advice of the Minister, is satisfied that any council has made default in the performance of any function conferred or imposed upon it by or under this Law or any other Law or Ordinance for the time being in force, he may make an order declaring the council to be in default and may, by the same or any other order:

(*a*) for the purpose of removing the default direct the council to perform such of its functions in such manner and within such time or times as may be specified in the order; or

(*b*) transfer to such person or body as he may deem fit such of the functions of the council in default as may be specified in the order.

(2) If a council with respect to which an order has been made under paragraph (*a*) of subsection (1) of this section fails to comply with any requirement thereof within the time limited thereby for compliance with that requirement, the Regional Authority may make an order under paragraph (*b*) of that subsection.

(3) Where an order has been made under paragraph (*b*) of subsection (1) of this section, the Regional Authority may, by the same or any other order, dissolve the council or suspend the council for such time as he may think fit from the performance of such of its functions as may be specified in such order.

(4) Nothing in this section shall apply in relation to any function conferred or imposed upon a council under the provisions of the Education Law, 1954.

NOTE. For the references to Local Government Inspector in sections 74 and 75 as originally enacted there were substituted references to the Minister by Law No. 13 of 1955; subsection (4) of section 75 was inserted by Law No. 6 of 1955.

Expenses in respect of transferred functions

76. Where any functions of a council are transferred to any person or body under the provisions of subsection (11) of section 75 of this Law, the expenses incurred by such person or body in discharging those functions shall be a debt due from the council in default of such person or body, as the case may be.

PART VIII. BYE-LAWS

Bye-laws [see p.121]

77. (1) A council may make bye-laws for the carrying into effect and for the purposes of any function conferred upon it by virtue of this Law or any other Law and may in such bye-laws specify a fine not exceeding fifty pounds or in default of payment imprisonment not exceeding six months for any breach of any such bye-law, and, in the case of a continuing offence, a further penalty not exceeding five pounds for each day on which the offence is continued after written notice of the offence has been served on the offender.

(2) The Regional Authority may by Instrument declare that subject to such limitations and conditions as he may impose, a council may make bye-laws relating to the use and alienation whether upon devolution by will or otherwise of interests in land of any description whatever within the area of the authority of the council and without derogation from the generality of these provisions specially in respect of any or all of the following matters:

(i) the control of any or all powers of alienation of land or of any interest therein to strangers or to persons other than strangers;

(ii) the control and use of communal land and of family land either generally or specifically and with special reference to the cultivation thereof and the type of crops which may be grown thereon;

(iii) the control of mortgaging with special reference to the approval of the mortgagee and the use to which the land may be put when mortgaged;

(iv) the control of the borrowing of money or money's worth secured upon standing crops;

(v) making the purchaser at any sale, whether such sale is by order of any court whatsoever or not, subject to the approval of the council or of a specified individual or individuals and providing, in the case of a sale by a court, that the land shall again be sold if the vendor is not approved under the bye-laws;

(vi) for the recording or filing of documents relating to the alienation of land or interest therein;

(vii) for the control either generally or specifically of the size or extent of communal land or family land over which any individual or group of persons may exercise rights or be permitted to exercise rights; and

(viii) the regulating of the allocation of communal land or family land and specifying the person or persons who may allocate such communal land subject to such special or general directions as the council may require.

In this subsection:

'land' means all land including everything attached to the earth in the Western Region other than land which is for the time being:

(a) freehold land the tenure of which is regulated exclusively by English law;

(b) Crown land;

(c) land subject to any interest conferred by any Instrument approved under the provisions of the Native Lands Acquisition Ordinance (Cap. 144) or any Ordinance or Law replacing those provisions;

(d) land vested for any interest in a body corporate which is established by any Ordinance or Law and is empowered to acquire and hold land;

(e) land which is the subject of a right of occupancy granted by the Governor in accordance with the Land and Native Rights Ordinance (Cap. 105).

(f) land within the area of a planning authority established under the provisions of the Nigeria Town and Country Planning Ordinance (Cap. 155) or any Ordinance or Law replacing those provisions;

(g) land held under a title which has been registered in accordance with the provisions of the Registration of Titles Ordinance (Cap. 197);

'stranger' means any native of Nigeria or native foreigner who is not eligible by local customary law to inherit land or the use of land within the area of jurisdiction of the council making the bye-law.

(3) A bye-law may make provision for the payment of such fees or charges as shall to the council seem fit.

(4) A council may authorise the remission of any fee or charge imposed under the provision of any bye-law.

(5) Any bye-law made by a council under the provisions of this section shall be read and construed subject to the provisions of this and any other Law or Ordinance.

(6) A bye-law made by a District or Local Council shall not be inconsistent with any bye-law made by a Divisional Council which is in force within the area of authority of such District or Local Council.

NOTE. Subsection (2) was inserted by Law No. 8 of 1953 and the definition of 'land' therein was substituted by Law No. 2 of 1954.

Method of making bye-laws [see pp.123-4]

78. (1) Bye-laws shall be made under the common seal of the council and shall not have effect until they are approved by the Regional Authority who, before approving, may amend the same.

(2) No bye-law shall be made by a council unless reasonable notice, in such manner as the Regional Authority may approve, of the intention of the council to make such bye-law has been given to the inhabitants of the area to be affected thereby.

(3) The Regional Authority may approve or refuse to approve any bye-law submitted and may, upon the date of its approval, fix the date on which the bye-law is to come into operation.

(4) The provisions of subsections (3) and (4) of section 19 of the Interpretation Ordinance (Cap. 94) shall have no application to any bye-law made under the provisions of this Law.

Adoptive bye-laws [see p.126]

78A. (1) The Minister may by order make adoptive bye-laws for the carrying into effect and for the purposes of any function which is or may be conferred on a council by or under the provisions of this Law or any other Law, and may in such order provide that the adoption of such bye-laws may be either as a whole or in such parts as may be therein specified.

(2) Subject to the provisions of this section and of any order made by the Minister under subsection (1), a council may adopt any bye-laws published as aforesaid which relate to any function of the council.

(3) The following provisions shall apply with respect to the adoption of any bye-laws by a council:

(*a*) the adoption shall be by resolution passed at a meeting of the council;

(*b*) reasonable notice of the intention to adopt the bye-law in the manner approved for the purposes of subsection (2) of section 78 of this Law shall be given to the inhabitants of the area affected;

(*c*) notice of the resolution shall be published in the *Gazette* and shall be conclusive evidence of the resolution having been passed;

(*d*) the adoption of the bye-laws shall take effect from the date of the publication of the notice in the *Gazette*;

(*e*) bye-laws adopted in accordance with the provisions of this section shall have the same force and effect as if they have been made by the council and may be revoked by resolution of the council published in accordance with paragraph (*c*) of this subsection;

(*f*) bye-laws adopted in accordance with the provision of this section may be amended by the adoption of any amendment made thereto by the Minister;

(*g*) the approval of the Regional Authority shall not be required.

(4) The provisions of subsections (1) and (2) of section 19 and of section 20 of the Interpretation Ordinance (Cap. 94) shall apply in relation to any bye-laws contained in an order made by the Minister under this section.

(5) Any adoptive bye-laws adopted by a council shall, notwithstanding the revocation of such adoptive bye-laws or any part thereof by the Minister remain of full force and effect.

(6) Any amendment by the Minister of adoptive bye-laws shall not be of force within the area of any council by which such adoptive bye-laws have been adopted unless and until such amendment shall have been adopted in accordance with the provisions of subsections (2) and (3) of this section.

(7) The provisions of sections 79 and 82 shall not apply in relation to bye-laws adopted under this section.

NOTE. This section was inserted by Law No. 13 of 1955.

Publication [see p.124]

79. Bye-laws shall be published in such manner as the Regional Authority may approve.

Regional Authority may make bye-laws [see p.125]

80. The Regional Authority may at any time after having given to a council reasonable notice and having considered the representations of the council thereon, make or amend any bye-law which such council is empowered by this Law to make, or revoke any bye-law made by such council.

Copy of bye-law to be deposited at council offices [see pp. 124-5]

81. (1) A copy of every bye-law when approved by the Regional Authority shall be deposited at the offices of the council by whom the bye-law was made, and shall at all reasonable times be open to public inspection without payment, and a copy thereof shall, on application, be furnished to any person on payment of such sum as the council may determine.

(2) A Divisional Council shall send a copy of every bye-law made by such council and approved by the Regional Authority to every other council to whose area the bye-law applies.

(3) Any council which receives a copy of a bye-law under the provisions of this section shall deposit such copy at its offices.

(4) The copy so deposited shall be open to inspection by the public without payment.

Evidence of bye-laws [see pp. 125-6]

82. A copy of a bye-law purporting to be made by a council, upon which is endorsed a certificate purporting to be signed by the chairman or other officer of such council authorised in that behalf, stating:

(*a*) that the bye-law was made and published by the council in the prescribed manner;

(*b*) that the copy is a true copy of the bye-law;

(*c*) that on a specified date the bye-law was duly approved by the Regional Authority and came into operation on a specified date; shall be admitted in evidence in any court without further proof and such certificate shall be evidence of the facts stated therein without further proof, and without proof of the handwriting or official position of the person purporting to sign the certificate.

Power of a District or Local Council to enforce bye-laws made by a Divisional Council

83. A District or Local Council authorised in that behalf by any bye-law made by a Divisional Council shall have power to enforce such bye-law within the area of its authority.

Power to engage staff [see p.115]

84. (1) Subject to the provisions of subsection (2) and of any regulations made under section 92 of this Law a council shall appoint a secretary or clerk to the council and may appoint such other officers and employ such other persons as it shall think necessary for the efficient discharge of the functions of the council, and may, subject as aforesaid, dismiss any person so appointed or employed.

(2) A council shall not appoint, engage or employ:

(*a*) a secretary, clerk to the council or treasurer, or

(*b*) any person at a salary of three hundred and fifty pounds per annum or above,

without the approval in writing of the Regional Authority.

(3) A person employed under the provisions of subsection (2) shall not be dismissed without the approval in writing of the Regional Authority.

(4) It shall be the duty of such council as the Regional Authority may by Instrument direct to engage and pay adequate staff (including clerks) for any Native Court which is established or situate within the area of its authority.

(5) Subject to the provisions of subsection (2) and of any such regulations as aforesaid a council may pay to any officer or person so employed such reasonable remuneration as it may determine.

Joint appointments

85. (1) Subject to the approval of the Regional Authority, a council may agree with any one or more councils, whether situated in the same area or not, on the joint employment of any staff or appointment of any officer.

(2) Where, due to shortage of staff or other reasonable cause, the Regional Authority deems it expedient so to do, he may require any two or more councils to concur in the joint employment of any staff or appointment of any officer and, if any such council fails to employ or appoint any person when required to do so under this section, the Regional Authority may exercise, on behalf of such council, the powers of employment and appointment conferred on a council by this Law.

(3) A council shall not agree with any other council to engage, employ or dismiss any person whose total salary under such agreement shall be three hundred and fifty pounds per annum or above without the approval in writing of the Regional Authority.

Age of retirement

86. (1) Without prejudice to other powers of terminating the employment of any officer, an officer shall normally retire from the service of a council when he attains the age of sixty years, and unless a council by resolution in a particular case, or with regard to any particular class of officers otherwise determine, all officers shall retire on attaining that age.

(2) An officer of a council may retire, or may be called upon by the council to retire, on his attaining the age of forty-five years.

Officers not to be interested in contract

87. Any officer of a council who is in any wise concerned or interested directly or indirectly by himself or his partner (otherwise than as a minority shareholder in a company) in any contract or work made with or executed for the council shall be incapable of holding any office or employment under this Law.

Appointment of seconded Government officers

88. (1) Notwithstanding the other provisions of this Part the council may, with the approval of the Governor, appoint to any office in its service a Government officer seconded to the service of the council for that purpose, for such period and on such terms and conditions as the Governor and the Regional Authority may approve.

(2) The Governor shall not be obliged to consult with the Executive Council in the exercise of his powers under subsection (1).

Security may be demanded by council of officers and others

89. A council may in the case of any officer in its employment, other than a Government officer appointed under the provisions of section 88, whether under this or any other Law or Ordinance whether employed jointly with another council or not, or in the case of a person not in its employment, but who is likely to be entrusted with the custody or control of money or property belonging to the council, either require him to give, or itself take, such security for the faithful execution of his office and for his duly accounting for all money or property which may be entrusted to him, as the council may think sufficient.

Accountability of officers

90. (1) Every officer employed by a council, whether under this or any other Law or Ordinance, shall at such times during the continuance of his office, or within three months after his ceasing to hold it, and in such manner as the council directs, make out and deliver to the council or as it directs, a true account in writing of all money and property committed to his charge, and of his receipts and payments, with vouchers and other documents and records supporting the entries therein, and a list of persons from whom or to whom money is due in connexion with his office, showing the amount due from or to each.

(2) Every such officer shall pay all money due from him to the council or otherwise as such council may direct.

(3) If any such officer:

(*a*) refuses or wilfully neglects to make any payment which he is required by this section to make; or

(*b*) after three days' notice in writing signed by the chairman of the council or by three members thereof, and given or left at his usual or last known place of residence, refuses or wilfully neglects to make out or deliver to the council, or as it directs, any account or list which he is required by this section to make out and deliver, or any voucher or other document or record relating thereto, or to give satisfaction respecting it to the council or as it directs;

a magistrate's court having jurisdiction where the officer is or resides may, on complaint, by order require him to make such payment or delivery or to give such satisfaction.

(4) Nothing in this section shall affect any remedy by action against any such officer or his surety, except that the officer shall not be both sued by action and proceeded against under the provisions of this section for the same cause.

Power of interdiction

91. Subject to the provisions of any regulations made under section 92 a council may interdict any officer, other than a Government officer appointed under section 88, or employee of the council from the duties and emoluments of his office or employment for incapacity, neglect or misconduct pending the decisions of the council as to his removal and, in the event of his removal such officer or employee shall be deemed to have been removed from office or employment as from the date of interdiction.

Staff regulations [see p.115]

92. (1) The Regional Authority may make regulations to be known as Staff Regulations, for all or any of the following purposes relating to officers and employees or to any class or grade of officer or employee in the employment of councils established under this Law:

(a) establishing a body to advise the Regional Authority on staff matters, which shall be known as the Local Government Service Commission, and prescribing the powers and duties of such body;

(b) maintaining discipline;

(c) regulating appointments, remuneration, promotion, termination of appointments, dismissals and leave;

(d) regulating the payment of allowances, the grant of advances, and the terms and conditions of service generally; and

(e) such other matters relating to departmental procedure and the duties and responsibilities of officers and employees, as the Regional Authority considers can be best regulated by such regulations.

(2) Any such regulations in so far as they relate to discipline may in particular, provide for:

(a) withholding or deferring of increments, or reduction in rank or salary either permanently or for a stated period; and

(b) the deduction from salary due or about to become due of such sum as may be appraised in respect of damage to property of the council by misconduct or breach of duty on the part of an officer.

NOTE. For regulations made under this section see Western Region Legal Notice No. 62 of 1955.

Pensions Regulations

93. (1) The Regional Authority may make regulations as to the pensions and gratuities which are to be paid, whether as of right or otherwise, to officers and persons who have been employed by a council or councils, to the legal personal representatives, estates or dependants of officers who die while so employed, and to the widows and children of deceased persons who have been so employed.

(2) Without prejudice to the generality of subsection (1) of this section regulations made under this section may contain such provision as appears to the Regional Authority to be necessary or expedient in relation to a person who transfers to or from employment with a council from or to employment with another council or with the Government.

NOTE. This section was substituted by Law No. 18 of 1955 for the section originally enacted.

General pension schemes

94. (1) Notwithstanding the provisions of section 93 of this Law, the Regional Authority may establish and maintain any scheme for

the payment of pensions and gratuities to officers and persons who have been employed by any council which elects to participate in such scheme, to the legal personal representatives, estates or dependants of officers and persons who die while so employed, or to the widows and children of deceased persons who have been so employed, and any such scheme may, with the approval of the Regional Authority, be altered, varied, amended or wound up from time to time, due regard being had to the existing rights of any officer or person coming within the scope of any such scheme.

(2) Where any such scheme as is mentioned in subsection (1) of this section has been established, any council may by resolution, which shall be irrevocable except with the consent of the Regional Authority, elect to participate in such scheme and thereupon:

(*a*) any scheme having similar objects previously maintained by the council under section 93 of this Law shall be merged in the scheme maintained under this section in such manner as may be prescribed by regulations made under this section; and

(*b*) such council shall be liable to make such contributions to, and the officers and persons employed by such council shall be entitled to such benefits under, such scheme as may be prescribed by regulations made under this section.

(3) The Regional Authority may make regulations for the maintenance, control and management of any scheme established under this section.

Persons employed may be required to contribute

95. It shall be lawful for a council to require any officer or person employed by it to make contributions under the provisions of any pensions scheme established under section 93 or 94 of this Law.

Gratuities and allowances

96. A council may, subject to the approval of the Regional Authority, grant gratuities and allowances to officers and persons who have been employed by the council and who are not qualified for benefit under the provisions of section 93 or 94 of this Law, or to the legal personal representatives, estates or dependants of such officers and persons.

Gratuities, etc., not liable to attachment

97. No pension or gratuity or other allowance granted in pursuance of the provisions of this Part of this Law, and no rights acquired by any officer or person in respect of contributions made in pursuance of provisions for the grant of pensions to widows and children of deceased officers and employees, shall be assignable or transferable, or liable to be attached or sequestered or levied upon, for or in respect of any debt or claim whatsoever:

Provided that the provisions of this section shall not affect the right of the council or the Government to recover from any sums due or payable to or in respect of any officer or employee any amount owing to the council or the Government by such officer or employee.

Protection of councillors, officers and employees

98. No matter or thing done and no contract entered into by a council, and no matter or thing done by any member, officer or employee of a council or other person whomsoever acting under the direction of a council, shall, if the matter or thing was done or the contract was entered into *bona fide* for the purposes of this Law, subject any member, officer or employee of the council, or any person acting under the direction of the council, personally to any action, liability, claim or demand whatsoever.

PART X. GENERAL FINANCIAL PROVISIONS

Declaration of revenue and funds of councils [see p. 94]

99. (1) The revenue and other funds of a council are hereby declared to be as follows:

(a) All sums of money or funds as are granted to a council by the Regional Authority under the provisions of section 221.

(b) Revenue accruing to a council from the following sources:

(i) moneys derived from any rate imposed by the council by virtue of the provisions of this Law;

(ii) moneys derived from licences, permits, dues, charges or fees specified by any bye-laws made by a council;

(iii) moneys payable to a council under the provisions of any other Law or Ordinance;

(iv) receipts derived from any public utility concern, or any service or undertaking belonging to or maintained by a council either in whole or in part;

(v) rents derived from the letting or leasing of any building or land belonging to a council;

(vi) grants-in-aid out of the general revenue of Nigeria, or of the Western Region, or other public revenue;

(viii) any particular public revenue which may lawfully be assigned to a council;

(viii) any sums of money which may lawfully be assigned to a council by any public corporation;

(ix) interest on the invested funds of a council;

(x) such sums of money as are payable to a council in satisfaction of a precept issued by the council on a rating authority in accordance with the provisions of section 129;

(xi) any amount of money transferable to a council under the provisions of section 20 of the Direct Taxation Ordinance;

(xii) to such extent as the Regional Authority may by the Instrument direct, the fees, fines and penalties payable in respect of or as a result of proceedings in native courts within the area of the authority of a council and the proceeds of the sale of any forfeitures ordered by such native courts;

(xiii) such sums of money as may be granted to a council by any other council.

(2) In addition to the revenue and funds specified in subsection (1) such sums of money as are payable to a Local Council by a rating authority in satisfaction of a precept issued by such Local Council under the provisions of section 131 shall form part of the revenue and funds of such council.

(3) Any other moneys lawfully derived by a council from any other source whatever not hereinbefore specifically mentioned shall be and form part of the revenue and funds of such council.

(4) All revenues of a council shall be paid into the general funds of the council and shall be applied to the administration, development and welfare of the area over which its authority extends and to the welfare of the inhabitants thereof.

Expenditure

100. Subject to the provisions of this Law, a council may incur all expenditure necessary for, and incidental to, the carrying out of any functions conferred upon it under this or any other Law or Ordinance, or by the Instrument.

Power to borrow [see p.100]

101. (1) A council may from time to time raise loans within Nigeria of such amounts, from such sources, in such manner, upon such conditions and for such purposes in fulfilment of their lawful functions as the Regional Authority may approve.

(2) Such loans shall be secured upon the property and the revenues of the council.

(3) Where any interest or any payment of capital due on any loan remains unpaid for three months after a demand therefor has been served on the council in writing by the person entitled thereto, the Regional Authority may:

(*a*) order that a rate necessary to produce the sum due shall be levied upon and collected from the ratepayers of the area of the authority of the council either immediately or at such date as he shall order, and for the purpose of raising such sum the Regional Authority shall in addition have the same power as the council concerned, of making and levying a general or special rate or of issuing a precept; or

(*b*) order the sale of any property including land on which the loan is secured.

(4) The power of the Regional Authority under this section of making and levying a general or special rate may be exercised at any time.

NOTE. For the powers of a council which is a local education authority to raise loans for the purposes of its functions under the Education Law, 1954, see section 86 of that Law.

Overdrafts

102. It shall be lawful for a council to obtain advances from banks by overdraft upon the credit of such council:

Provided that no such overdraft shall at any time in any circumstances exceed the income of such council in the preceding financial year.

Investment of funds

103. A council may invest all or any portion of the moneys of the council in such manner as may be approved by the Regional Authority.

Financial year

104. The financial year for each council shall begin on the 1st day of April in one year and end on the 31st day of March in the year next following.

Accounts to be kept and to be made up yearly

105. (1) Every council shall keep proper accounts and other records in relation thereto and immediately after the end of each financial year shall cause its accounts for that year to be brought to a balance and a balance sheet prepared with respect thereto together with a statement or abstract of such accounts.

(2) A Divisional Council or District Council shall keep a separate account for any rate which may be made and levied by it at the request of a Local Council.

NOTE. The reference to a Divisional Council in subsection (2) was inserted by Law No. 13 of 1955.

Deposit and suspense accounts

106. A council may make advances and loans and operate deposit and suspense accounts within such limits and upon such conditions as shall be approved in writing by the Regional Authority, and such approval may be given either generally or with respect to any particular council or with respect to the councils in any particular area.

Financial Memoranda [see p. 91]

107. The Regional Authority may issue written instructions (to be called Financial Memoranda), not inconsistent with any of the provisions of this Law, for the better control and management of the financial business of councils, and for the regulation of the procedure of Finance Committees; and such instructions may be issued either generally or with respect to any particular council or with respect to the councils in any particular area and shall be observed and obeyed by the council or councils with respect to which such instructions have been issued.

Estimates [see pp. 104-6]

108. (1) Every council shall submit to the Regional Authority, at such time and in such manner as the Regional Authority may direct, a detailed estimate of its revenue and expenditure for the next ensuing financial year.

(2) The Regional Authority shall consider such estimate as is submitted and may either approve or disapprove such estimate as a whole or disapprove of any item or items contained therein, and shall notify the council accordingly:

Provided that if such estimate is not approved or disapproved by the Regional Authority before the commencement of the financial year for which such estimate is prepared, the council may by resolution authorise expenditure, in accordance with such estimate, on such items as had received approval in the Estimates for the previous financial year so long as the total expenditure so authorised by resolution does not exceed twenty-five per centum of its revenue for the preceding year.

(3) Where the Regional Authority approves the estimate as a whole, the council may incur the expenditure, collect the revenue, and generally put into operation the provisions of the approved estimate, but where the estimate is disapproved as a whole, no expenditure shall be incurred, no revenue collected nor shall any of the provisions of the estimate be put into operation without the prior approval of the Regional Authority.

(4) Where the Regional Authority disapproves of any item or items of expenditure or revenue in an estimate submitted for approval, the remainder of any such estimate excluding such item or items so disapproved shall be deemed to be an approved estimate, but the council shall not incur any expenditure or collect revenue, as the case may be, in respect of the item or items disapproved.

(5) Where the Regional Authority has disapproved of an estimate as a whole or has disapproved of any item or items in an estimate and subsequently approves such estimate or such item or items, or subsequently approves an amended or varied estimate or amended or varied item or items then such estimate or such item or items shall, unless the Regional Authority otherwise directs, be deemed to be and to have been an approved estimate or an approved item or items from the beginning of the financial year to which such estimate or items relate.

(6) Subject to the provisions of any Financial Memoranda relating thereto, a council may by resolution authorise the expenditure of money appropriated for any one purpose in an approved estimate on any other purpose therein contained, but no such expenditure shall be incurred for any purpose in respect of which provision has not been made in such approved estimate without the prior consent of the Regional Authority, and no expenditure shall in any case be so incurred in respect of any purpose where the item in the estimate relating thereto has been disapproved by the Regional Authority.

(7) Where it appears to a council in any financial year that expenditure for any specified purpose is desirable and no, or insufficient, provision therefor has been made in the estimate for such year, a council may submit a supplementary estimate to the Regional Authority for approval and the provisions of subsections (3), (4), (5) and (6) of this section shall apply to such supplementary estimate.

(8) Notwithstanding the provisions of section 99 of this Law, to arrive at the estimated revenue, for the purpose of this section, of a

council which is a rating authority, any sum payable by such council to any other council in satisfaction of a precept shall first be deducted.

(9) The Regional Authority may direct that any council shall have authority to control its own finances, in which case the council shall forward to the Regional Authority any estimate or supplementary estimate of revenue or expenditure required to be submitted in accordance with the foregoing provisions of this section, but the power of approval or disapproval of such estimate or supplementary estimate or of any item thereof, shall not, during the continuation of such direction, be exercised by the Regional Authority.

NOTE. Subsection (9) was inserted by Law No. 13 of 1955.

PART XI. RATES AND RATING

Rating authority [see p. 91]

109. For the purposes of this Law, the rating authority for an area shall be such Divisional or District Council as the Regional Authority may by instrument direct and, subject to the provisions of sections 101 and 139 of this Law, or except as may be otherwise specifically provided in any other Law or Ordinance, no authority other than the rating authority shall have power to make or levy any rate in the area of the authority of such council, notwithstanding any customary law to the contrary.

NOTE. Law No. 13 of 1955 amended this section so that it refers only to Divisional or District Councils.

Duty to make sufficient rates

110. Every council shall make such rates or issue such precepts as will be sufficient to provide for such part of the total estimated expenditure to be incurred by the council during the period in respect of which the rate is made or precept is issued as is to be met out of moneys raised by rates, including in that expenditure any sums payable to any other council under precepts issued by that council, together with such additional amount as is, in the opinion of the council, required to cover expenditure previously incurred, or to meet contingencies or to defray any expenditure which may fall to be defrayed before the date on which the money to be received in respect of the next subsequent rate or precept will become available.

111. (1) In any area in which the Assessment Ordinance applies a rating authority shall have power to impose an annual rate on any tenements within its area which are assessed in accordance with that Ordinance and such rate shall be a uniform amount per pound of the assessed value of such tenements.

(2) The following persons shall be liable for the payment of the rate:

(*a*) in respect of all land which is 'native lands' for the purposes of the Land and Native Rights Ordinance (Cap. 105), the occupier of any tenement not exempt from the rate;

(*b*) in respect of all other tenements, the owner and occupier of every such tenement not exempt from the rate but the same shall be deemed to be an owner's rate, and as between the occupier and the owner of any tenement, shall, in the absence of any agreement to the contrary, be borne by the owner, and the amount thereof, if paid by the occupier, may be recovered by him from the owner in an action for money paid to his use or may be deducted from any rent due or to become due in respect of the tenement.

(3) In this section:

'assessed value' in relation to any tenements means the value at which such tenements are for the time being assessed in the current valuation list (Cap. 16);

'current valuation list' means a valuation list prepared in accordance with the Assessment Ordinance (Cap. 16) and for the time being in force;

'owner', 'occupier' and 'tenement' have the meanings assigned to them respectively in section 2 of the Assessment Ordinance.

NOTE. Law No. 13 of 1955 amended subsection (1) to refer to assessed value instead of annual value and substituted subsection (3) for that subsection as originally enacted.

System of rating where Assessment Ordinance does not apply (Cap. 16)
[see pp. 97-9]

112. (1) (i) In any area to which the Assessment Ordinance does not apply, if it is so stated in the Instrument by which it is established, a rating authority may with the approval of the Regional Authority impose an annual rate on any tenements within the area of its authority which are assessed in accordance with the regulations made

under section 128 of this Law and such rate shall be a uniform amount per pound of the assessed value of such tenements.

(ii) The following persons shall be liable for the payment of the rate:

(*a*) in respect of all land which is 'native lands' for the purposes of the Land and Native Rights Ordinance (Cap. 105), the occupier of any tenement not exempt from the rate;

(*b*) in respect of all other tenements, the owner and occupier of every tenement not exempt from the rate but the same shall be deemed to be an owner's rate, and as between the occupier and the owner of any tenement, shall, in the absence of any agreement to the contrary, be borne by the owner, and the amount thereof if paid by the occupier, may be recovered by him from the owner in an action for money paid to his use or may be deducted from any rent due or to become due in respect of the tenement.

(iii) In this subsection:

'assessed value' in relation to a tenement means the value at which the tenement is, for the time being, assessed in accordance with regulations made under this Part;

'occupier', and 'owner' have the meanings assigned to them, respectively, by section 2 of the Assessment Ordinance (Cap. 16);

'tenement' means any land with buildings which is held or occupied as a distinct or separate holding or tenancy or any wharf or pier, but does not include any land without buildings.

NOTE. Law No. 13 of 1955 amended subsection (1) (i) to refer to assessed value instead of annual value and substituted paragraph (iii) for that paragraph as originally enacted.

(2) (i) In any area to which the Assessment Ordinance (Cap. 16) does not apply, a rating authority, if it is so stated in the Instrument by which it is established, may make and levy an annual rate upon the annual income of any person who, or community which, is liable for the payment of tax within the area of its authority under the provisions of the Direct Taxation Ordinance (Cap. 54) and such rate shall be at such amount per pound of the income of the person assessed as the rating authority may direct provided that the rates per pound shall be uniform throughout the area of the rating authority:

Provided that any person who is taxed in respect of any cattle in lieu of any other tax under the provisions of section 10 of the Direct Taxation Ordinance (Cap. 54), shall not for that reason be liable for the payment of rate under this subsection.

(ii) In addition, such rating authority may by resolution make and levy an annual rate upon any other person who, or class of persons which, is taxable within the area of its authority by virtue of the provisions of the Direct Taxation Ordinance (Cap. 54), and such rate shall be a uniform amount per person:

Provided that the amount of such rate shall not exceed the lowest amount of rate payable by any person rated under the provisions of subparagraph (i) of this subsection.

(iii) The annual income of any person who is rateable under the provisions of this subsection shall be deemed to be the annual income of such person ascertained under the provisions of section 7 of the Direct Taxation Ordinance (Cap. 54), for the purposes of taxation under that Ordinance.

(3) In any area to which the Assessment Ordinance (Cap. 16) does not apply, a rating authority if it is so stated in the Instrument by which it is established may make and levy an annual rate upon any person or class of persons over the age of sixteen years ordinarily resident within the area of its authority.

Assessment committees

113. A rating authority may appoint such assessment committee or committees as it thinks fit for the purpose of assessing the liability of any person or persons for payment of any rate levied or to be levied under this Law.

Different systems of rating

114. (1) An Instrument relating to a council which is a rating authority may authorise that Council:

(a) to apply different systems of rating to different parts of the area of its authority; and

(b) to apply different systems of rating to different descriptions of property.

(2) Except as provided in subsection (1) of this section a rating authority shall not, at any time, apply more than one system of rating within its area.

NOTE. This section was substituted by Law No. 13 of 1955 for section 114 as originally enacted.

Publication of rate

115. (1) Notice of every rate shall be given by the rating authority within ten days after the passing of a resolution making such rate, and the rate shall not be valid unless notice thereof is duly given in manner for the time being required by law.

(2) Notice may be given in such manner as the rating authority may resolve and may if the rating authority think fit be given either by affixing a copy of the resolution or a notice at any time within the said period of ten days in such public or conspicuous places or situations within the area of its authority as it deems necessary, or by publishing a copy of the resolution or notice in one or more newspapers circulating in the area of the authority of the rating authority, and different methods of publication may be used as respects different parts of the area of the authority of the rating authority.

General and special rate

116. (1) For the purpose of raising revenue a rating authority may make and levy a general rate.

(2) In addition to a general rate a rating authority may make and levy a special rate for the purposes of raising revenue for any special purposes, or from any particular part of the area of its authority. Such rate shall be termed a 'special rate'.

Date and place of payment of rate

117. When a rating authority has given notice of a rate in accordance with the provisions of section 115 of this Law, it shall be the duty of every person liable for such rate to pay the amount thereof to a rate collector or other person duly appointed or authorised by the rating authority to collect and receive the same at such time and at such place as may be specified by the rating authority from time to time.

Exemptions from assessment and rating

118. (1) Notwithstanding any other provision of this Law the following tenements shall be exempt from assessment and rating under this Law:

(i) all lands and buildings appropriated exclusively for the purposes of public worship;

(ii) cemeteries and burial grounds;

(iii) charitable and educational institutions;

(iv) any tenements specifically exempted by the Regional Authority by notice in the *Regional Gazette*.

(2) The rating authority may reduce or remit payment of any rate on account of the poverty of any person liable to the payment thereof.

Claim for amount of rate

119. (1) The claim for the amount of any rate payable under the provisions of this Law shall be prior to all other claims against the person liable to pay the same, except claims by the Crown or the Government.

(2) If any person fails to pay any rate for which he is liable on or before the date on which it is payable the rating authority may recover the same as a civil debt with costs and interest at the rate of ten per centum per annum from the day when such rate ought to have been paid until the date of payment.

Penalty for refusal to pay rates and wilful misrepresentation

120. (1) Any person who, without lawful justification or excuse, the proof of which shall lie on the person charged, refuses to pay any rate payable by him under this Law on or before the date on which it is payable, shall be guilty of an offence and shall be liable to a fine not exceeding one hundred pounds or in default of payment to imprisonment for a term not exceeding one year.

(2) Any person who wilfully misrepresents in any way his rateable capacity shall be guilty of an offence and shall be liable to a fine not exceeding one hundred pounds or to imprisonment for a term not exceeding one year or to both such fine and imprisonment.

Penalty for inciting a person to refuse to pay rates, etc.

121. Any person who without lawful justification or excuse, the proof of which shall lie on the person charged, incites any person to refuse to pay any rate payable by him under this Law on or before the day on which it is payable or who incites or assists any person to misrepresent in any way his rateable capacity, shall be guilty of an offence, and shall be liable to a fine not exceeding one hundred pounds or to imprisonment for a term not exceeding one year or to both such fine and imprisonment.

Penalty for unauthorised collection of rates

122. Any person who:

(a) not being authorised under this Law or by the council concerned or by a rate collector so to do, collects or attempts to collect any rate under this Law;

(b) collects or attempts to collect any rates other than the rates described in this Law or authorised by any other Law;

shall be guilty of an offence and shall be liable to a fine not exceeding one hundred pounds or to imprisonment for a term not exceeding one year or to both such fine and imprisonment.

Duty to give information

123. Any person who may be required so to do shall give all such information as may reasonably be required of him by any rating authority, rate collector, assessment committee, or appraiser appointed under this Law, with a view to obtaining information for the assessment or collection of the rate.

Penalty for refusing to give information

124. Any person having been required to give information under the provisions of section 123 who shall neglect or refuse to give such information or who shall wilfully mislead or attempt to mislead any rating authority or rate collector or their agents in any matter connected with the collection of the rate shall be liable to a fine of one hundred pounds or to imprisonment for one year or to both such fine and imprisonment.

Appointment of rate collectors

125. (1) A rating authority may, in writing, appoint any council or any suitable person to be a rate collector in respect of any specified area.

(2) It shall be the duty of every rate collector:

(*a*) to furnish orally or in writing to the rating authority a nominal roll of all rateable persons or tenements as the case may be in the area to which he has been appointed;

(*b*) to collect and receive from each person liable for the payment of rates in the area to which he has been appointed the rates payable by each such person;

(*c*) to pay all amounts so collected to the rating authority; and

(*d*) to report to the rating authority the name of any person who has failed to pay the amount due from him for rates.

Penalty in respect of offences by rate collector

126. Any rate collector or individual member of a rate collector who:

(*a*) fails to deposit with the rating authority any sum of money collected by him as rates;

(*b*) demands from any community or any person an amount in excess of the duly assessed rates;

(*c*) renders false returns, whether orally or in writing, of the number of the ratepayers or the amounts of rates collected or received by him;

(*d*) fails to carry out any duty imposed upon him, either individually or as a member of a rate collector,

shall be guilty of an offence and shall be liable to a fine of one hundred pounds or to imprisonment for two years or both such fine and imprisonment.

Legal proceedings

127. Proceedings either to enforce the payment of any rate payable under the provisions of this Part or for the imposition of penalties under the provisions of this Part may be taken either by the rating authority or by a rate collector as the case may be, before any court of competent jurisdiction.

Regulations relating to rates and rating

128. (1) The Regional Authority may make regulations:

(*a*) prescribing the procedure for the appointment of assessment committees under section 113 of this Law and the procedure, powers and duties of such committees;

(*b*) prescribing the method of assessment of property or possessions for the purposes of any rate to be levied under this law;

(*c*) providing for the hearing of appeals against any such assessment.

(2) Regulations made under this section shall provide that the assessment of the properties of any body directly incorporated by any Ordinance or Law shall be in accordance with the provisions of that Ordinance or Law, and in so far as provision is not made therein, in accordance with the provisions of the Assessment Ordinance.

NOTE. Law No. 13 of 1955 inserted subsection (2) and deleted paragraph (*d*) of the section as originally enacted.

For provisions relating to the rating of statutory corporations see section 54 of the Electricity Corporation of Nigeria Ordinance, 1950, and section 118 of the Ports Ordinance, 1954.

PART XII. PRECEPTS

Divisional council may precept [see p. 91]

129. (1) Except where it is itself the rating authority a Divisional Council shall have power to issue precepts for the purpose of meeting liabilities in respect of expenditure for which the whole of the area of the authority of the council is liable or for the purpose of meeting

liabilities in respect of expenditure for which only part of the area of its authority is liable.

(2) A precept issued by a Divisional Council for the purpose of meeting liabilities in respect of expenditure for which the whole area of its authority is liable shall be addressed to all the rating authorities situate in the area of the authority of such Divisional Council.

(3) A precept issued by a Divisional Council for the purpose of meeting liabilities in respect of expenditure for which part only of the area of its authority is liable shall be addressed to such rating authorities as are situate within the area chargeable with such expenditure.

(4) A precept issued by a Divisional Council shall be expressed as a lump sum and shall be satisfied by the rating authority to which it is addressed.

(5) Where a Divisional Council issues a precept to more than one rating authority under the provisions of this section the sum required from a rating authority shall bear to the total sum required by the Divisional Council the same proportion as the taxable population within the area of the rating authority, as assessed by the Regional Authority, bears to the taxable population within the area of authority of the Divisional Council as assessed by the Regional Authority:

Provided that the Regional Authority may, in any particular case, direct that a Divisional Council may issue precepts to rating authorities under which the total sum required is to be met by such rating authorities in such proportions as may be specified in the direction instead of in the proportions specified in this subsection.

NOTE. Law No. 13 of 1955 substituted this section for the section originally enacted as section 129.

District council may precept [see p. 91]

130. (1) Except where it is itself the rating authority a District Council shall have power to issue precepts for the purpose of meeting liabilities in respect of expenditure for which the whole of the area of the authority of the council is liable or for the purpose of meeting liabilities in respect of expenditure for which part only of the area of its authority is liable.

(2) A precept issued by a District Council shall be addressed to the Divisional Council within whose area of authority it is situated.

(3) A precept issued by a District Council shall be expressed as the rate to be levied on behalf of such council and shall be satisfied by the Divisional Council to which it is addressed.

NOTE. Law No. 13 of 1955 substituted this section for the section originally enacted as section 130.

Local Council may precept

131. (1) Subject to the provisions of section 132 a Local Council shall have power to issue precepts for the levying of rates to the rating authority in the area of the authority in which it is situate to meet all liabilities falling to be discharged by such Local Council.

(2) Any precept issued by a Local Council shall be satisfied by the rating authority.

Precepts by Local Council

132. (1) Any precept issued by a Local Council shall be passed by the council by a resolution of three-fourths of the Councillors present and voting at a meeting of the council, and be approved by the Local Government Inspector unless the Instrument by which the council is established otherwise provides.

(2) A precept may be issued by a Local Council for the purposes of meeting liabilities in respect of expenditure for which the whole of the area of the authority of the council is liable or for the purpose of meeting liabilities in respect of part of the area of its authority.

(3) A precept issued by a Local Council shall be so issued as to secure that any rate is levied:

(*a*) in the case of a rate to meet liabilities in respect of expenditure for which the whole area of the authority of the council is chargeable, on the whole of the area of the authority of such Local Council; and

(*b*) in the case of a rate to meet liabilities in respect of expenditure for which part of the area of the council is chargeable, on that part of the area of the authority of the council chargeable therewith.

(4) A precept issued by a Local Council shall indicate the purpose for which the precept is issued, and may indicate the ratepayers or classes of ratepayers upon whom the rate is to be levied by the rating authority.

(5) In an area in which the Assessment Ordinance (Cap. 16) applies a precept issued by a Local Council shall not require the rating authority to make and levy in any one year:

(*a*) a general rate in excess of ten per centum of the annual value of any rateable tenement; and (*b*) a special rate in excess of ten per centum of the annual value of any rateable tenement.

(6) In an area in which the Assessment Ordinance (Cap. 16) does not apply a precept issued by a Local Council shall not require the rating authority to make and levy in any one year a general rate in excess of:

(*a*) ten per centum on the annual value of any rateable tenement, rated under the provisions of subsection (1) of section 112; or

(*b*) threepence in the pound of a rateable income rated under the provisions of paragraph (i) of subsection (2) of section 112;

(*c*) the lowest sum of money payable by a ratepayer under paragraph (*b*) rated under the provisions of paragraph (ii) of subsection (2) of section 112; or

(*d*) a capitation rate of four shillings per person rated under the provisions of subsection (3) of section 112.

(7) In addition to the provisions of subsection (6) in an area to which the Assessment Ordinance (Cap. 16) does not apply a Local Council may issue precepts to the rating authority requiring it to make and levy a special rate in any one year not in excess of the amounts of rate specified in subsection (6).

(8) The Rating Authority from time to time may increase, reduce, revoke or alter the amounts of rate specified in subsections (5) and (6) of this section.

Precepts may include general and special contributions

133. A precept issued by a council may include as separate items a contribution for purposes for which the whole area of its authority is chargeable and a contribution for special purposes.

Matters to be contained in precepts

134. (1) A council shall on issuing a precept inform the rating authority of the purpose for which such precept is issued and give such other information as is reasonably necessary to enable the rating authority to satisfy such precept and to ascertain if the precept shall be satisfied by a general rate or by a special rate.

(2) A precept shall state the date or dates on or before which payment is required to be made.

NOTE. Law No. 13 of 1955 substituted this section for the section originally enacted as section 134.

Time of service of precept

135. Unless otherwise stated in the Instrument, any precept issued by a council shall be served on the rating authority concerned before the 1st day of December in the year preceding the financial year in which the demand is to be satisfied, or before such other date as the Regional Authority may direct.

Rating Authority to furnish information to councils concerned

136. It shall be the duty of a rating authority to furnish to every council concerned such information as may be required by such council in order to enable it to issue precepts upon such rating authority.

Amount due under precept

137. For the purposes of estimating and ascertaining the amount due under a precept the cost of collection and losses in collection shall not be considered.

NOTE. Law No. 13 of 1955 deleted subsections (1) and (2) of the section as originally enacted.

Interest on unsatisfied precepts

138. Where the amount due under a precept or any part of that amount is not paid on or before the date specified in the precept for payment, the council by which the precept was issued may, if it thinks fit, require the rating authority to pay interest at five per centum per annum on that amount or part of that amount and any interest so payable shall be paid by the rating authority to the council by which the precept was issued in like manner as if it were due under the precept.

Power to enforce precepts

139. Where a council fails to pay the amount or any part of the amount due under a precept on or before the date specified in the precept for payment, the Regional Authority may, on application by the council by which the precept was issued, exercise any of the powers conferred upon him by section 75 of this Law.

PART XIII. AUDIT

Inspection and audit of accounts [see p.108]

140. (1) The accounts kept by a council in accordance with section 105 of this Law, together with all books, vouchers, papers and moneys relating thereto shall be made available by the council at all times for inspection by an auditor to be appointed in respect of the council by the Minister.

(2) Such accounts shall be audited at such intervals as the Minister may direct and, for that purpose, a council shall prepare and submit to the auditor statements or abstracts containing such particulars and relating to such periods as the Minister may specify.

(3) For the avoidance of doubt it is hereby declared that the Minister may appoint a Local Government Inspector or any member of the staff of the Ministry of Local Government to be an auditor in respect of any council [see p.109].

(4) The Minister may exempt any Local Council from the requirements of this section.

NOTE. Law No. 13 of 1955 substituted this section for the section originally enacted as section 140.

Liability for payment of remuneration of auditors

141. Payment shall be made by a council in respect of the remuneration and expenses of any auditor appointed under this Law, including the staff of such auditor, to such amount as the Regional Authority shall determine.

Powers and duties of auditor [see pp.109-10]

142. (1) An auditor appointed by the Minister at every audit held by him may:

(*a*) disallow any item of expenditure which is contrary to law or Financial Memoranda issued under section 107 of this Law, or is unsupported by proper records or accounts, or which he considers unreasonable;

(*b*) surcharge the amount of any expenditure disallowed upon the person responsible for incurring or authorising the expenditure;

(*c*) surcharge any sum which has not been duly brought into account upon the person by whom that sum ought to have been brought into account;

(*d*) surcharge the amount of any loss or deficiency upon any person by whose negligence or misconduct the loss or deficiency has been incurred:

Provided that no item of expenditure incurred by a council shall be disallowed by the auditor, if it has been sanctioned by the Regional Authority

(2) It shall be the duty of any such auditor:

(*a*) to certify the amount due from any person upon whom he has made a surcharge; and (*b*) to certify at the conclusion of the audit his allowance of the accounts, subject to any disallowances or surcharges which he may have made.

NOTE. Law No. 13 of 1955 substituted paragraph (*a*) of subsection (1) for that paragraph as originally enacted.

Special relief [see pp.111-12]

143. Notwithstanding any of the provisions of the last preceding section, no liability to surcharge shall be incurred by an officer or servant of the council who can prove to the satisfaction of the auditor that he acted in pursuance of, and in accordance with, the terms of a resolution of the council or of a committee duly appointed by the council, or on the written instructions of any senior officer of the council.

Auditor may take evidence [see p.110]

144. (1) For the purpose of any examination under the provisions of this Part, the auditor may take evidence and examine witnesses, upon oath or affirmation (which oath or affirmation the auditor is hereby empowered to administer), and may, by summons under his hand, require all such persons, as he may think fit, to appear personally before him at a time and place to be stated in such summons and to produce all such books and papers, including the minutes of the proceedings of the council or of any committee thereof, as he may consider necessary for such examination.

(2) Any person who, when so required, without reasonable excuse:

(*a*) neglects or refuses to comply with the terms of such summons;

(*b*) having appeared, refuses to be examined on oath or affirmation or to take such oath or affirmation; or

(*c*) having taken such oath or affirmation, refuses to answer such questions as are put to him;

shall be guilty of an offence and shall be liable, on conviction therefor for every such neglect or refusal, to a fine not exceeding twenty-five pounds or to imprisonment for a term not exceeding three months.

Payment of sums due

145. Every sum certified by the auditor to be due from any person shall be paid by that person to the treasury of the council concerned within sixty days after it has been so certified or, if an appeal with respect to that sum has been made, within thirty days after the appeal is finally disposed of or abandoned or fails by reason of the non-prosecution thereof.

Recovery

146. (1) Any sum which is certified by the auditor to be due and has become payable shall, on complaint made or action taken by or under the direction of the Regional Authority, be recoverable as a civil debt.

(2) In any proceedings for the recovery of such a sum, a certificate signed by the auditor shall be conclusive evidence of the facts certified, and a certificate signed by the chairman of the council concerned or other officer whose duty it is to keep the accounts that the sum certified to be due has not been paid to him shall be conclusive evidence of non-payment, unless it is proved that the sum certified to be due has been paid since the date of the certificate.

(3) Unless the contrary is proved, a certificate purporting to be signed by the auditor, or by the chairman of the council or other officer whose duty it is to keep the accounts, shall be deemed to have been signed by such auditor, chairman or other officer, as the case may be.

Appeals [see p.110]

147. (1) Any person who is aggrieved by a decision of the auditor on any matter with respect to which he made an objection at the audit, and any person aggrieved by a disallowance or surcharge made by the auditor may, where the disallowance or surcharge or other decision relates to an amount not exceeding two hundred pounds appeal to the Regional Authority and may in any other case appeal either to the Regional Authority or to the High Court.

(2) The High Court or Regional Authority on such appeal shall have power to confirm, vary or quash the decision of the auditor, and to remit the case to the auditor with such directions as the High Court or Regional Authority thinks fit for giving effect to the decision on appeal, and if the decision of the auditor is quashed, or is varied so as to reduce the amount of the surcharge to one hundred pounds or less, the appellant shall not by reason of the surcharge be subject to the disqualification imposed by section 24 (*b*) of this Law.

(3) Where an appeal is made to the Regional Authority under the section, he may at any stage of the proceedings state in the form of a special case for the opinion of the High Court any question of law arising in the course of the appeal, but save as aforesaid the decision of the Regional Authority shall be final.

NOTE. Legal Notice No. 76 of 1955 substituted references in this section to the High Court for references to the Supreme Court.

Annual statements of account

148. Every council shall render to the Regional Authority an annual financial statement, duly certified by the auditor, in such form as the Regional Authority may direct and unless the Regional Authority shall otherwise direct shall before the first day of September in each year publish the same at its own offices, and in any other manner customary in the area.

NOTE. The requirement that the annual statement of accounts should be published at the treasury of the Divisional Council was deleted by Law No. 13 of 1955.

With regard to joint committees for police purposes see now the Local Government Police Law, 1955.

PART XIV. ASSOCIATIONS OF COUNCILS

Establishment of joint committees to operate joint services

149. (1) Where two or more councils desire to make provisions for the joint operation of services of any kind (which term shall include police, prisons, a treasury and any other service which a single council may lawfully (operate) and have provided therefor by joint estimates, they may, with the approval of the Minister, jointly and severally establish a committee for the purpose (hereinafter referred to as a 'joint committee'), to consist of a person or persons appointed in manner agreed between the councils concerned, and, subject to the provisions of sections 151, 154, and 155, jointly and severally delegate to such joint committee all or any of their functions in respect of the operation of such services.

(2) Where the Regional Authority deems it expedient so to do, he may require any two or more councils to establish a joint committee for the purpose of the joint operation of services of any kind and, subject to the provisions of sections 151, 154, and 155, require such councils to delegate to such joint committee all or any of their functions in respect of the operation of such services.

(3) Nothing in this section shall authorise the establishment of a joint committee for the purpose of any service for which provision is made in the Education Law, 1954, by a Council which is a local education authority appointed under that Law.

NOTE. Law No. 13 of 1955 amended subsection (1) to confer the power of approval on the Minister instead of on the Local Government Inspector. Subsection (3) was inserted by Law No. 6 of 1955.

Appointment, removal and remuneration of members of joint committees

150. (1) The Instrument establishing the joint committee shall contain provision for the appointment and removal of members of the joint committee, and for the duration of their appointments.

(2) The members of a joint committee shall be deemed to be employed, for the purpose of the joint committee, by the councils concerned jointly, and shall receive such remuneration as may be jointly determined by the councils concerned.

Functions which may be delegated

151. The Instrument establishing a joint committee may delegate to it with or without restrictions or conditions any powers or functions of the councils concerned relating to the purpose for which the joint committee is formed except the power of making bye-laws, or levying a rate or issuing a precept or borrowing money.

Joint committees may sue and be sued

152. The establishment of a joint committee shall be notified in the *Regional Gazette,* and thereupon the joint committee may sue, and be sued as such, and the provisions of section 205 to 205c shall apply, *mutatis mutandis,* to civil legal proceedings by or against the joint committee.

NOTE. The words 'to 205c' were added by Law No. 8 of 1955.

Joint committees to be bodies corporate

153. Every joint committee shall be a body corporate by the name designated in the instrument establishing such committee, and shall have perpetual succession and a common seal and may sue and be sued.

Exercise of delegated powers

154. A joint committee shall exercise the powers delegated to it subject to such joint directions, whether general or particular, as it may from time to time receive from the councils concerned but so long as the delegation remains in force none of the councils concerned shall itself exercise any of the delegated powers, with the exception of the powers referred to in section 58.

Revocation or modification of delegated powers

155. (1) A council which has delegated any of its powers to a joint committee shall not revoke or modify the delegation without the prior consent of the Minister, which shall be subject to such conditions as to financial or other matters as the Minister may deem just, and, without prejudice to the generality of the foregoing, the Minister may direct that such revocation or modification shall not take effect until the last day of a financial year, as defined in section 104.

(2) Any such revocation or modification shall be notified in the *Regional Gazette*.

NOTE. Law No. 13 of 1955 amended subsection (1) by substituting references to the Minister for references to the Local Government Inspector.

Services operated by joint committees and employees of joint committees

156. (1) Where the management of one or more existing police forces or prisons or other services is delegated to a joint committee, the joint force or service shall be deemed to have been constituted by the joint committee.

(2) All persons employed in any service which is operated by a joint committee shall, from the date of the delegation to the joint committee of power to operate the service, be deemed to be employed by the joint committee:

Provided that for the purpose of computing seniority of service, any period of service spent in the employment of any of the councils concerned shall be deemed to be service in the employment of the joint committee and *vice versa*.

[PART XV. POLICE, containing sections 157–167, was repealed by the Local Government Police Law, 1955]

PART XVI. PRISONS

Council may by order constitute or take over a prison

168. (1) A council with the approval of the Regional Authority may by order declare any building within the area of its jurisdiction to be a prison under this Law and by the same or any subsequent order declare the district or place for which any such building shall be used for the purposes of a prison and may likewise order that any building declared a prison under this Law shall cease to be a prison.

(2) A council with the approval of the Regional Authority may by order take over any native authority prison existing within the area of its authority.

Extent of prison

169. Every prison shall include the grounds and buildings within the prison enclosure.

Who may be confined in a prison

170. Any prisoner may be confined in a prison constituted under this Law who:

(*a*) is awaiting trial before any native court or who has been convicted by such court;

(*b*) has been committed to custody by the High Court, or any magistrate's court, when the Governor-General or the Governor in Council, in exercise of the powers conferred upon him by section 26 of the Prisons Ordinance, has so ordered.

Council may by order constitute a lock-up

171. A council with the approval of the Local Government Inspector may within the area of jurisdiction of the council and of any one native court declare any one building, part of a building, or collection of buildings together with the enclosure, if any, relating thereto to be a lock-up and such declaration shall be made known within the area of the council in such manner as is customary.

Period of detention in a lock-up

172. Subject to such regulations as may be made by the Governor under section 180, a prisoner who is awaiting trial or who has been convicted or who has been adjudged a debtor, may be detained in a lock-up for a period not exceeding fourteen days.

Prison and lock-up officers

173. The council shall appoint:

(*a*) for each prison a head warder, a prison clerk and such number of warders and wardresses as shall be necessary for the proper administration of the prison; and

(*b*) for each lock-up such officers as may be necessary.

Superintendence and visitation of prisoners

174. (1) The Director of Prisons shall have the general superintendence of prisons established under this Law, shall advise the councils thereon, and shall submit to the Regional Authority an annual report on the administration of the prisons and such other reports as the Regional Authority or the Director of Prisons may consider necessary.

(2) The Chief Justice, Members of the Executive Council, Judges of the High Court, the Commissioner of Police, and officers of or above the rank of field officer in the Royal West African Frontier Force shall *ex officio* be visitors of all prisons established under this Part of this Law.

(3) In addition to the *ex officio* visitors hereinbefore mentioned a magistrate shall be an *ex officio* visitor in respect of each prison within

the district in which he is officiating as a magistrate and there shall also be appointed by the Local Government Inspector not less than five other persons to be visitors in respect of any or all such prisons within the particular province or the Colony, as the case may be.

(4) The Local Government Inspector shall appoint one or more of such visitors to be a visiting committee for each prison, but the appointment of such committee shall not interfere with the general right of visitation on the part of the visitors.

(5) For the purposes of this section the expression 'prison' includes a lock-up.

NOTE. Law No. 8 of 1953 inserted subsection (1) of this section, which was further amended by Law No. 2 of 1954.

Prisoners in legal custody of head warder

175. Subject to such regulations as may be made by the Regional Authority under section 180 relating to prisoners under sentence of death, every prisoner shall be deemed to be in the custody of the head warder.

Provisions in the case of lunacy of prisoners

176. (1) The head warder shall report to the council and also to a medical officer or to an Assistant Local Government Inspector any prisoner who appears to be of unsound mind. If the prisoner shall be certified by a medical officer to be of unsound mind, the Local Government Inspector, after consultation with the council constituted for the area within which the prison is situated, shall by order in writing under his hand authorise the removal of the prisoner to a lunatic asylum to which the Lunacy Ordinance (Cap. 121) applies and which may have been appointed by the Governor for that purpose.

(2) Any prisoner removed as aforesaid shall remain in such asylum until the term of imprisonment to which he is subject determines or until it shall be certified by a medical officer that he has become of sound mind in which latter case he shall by order of the Local Government Inspector be redelivered into the custody of the aforesaid head warder.

(3) Where a prisoner has been removed to a lunatic asylum in accordance with the provisions of subsection (1) and it has been certified by a medical officer that he has become of unsound mind and his term of imprisonment is about to determine, it shall be the duty of the head warder to give information on oath to a magistrate as in the terms of Form B in the Schedule to the Lunacy Ordinance (Cap. 121) for the purpose of the adjudication of such person as a lunatic as from the date of the determination of his sentence.

177. (1) The head warder, upon receiving the order of a court directing him to bring up a prisoner before the court at the time and place stated therein, shall obey such order and may, for the purpose of carrying out such order, cause the prisoner to be removed to another prison established under this Law or under the Prisons Ordinance (Cap. 177).

(2) If the prisoner shall be remanded, committed for trial, imprisoned, or detained by such court, he shall be so dealt with either in the prison whence he came, or in such other prison as such court may direct.

Removal of prisoners in other cases

178. A Local Government Inspector or any officer who may have been authorised in that behalf by a Local Government Inspector may order any person imprisoned under the sentence of any court for an offence committed by him to be removed from the prison in which he is confined to any other prison within the meaning of this Law, and whenever any prisoner is removed to any other prison than that named in the warrant or order under which he may have been imprisoned, the said warrant or order, together with an order of removal, either endorsed on the warrant or order, or separate therefrom, shall be sufficient authority for the removal of such prisoner to the prison named in the order of removal, and his detention therein, and for carrying out the sentence described in the warrant or order of imprisonment, or any part thereof which may remain unexecuted.

Provided that where a prisoner who has been committed to custody by the High Court or a magistrate's court and is confined in a prison authorised by the Governor-General or the Governor by Order in Council made under section 26 of the Prisons Ordinance (Cap. 177) as being a prison in which persons so committed to custody may be detained, such prisoner shall not be transferred to another prison except one so authorised.

Rules

179. (1) The Regional Authority and, subject to the provisions of any Law or Ordinance for the time being in force, a council subject to the approval of the Regional Authority may, in respect of a prison established within its jurisdiction make rules for all or any of the following purposes:

(*a*) relating to prison staff:

(i) the engagement, discharge and service of members of a prison staff;

(ii) the titles or grades of which a prison staff shall consist;

(iii) the uniform or equipment of a prison staff;

(iv) the prevention of negligence or abuse on the part of members of a prison staff, and the maintenance of discipline;

(v) the efficient discharge of their duties by members of a prison staff;

(vi) generally for ensuring the proper administration of and control over prison staff;

(*b*) relating to the prisoners:

(i) the return of a discharged prisoner to his ordinary place of abode and the necessary and proper precaution to ensure such return;

(ii) the release of prisoners on the day preceding such holidays or other days as may be specified in the rules;

(iii) the regulation of the work or labour of convicted persons;

(iv) the remission of sentences for good conduct;

(v) the discipline of the prisoners.

(2) Where a council has with the approval of the Regional Authority made rules in respect of any of the matters referred to in subsection (1), any regulations made by the Regional Authority in respect of the same matters shall cease to have effect in respect of the prisons to which such council rules apply.

Power to make regulations

180. (1) The Regional Authority may make regulations in respect of prisons to which this Part applies for any or all of the following purposes:

(*a*) for regulating the legal custody of prisoners under sentence of death;

(*b*) for the removal of prisoners in case of infectious disease and the removal of sick prisoners to a hospital outside the prison and the custody of prisoners so removed;

(*c*) the grant of licences to prisoners to be at large, the conditions of such licence and the penalties and procedure upon a breach of such conditions;

(*d*) the health and diet of the prisoners;

(*e*) the length of time and conditions under which a person awaiting trial or a judgement debtor may be kept in custody in a lock-up;

(*f*) notwithstanding the particularity of the powers hereinbefore

vested in such council for the estate or interest claimed, free from all adverse or competing rights, titles, interests, trusts, claims and demands whatsoever.

NOTE. The period of five years specified in subsection (1) was substituted for the period of two years by Law No. 13 of 1955. Subsection (3) was substituted by Law No. 13 of 1955 for that subsection as originally enacted. Subsection (5) was inserted by Law No. 8 of 1953 and amended by Law No. 13 of 1955.

Council may file documents in Land Registry

186. (1) Where a council has deposited a list of properties in accordance with section 185 and published a notice in the *Gazette* in accordance with subsection (3) of that section, it may, after the expiration of two years from the publication in the *Gazette* of such notice file in the appropriate office of the Land Registry:

(a) a certificate signed by the Commissioner of Lands:

(i) stating that a plan was deposited in accordance with the provisions of subsection (2) of section 185;

(ii) specifying the rights or interests claimed by the council in respect of which no dispute has arisen; and

(iii) specifying the rights or interests of which the council has been adjudged the owner in accordance with subsection (4) of section 185; and

(b) a plan or plans showing the boundaries of the land referred to in the certificate.

(2) Where a council has filed a certificate and plan in accordance with subsection (1) of this section, the proceedings of the council under section 185 shall not be questioned on the grounds that the council has failed to comply with any of the provisions of that section.

NOTE. Law No. 13 of 1955 substituted this section for the section originally enacted as section 186.

Power of councils to acquire land compulsorily [see p.127]

187. A council may, with the consent of the Regional Authority previously obtained, acquire compulsorily any lands within the area of its jurisdiction required for local government purposes either absolutely or for a term of years or for such time as it may be required for local government purposes.

Preliminary investigation [see p.128]

188. (1) Whenever it appears to any council that any land within the area of its jurisdiction is likely to be needed for any local government purpose it shall be lawful for any council in this behalf and for their servants and workmen to do all or any of the following things:

(*a*) to enter upon and survey and take levels of any land in such locality;

(*b*) to dig or bore under the sub-soil;

(*c*) to do all other acts necessary to ascertain whether the land is adapted for such purpose;

(*d*) to clear, set out and mark the boundaries of the land proposed to be acquired and the intended line of the work (if any) proposed to be made thereon: provided that no person shall enter into any building or upon any enclosed court or garden attached to a dwelling house (except with the consent of the occupier thereof) without previously giving such occupier at least seven days' notice of his intention to do so.

(2) As soon as conveniently may be after any entry made under subsection (1) the person so authorised as aforesaid shall pay for all damage done and in the case of dispute as to the amount to be paid either such person or the person claiming compensation may refer such dispute to the native court having jurisdiction in the area.

Notice to be given [see p.128]

189. (1) When a council decides that any lands shall be acquired for local government purposes and the Regional Authority has given his consent thereto, the council shall give notice to the persons interested or claiming to be interested in such lands or to such of them as shall after reasonable enquiry be known to the council.

(2) The notice to be given under subsection (1) hereof may be in the Form A in the First Schedule hereto or to the like effect and shall specify:

(*a*) the purpose for which the land is being acquired; and

(*b*) whether the land is being acquired absolutely or for a term of years or for such time as it may be required for the purpose aforesaid.

(3) If under the provision of section 197 the council shall decide to allocate other land to the person entitled to the lands acquired the notice shall state in addition to the matters specified in Form A the fact that other land is to be allocated to the persons entitled and the situation of such land.

(4) All notices required to be served in accordance with subsection (1) hereof shall be displayed at the office of the council by whom such lands are acquired and upon the land to be acquired and shall be made known in such manner as is customary in the area of the authority by which the notice is issued.

Power to take possession

190. (1) The council may by such notice aforesaid or by any subsequent notice direct the persons aforesaid to yield up possession of such lands after the expiration of the period specified in the notice which period shall not be less than six weeks from the service of such notice.

At the expiration of such period the council and all persons authorised by it shall be entitled to enter into and take possession of such lands accordingly.

(2) A duplicate of such notice shall be served on the occupier or occupiers of such lands.

Vesting of land acquired

191. (1) Any lands acquired as aforesaid by a council shall vest in such council at the date of the entry of the council into possession thereof for the estate or interest specified in the notice published in accordance with section 189 against all persons free from all adverse or competing rights, titles, interests, trusts, claims and demands whatsoever.

(2) Upon the entry of a council into possession all leases and all rights of occupancy in respect of the lands acquired which are existing at the time of entry shall be deemed to be terminated but without prejudice to any lessees or occupiers rights in any compensation payable under section 198.

Claims by persons on whom notices served

192. (1) If for six months after the service of a notice under section 189 (2) no objection to the offer made in such notice shall have been lodged with the council and no other claim shall have been made the amount specified in such offer shall be paid forthwith to the person specified in the notice in full discharge of any claim for compensation.

(2) If an objection is lodged within the prescribed time any question as to the amount of compensation payable in respect of the land acquired and any questions as to the apportionment of such compensation among the persons having an interest in the land shall in default of agreement be determined by the native court or an arbitrator in manner hereinafter mentioned.

Claims by persons not served

193. (1) All persons not served with a notice in accordance with section 189 claiming any interest in any lands acquired shall within six months of the publication of the notice acquiring the land notify the council either in writing or by attending personally at the office of the council of:

(*a*) the interest of the claimant in the said land; and
(*b*) the amount of compensation claimed.

(2) No person claiming after the expiration of the period of six months shall be entitled to recover compensation by way of land or money.

Matters of dispute to be referred

194. If the person who may have lodged any claim and the council shall not agree as to the amount of the compensation by way of land or money to be given for the estate or interest in such lands belonging to such person, or if such person has not given satisfactory evidence of such claim or if separate and conflicting claims are made in respect of the same lands the amount of compensation due, if any, and every such case of disputed interest or title shall be settled by a court or an arbitrator in manner hereinafter provided.

Tribunal for settlement of disputes

195. (1) All matters which shall be referred to a court for determination in accordance with sections 192 (2) and 194 shall be determined by a native court upon which courts necessary jurisdiction is hereby conferred or at the option of the claimant concerned, by an arbitrator appointed in manner hereinafter provided.

(2) When a matter is referred to a native court the steps to be taken for the appearance of the parties the proceedings in court and the right of appeal shall be the same as if it were a suit for determination by that court between two persons normally subject to the jurisdiction of that native court.

(3) If any claimant shall require that the matter shall be referred to an arbitrator, such arbitrator shall be appointed by agreement between the council and the person claiming compensation. In the absence of such agreement or in the event of the person claiming compensation failing to nominate an arbitrator within one month of being called upon by the council the arbitrator shall be appointed by the Regional Authority upon the application of the council.

(4) The award of an arbitrator under the provisions of this section shall be final.

Written report of Government officer to be evidence

196. (1) The written report of any officer of the Public Works, Land Survey, Agriculture, Forestry, or Railway Departments as to the value of the lands or of any buildings or trees or crops thereon shall be evidence thereof.

(2) Any such officer may on giving three days notice in writing to the occupier enter upon any such lands or into any buildings thereon for the purposes of ascertaining the value of such land and the buildings, trees, and crops thereof.

(3) Any party having an interest in such lands or the court or an arbitrator may require the attendance of such officer as a witness.

(4) The report of such officer may be proved by a copy thereof under his hand, and proof of the signature on such copy shall not be required unless the court sees reason to doubt the genuineness thereof.

Council may offer alternative land

197. (1) If there shall be any land subject to the disposition of the council available for allocation the council may allocate to the persons entitled to the land acquired land equivalent in value and interest to the holdings of such persons over the land acquired.

(2) In addition to any land allocated in accordance with subsection (1) thereof the person entitled to the land acquired shall be entitled to compensation for the value at the date of acquisition of the land of his unexhausted improvements and for the inconvenience caused by his disturbance.

Rules for assessment of compensation

198. If no land shall be allocated to the person entitled to the land acquired under the provisions of section 197 the court or an arbitrator shall in estimating the compensation to be given for any land or any estate or interest therein act on the principles laid down for the assessment of compensation in the Public Lands Acquisition Ordinance (Cap. 185) from time to time.

Council may withdraw from completing acquisition

199. Nothing in this Law shall be taken to compel a council to complete the acquisition of any land unless it shall have entered in possession or has failed within one month of the judgement of the arbitrator to intimate to the person entitled to the land that it does not intend to proceed to acquire the land.

Provided however that the owner of the land and all persons entitled to any interest therein shall be entitled to receive from the council all such costs as may have been incurred by them by reason or in consequence of the proceedings to acquire the land.

Council not responsible for application of compensation

200. The payment to any person to whom any compensation shall be paid or the payment into court of any compensation upon the decision of a court shall discharge a council from seeing to the application or being answerable for the misapplication thereof.

Documents may be filed in Land Registry and effect thereof

201. (1) A council may after entering into possession of any land acquired under the provisions of this Law file in the appropriate office of the Land Registry of Nigeria a copy of the notice published in accordance with section 189 together with:

(i) a plan on which is delineated as accurately as may be practicable the boundaries of the land affected; and

(ii) a certificate signed by the Commissioner of Lands:

(*a*) that the approval of the Regional Authority has been given; and

(*b*) that notice was published as required by section 189; and

(*c*) that notice was served upon the persons required to be served under this Law.

(2) After the date of the filing of such documents the proceedings previous thereto shall not be questioned or defeasible by reason of any irregularity or error or defect in the notice or want of notice, or of any other irregularity, error or defect.

NOTE. Law No. 13 of 1955 substituted the reference in this section to the Commissioner of Lands for a reference which appeared in the original section to the Local Government Inspector.

Divesting of land no longer required

202. (1) Any lands vested in a council by virtue of the provisions of section 191 shall, subject to the provisions of subsection (2) hereof, remain so vested notwithstanding that the particular purpose for which the land was acquired shall have failed.

(2) (i) If in the opinion of a council any land acquired for such term as it may be required for a council purpose is no longer required for the purpose for which it was acquired the council shall give notice to the persons entitled to the reversion of the land.

229

(ii) Such notice shall be in Form B in the First Schedule hereto and shall be published once in the *Regional Gazette* and displayed at the office of the council.

(iii) From the date of the publication of the notice in the *Regional Gazette* the land shall cease to be vested in the council.

Penalty for obstructing authority

203. Every person who shall wilfully hinder or obstruct any person duly authorised by a council from entering upon or taking possession of or using any land in pursuance of the provisions of this Law; or who shall molest, hinder or obstruct such person when in possession of such lands shall be liable on summary conviction before any court to a fine of twenty-five pounds or to imprisonment for three months.

Notice not to be admission that land not council land

204. The fact that a notice has been served upon any person under section 189 shall not be taken as an admission by a council that the person on whom such notice has been served or any other person has any estate or interest in the land or any part of the land specified in the notice or debar the council from alleging in any proceedings under this Law or otherwise that such land is subject to the disposition of the council.

Service of notices

205. Every notice required by this part of the Law to be served on any person may be served:

(*a*) by delivering the same to such person or by delivering the same at the abode where such person ordinarily resides to some adult members or servant of his household; or

(*b*) if the abode where such person ordinarily resides is not known by forwarding the same by registered post addressed to such person at his last known place of abode or business; or

(*c*) if the name of such person is not known or if service cannot with reasonable diligence be effected under paragraph (*a*) or (*b*) of this section, by fixing the same on a conspicuous part of the premises in respect of which the notice is issued.

Notice of suit to be given to council by intending plaintiff

205a. (1) No suit shall be commenced against a council until one month at least after written notice of intention to commence the same has been served upon the council by the intending plaintiff or his agent.

(2) Such notice shall state the cause of action, the name and place of abode of the intending plaintiff and the relief which he claims.

Limitation of suits against council

205b. When any suit is commenced against any council for any act done in pursuance or execution or intended execution of any Law or Ordinance or of any public duty or authority, or in respect of any alleged neglect or default in the execution of any such Law or Ordinance, duty or authority, such suit shall not lie or be instituted unless it is commenced within six months next after the act, neglect or default complained of, or in the case of a continuance of damage or injury, within six months after the ceasing thereof.

Mode of service on council

205c. The notice referred to in section 205A of this Law and any summons, notice or other document required or authorised to be served on a council in connection with any suit by or against such council, shall be served by delivering the same to, or by sending it by registered post addressed to, the chairman of the council at the principal office of the council.

Provided that the court may with regard to any particular suit or document order service on the council to be effected otherwise, and in that case service shall be effected in accordance with the terms of such order.

Appearance of council in legal proceedings

205d. In any prosecution by or on behalf of a council and in any civil cause or matter in which a council is a party the council may be represented by any councillor, officer or employee duly authorised in that behalf by the council.

NOTE. Sections 205A, 205B, 205C and 205D were inserted by Law No. 8 of 1953.

PART XVIII. LEGAL PROCEEDINGS, NOTICES, ETC.

Trial of persons

206. Save as is otherwise expressly provided, any person accused of an offence against this Law or any regulations or bye-laws made thereunder may be tried by any court, including any native court of competent jurisdiction.

Preservation of jurisdiction of native courts in certain matters

207. No native court shall be precluded from trying an offence under this Law by reason of the fact that such offence, if committed, was a breach of an order, resolution, bye-law, direction or rule issued or made by any member of the court as a member of a council or by reason of the fact that the proceedings have been instituted by or on behalf of any member of the court as a member of or agent for a council.

Description of property

208. Wherever in any criminal process or proceeding it is necessary to refer to the ownership or description of property belonging to or under the management of a council, such property may be described as the property of the council.

Onus of proof in certain cases

209. Where in any proceedings under this Law any person is summoned or otherwise dealt with as the occupier of any tenement or building and such person shall allege that he is not the occupier, the proof of such allegation shall be upon such person.

Name of council, etc., need not be proved

210. In any proceedings instituted by or against a council it shall not be necessary to prove the corporate name of the council or the constitution and limits of its area.

Powers of entry

211. Subject to the provisions of this Law, any member of a council, officer or servant of a council duly authorised in writing for the purpose by the council, may at all reasonable times, enter into or upon any land, buildings or premises within the area in which such council is established for the purpose of carrying out any inspection, inquiry or the execution of works under the provisions of this Law or of any bye-law or regulation in force made by a council having jurisdiction in the area.

Publication of notices

212. Save as in this Law is otherwise expressly provided, the publication of any notice or other document required by this Law to be published shall be deemed to be duly made if it is fixed, for a reasonable time, in some conspicuous place on or near the outer door of the office of the council during office hours, and also in some other conspicuous place or situation within the area of the authority of the council.

213. (1) Subject to the provisions of this section, any notice, order or other document required or authorised by this or any other Law or Ordinance to be served by or on behalf of a council, or by an officer of the council, on any person shall be deemed to be duly served:

(*a*) where the person to be served is a company, if the document is addressed to the secretary of the company at its registered office or at its principal office or place of business, and is either:

(i) sent by registered post; or

(ii) delivered at the registered office, or at the principal office or place of business, of the company;

(*b*) where the person to be served is a partnership, if the document is addressed to the partnership at its principal place of business, identifying it by the name of the style under which its business is carried on, and is either:

(i) sent by registered post; or

(ii) delivered at that office;

(*c*) where the person to be served is a public body, a local or native authority, or a corporation, society or other body, if the document is addressed to the chairman, clerk, president, secretary, treasurer or other principal officer of that body, authority, corporation or society at its principal office and is either:

(i) sent by registered post; or

(ii) delivered at that office;

(*d*) in any other case, if the document is addressed to the person to be served, and is either sent to him by registered post or delivered at his residence or place of business.

(2) Any document which is required or authorised to be served on the owner or occupier of any premises may be addressed 'the owner' or 'the occupier', as the case may be, of those premises (naming them) without further name or description, and shall be deemed to be duly served:

(*a*) if the document so addressed is sent or delivered in accordance with paragraph (*d*) of subsection (1) of this section; or

(*b*) if the document so addressed or a copy thereof so addressed is affixed to some conspicuous part of the premises.

(3) Where a document is served on a partnership in accordance with this section, the document shall be deemed to be served on each partner.

(4) For the purpose of enabling any document to be served on the owner of any premises, the council may by notice in writing require the occupier of the premises to state the name and address of the

owner thereof, and if the occupier refuses or wilfully neglects to do so, or wilfully mis-states the name and address of the owner he shall, unless in the case of a refusal he shows cause to the satisfaction of the court for his refusal, be guilty of an offence and shall be liable in respect of each offence to a fine not exceeding twenty-five pounds or in default of payment to imprisonment for a term not exceeding three months.

(5) In this section the word 'document' means any notice, order or other document which is required or authorised to be served as specified in subsection (1) of this section.

Instruments executed or issued by council

214. (1) Any contract or instrument which, if entered into or executed by a person not being a body corporate, would not require to be under seal, may be entered into or executed on behalf of a council by any person generally or specially authorised by such council for that purpose.

(2) Any document purporting to be a document duly executed or issued under the seal of a council or on behalf of a council shall, unless the contrary is proved, be deemed to be a document so executed or issued, as the case may be.

PART XIX. MISCELLANEOUS

Obstruction of officers, etc.

215. Any person who:

(*a*) wilfully obstructs any member of a council or any officer or servant of a council in the execution of his duty as such:

(*b*) being the occupier of any premises, prevents the owner of such premises from complying with any of the requirements of a council; shall be guilty of an offence and shall be liable to a fine not exceeding twenty-five pounds or to imprisonment for a term not exceeding three months or to both such fine and imprisonment.

Penalty of unqualified person sitting or voting

216. (1) Any person who:

(*a*) having been elected or appointed as a member of a council but not having been, at the time when he was elected or appointed, qualified to be so elected or appointed, sits or votes in the council; or

(*b*) sits or votes in a council after his seat therein has become vacant or he has become disqualified from sitting or voting therein, knowing or having reasonable grounds for knowing, that he was so disqualified, or that his seat has become vacant, as the case may be, shall be liable to a penalty not exceeding five pounds for every day upon which he so sits or votes.

(2) Such penalty shall be recoverable by action in the High Court at the suit of any person entitled to vote at an election or an elected member of the council.

NOTE. Law No. 13 of 1955 substituted subsection (2) for that section as originally enacted.

Transfer to council of powers and duties of Government officers

217. A council may exercise any powers and may perform any duties for the time being vested in or imposed upon any Government officer which the Regional Authority may by order declare to be transferred to such council.

Delegation of powers by Regional Authority

218. (1) The Regional Authority may, by notice in the *Regional Gazette*, depute any person by name or office to exercise or perform on his behalf, subject to such conditions, exceptions and qualifications as may be specified in the notice, such of the powers and duties conferred upon him by this Law as may be so specified other than the powers conferred by sections 3, 4, 33, 94 and 217 of this Law, and thereupon or from the date specified in the notice the person so deputed shall have and exercise such powers and perform such duties subject as aforesaid.

(2) The Regional Authority may, in the like manner, revoke any such notice, and may exercise any powers or perform any duties conferred upon him by this Law notwithstanding the delegation by him of such powers or duties.

NOTE. Law No. 13 of 1955 deleted the restriction on the delegation of powers under sections 92 and 128 which appeared in subsection (1) as originally enacted.

For delegations in force under this section on September 1st, 1955, see Western Region Legal Notice No. 14 of 1954.

Supply of information to Regional Authority

219. It shall be the duty of every council to furnish the Regional Authority with such information as he may require in relation to his functions under this Law.

Crown rights

220. Save as is otherwise expressly provided, nothing in this Law shall affect prejudicially any estate, right, power, privilege or exemption of the Crown.

Property of local and native authorities to vest in council as directed
by Regional Authority [see pp.17-18, 92-3]

221. Upon the establishment of a council all sums of money, streets, open places, lands, buildings, waterworks, bridges, piers, ferries, vehicles, goods and all other property whatsoever vested in, belonging to, held by, or purporting to belong to or to be held by any local authority or native authority formerly constituted within the area of the authority of such council shall be transferred to and vest in such council as the Regional Authority may direct, in such proportions and upon such terms and conditions as the Regional Authority may determine.

Provided that the provisions of this section shall not apply to any lands, buildings or other property held by a local authority or a native authority solely or mainly for the purposes of its functions as a local education authority under the Education Law, 1954.

NOTE. The proviso to this section was inserted by Law No. 6 of 1955.
For the transfer of property referred to in the proviso see section 16 of the Education Law, 1954.

Subsisting contracts etc., of local and native authorities and
pending proceedings, etc. [see p.18]

222. (1) Upon the establishment of a council upon a direction by the Regional Authority given on that behalf whereof notice in writing shall be given to all interested parties, the rights, interests, obligations and liabilities of any local authority or native authority formerly constituted within the area of the authority of such council under any contract or instrument whatsoever (including contracts of service) subsisting immediately before the date of such direction shall be deemed to be and by virtue of this provision shall be assigned to the council specified in such direction as from such date as may be so specified; and any such contract or instrument in respect to which such direction as aforesaid is given shall be as of full force and effect against or in favour of the council so specified, and shall be enforceable as fully and effectually, as if, instead of the local authority or native authority concerned, the council so specified had been named therein or had been a party thereto.

(2) Any proceeding or cause of action, pending or existing, immediately before the date specified in any direction given pursuant to the provisions of subsection (1) of this section, by or against any such local authority or native authority as is referred to in such subsection in respect of any right, interest, obligation or liability under any such contract or instrument as is specified in such direction may be continued and enforced by or against the council specified in such

direction, as it might have been against the local authority or native authority concerned, if this Law had not been passed.

(3) For the purposes of this section the term 'obligations and liabilities' shall include the obligation and liability of any such local or native authority as is referred to in subsection (1) to pay any retiring allowance to any person who was formerly an officer of or in the employment of such local or native authority, granted in pursuance of its customary practice or under the provisions of any Superannuation Scheme for Native Administration Servants.

Notices, regulations, etc., made by local and native authorities to remain enforceable [see p.126]

223. (1) Any notice, order, rule, regulation or bye-law made by any local or native authority by virtue of the provisions of any Ordinance shall remain effective and in force until such time as it is revoked or replaced by a bye-law or notice made or issued under the provisions of this Law by any council established in the area of such local or native authority and which has the power to make or issue such bye-law or notice.

(2) Any such notice, order, rule, regulation or bye-law made by such local or native authority may be enforced by such council as though made by such council.

(3) Any licence, registration or permit issued, made or granted under the provisions of any Ordinance shall continue in force for the period specified in such licence, registration or permit unless the same is sooner suspended or cancelled under or in pursuance of any bye-law, lawfully made under the provisions of this Law.

(4) For the purposes of this section the Regional Authority, subject to the provisions of section 80, shall have the power to revoke, vary or amend any notice, order, rule, regulation or bye-law made by any local or native authority.

(5) The provisions of subsection (2) of section 19 of the Interpretation Ordinance (Cap. 94) shall have no application as regards this Law.

Native courts

224. (1) It shall be the duty of such council as the Regional Authority may direct, to maintain, repair and equip any native court, office, lock-up or other building required for or used in connection with the establishment and running of such court which is situate within the area of its authority and to acquire or provide land

237

for and to build any such court, office, lock-up or other building when requested to do so by the Local Government Inspector.

(2) Notwithstanding the provisions of section 84 a Local Government Inspector may require such council to remove any clerk employed in a native court from any particular court, who in his opinion is unsatisfactory, and upon the receipt of such request the council shall cause such clerk to be removed from such court forthwith and it shall be the duty of the council to engage or transfer another clerk to such court forthwith.

Native Court sitting fees

225. It shall be the duty of a council to pay such sitting fees to any member of a native court which is situated within its area as are laid down from time to time by the Regional Authority.

Native Court fees, fines, etc. (Cap. 142) [see p. 94]

226. Notwithstanding any provision in the Native Courts Ordinance, or in any warrant issued thereunder, all fees, fines and penalties payable in respect of or as a result of proceedings in any native court in the area of the authority of a council and the proceeds of sale of any forfeiture ordered by such native court shall be paid to and form part of the revenue of such council as the Regional Authority may direct.

Certain Ordinances not to have effect [see p. 8]

227. (1) Upon the establishment of a council the Ordinances set out in the first column of the Second Schedule shall cease to have effect in the area of such council to the extent set out in the second column thereof until the Instrument by which such council is established is revoked under the provisions of section 13.

(2) Such revocation shall not affect:

(a) anything lawfully done or suffered under this Law,

(b) any right, privilege, obligation or liability which has lawfully accrued or been incurred under this Law,

(c) any penalty, forfeiture or punishment lawfully incurred in respect of any offence committed against this Law,

(d) any investigation, legal proceeding or remedy in respect of any such right, privilege, obligation, liability, penalty, forfeiture or punishment as aforesaid; and any such investigation, legal proceeding or remedy may be instituted, continued or enforced and any such penalty, forfeiture or punishment may be imposed as if such Instrument had not been so revoked.

228. Upon the revocation of an Instrument establishing a council under the provisions of section 13:

(*a*) all sums of money, streets, open places, lands, buildings, water-works, bridges, piers, ferries, vehicles, vessels, goods and all other property whatsoever vested in, belonging to, held by or purporting to belong to or to be held by the council concerned shall be transferred to and vest in such council as the Regional Authority may direct;

(*b*) the rights, interest, obligations and liabilities of such council under any contract or instrument whatsoever subsisting immediately before the date of the said revocation shall be deemed to be and by virtue of this section shall be assigned to such council as the Regional Authority may direct and any such contract or instrument shall be as of full force and effect against or in favour of such council and shall be enforceable as fully and effectually as if, instead of the council concerned the council as directed by the Regional Authority had been named therein and had been a party thereto;

(*c*) any proceeding or cause of action, pending or existing, immediately before the date of such revocation by or against such council in respect of any right, interest, obligation or liability under any such contract or instrument as is referred to in paragraph (*b*) of this section may be continued and enforced by or against such council as the Regional Authority may direct as it might have been against the council concerned, if such revocation had not been effected.

Provided that nothing in this section shall apply to any assets or liabilities, of whatever nature, held or incurred by the council solely or mainly for the purposes of its functions as a local education authority under the provisions of the Education Law, 1954.

NOTE. The proviso to this section was inserted by Law No. 6 of 1955.

For the transfer of assets and liabilities referred to in the proviso see section 16 of the Education Law, 1954.

Regulations

229. The Regional Authority may make regulations with respect to the following matters:

(*a*) the collection of rates and the form of any precept, demand note, valuation list, or any other document;

(*b*) the submission of reports and returns;

(*c*) the display and publication of notices;

(*d*) generally for the proper and orderly conduct of the business of a council;

(*e*) the form of conditions in any contract of service;

(*f*) the borrowing of money by councils;

(*g*) the provision of machinery for negotiating conditions of service, salaries and wages between councils, their staffs, officers and employees; and

(*h*) generally for the better carrying out of the provisions of this Law.

FIRST SCHEDULE [see p.128]

Western Region Local Government Law, 1952

Form A

Notice is hereby given that the following lands (describe lands, giving measurements and showing boundaries whenever practicable) have been acquired for local government purposes to wit:............ by the.......................Council and the Regional Authority has given his consent thereto.

* The amount of compensation offered to.............................. in respect of the interest...as claimed in the said land, is the sum of..

Any person claiming to have any right or interest in the said land is required within six weeks from the date of this notice to send to ....Council a statement of his right and interest and of the evidence thereof, and of any claim made by him in respect of such right or interest.

* And notice is also hereby given that the.............................. Council intends to enter into possession of the said lands at the expiration of..................weeks from the date of this notice and is hereby directed to yield up possession of the said lands before expiry of such period.

Any person who shall wilfully hinder or obstruct any person authorised by the council from taking possession of the said lands is liable under the provision of the Law above-mentioned on conviction to a fine of twenty-five pounds or to imprisonment for three months.

* The.......................Council will allocate the following land (describe land, giving measurements and showing boundaries whenever possible) to...

The..........................day of.......................195 .

..........................Council

* Delete if not applicable

240

Form B

Notice is hereby given that the following lands (describe lands, giving measurements and showing boundaries wherever practicable) which were acquired for so long as they might be required for the purpose of a..are no longer required for the said purpose by the.............................Council.

The...........................day of...........................195 .

..................................Council

SECOND SCHEDULE [see p. 8]
(Section 227)

Ordinance	Section or Part
1. The Markets Ordinance (Cap. 127)	The whole Ordinance
2. The Native Authority Ordinance (Cap. 140)	The whole Ordinance
3. The Public Health Ordinance (Cap. 183)	Section 17, 18, 41, 42, and 43
4. The Townships Ordinance (Cap. 216)	The whole Ordinance

The Eastern Region Local Government Law, 1955, is printed as originally enacted. It must be read in conjunction with the Eastern Region Local Government (Amendment) Law, 1955, and the Eastern Region Local Government (Amendment) Law, 1956.

EASTERN REGION LOCAL GOVERNMENT LAW, 1955

ARRANGEMENT OF SECTIONS

PART I. PRELIMINARY

PART V. ELECTION OFFENCES

245

247

'court' includes the Supreme Court, a Magistrate's Court and a Native Court;

'functions' includes duties and powers;

'Instrument' means the Instrument by which a local government council is established under the provisions of this Law, and includes any Instrument varying or amending such Instrument;

'member of council' and 'member of a committee' include the chairman, vice-chairman and a councillor of that council or committe whether elected, appointed or co-opted;

'the Minister' means the Minister for the time being charged under section 119 of the Nigeria (Constitution) Order-in-Council, 1954, with responsibility for Internal Affairs;

'officer' includes servant;

'vice-chairman' includes the Deputy Mayor of a Municipality.

'Village Council' means any Village Council constituted and in existence under the provisions of any local customary law at the date of the commencement of this Law.

PART II.

ESTABLISHMENT OF LOCAL GOVERNMENT COUNCILS

Power to establish councils by Instrument [see p.15]

3. (1) After consulting the wishes of the inhabitants of the area concerned, the Minister with the prior approval of the Governor-in-Council may by Instrument establish such councils for the purposes of local government as he shall think fit.

(2) Such councils shall be County Councils, Municipalities, Urban District Councils, District Councils or Local Councils as the Minister may determine.

Publication and construction of Instrument

4. (1) Every Instrument shall be prepared in duplicate and shall be signed by the Minister; one copy shall be retained by the Minister and one by the council concerned.

(2) Every Instrument shall be published in the *Regional Gazette*.

(3) Every Instrument shall be read and construed as one with this Law and shall be of the same force and effect as if it were enacted in this Law.

Contents of Instrument [see p.17]

5. (1) In addition to any other matter which is required by this Law to be inserted in an Instrument, every Instrument establishing a council shall

(*a*) specify the name and type of council and the date it shall be established;

(*b*) describe the device of the seal of the council;

(*c*) define the limits of the area of the authority of the council; and

(*d*) provide for the constitution of the council, the number of councillors and the date for the first election of the council.

(2) An Instrument may:

(*a*) provide for the holding of the first election of a council before the date stated in the Instrument for the establishment of such council, notwithstanding any provision of this Law;

(*b*) provide for the election or appointment of a chairman of a council;

(*c*) specify the method of the election or the system of the appointment of a chairman of a council;

(*d*) provide for the election or appointment of councillors or the election of some and the appointment of other councillors of the same council;

(*e*) specify the method of election of councillors by reference to any regulations governing electoral procedure made by the Minister under the provisions of section 39 or the system of the appointment of councillors as the case may be;

(*f*) specify the qualifications of the persons or bodies of persons entitled to appoint a chairman or councillors as the case may be;

(*g*) provide for the division of the area of the authority of the council into wards; and specify the number of councillors to represent each ward;

(*h*) provide for the quorum of a council;

(*i*) subject to the provisions of this Law, empower the levying or collection of a rate and specify the system of rating or the systems of rating;

(*j*) require a council to set up a standing committee other than a Finance Committee for any specified purpose and specify the composition of such committee including the number and qualifications of any members of such committee who are not members of the council;

(*k*) specify the date or dates for the election of councillors; and

(*l*) require a council to establish, maintain, repair or equip a Native Court established under the provisions of the Native Courts Ordinance (Cap. 142), and to pay sitting fees to the members of such courts.

(3) In so far as the Instrument provides for the appointment of a councillor it may further provide that such appointment shall be

subject to the approval of the Minister, some other council or of some person or persons named or designated in the Instrument.

(4) An Instrument may further declare that subject to such limitations and conditions as may be specified therein, the council either shall perform or may perform all or any of the functions specified in section 80.

Incorporation of councils. Seal

6. Every council established under the provisions of this Law shall be a body corporate having perpetual succession and a common seal and power to hold land.

PART III. POWERS OF THE MINISTER

Power to amend Instrument [see pp.18-19]

7. (1) After consulting the wishes of the inhabitants of the area concerned the Minister with the prior approval of the Governor-in-Council may by Instrument amend an Instrument in all or any of the following ways:

(*a*) change the name or seal of the council;

(*b*) add to, take away from or impose any condition upon the exercise of any of the functions of the council subject to the provisions of this Law; or

(*c*) alter the constitution of the council, the method of election or appointment of the chairman, or the appointment of councillors, or the system of rating within the provisions of this Law.

(2) The Minister shall cause to be published in the area concerned thirty clear days' notice of his intention to exercise his powers under this section and shall give an opportunity to the council concerned to make representations to him in writing.

Alteration of the area of the authority of a council

8. (1) Where the Minister considers, either on the receipt of proposals from the council concerned, or otherwise, that a *prima facie* case exists for any of the following changes, namely:

(*a*) an alteration or definition of the boundaries of the area of the authority of a council;

(*b*) the transfer of any part of the area of the authority of a council to another council;

(*c*) the union of the area of the authority of a council with the area of the authority of another council;

(*d*) the formation of a new County Council, Municipality, District Council or Local Council in the area of or part of the area of the authority of an existing council;

(*e*) an alteration of the status of a council;
the Minister shall cause an inquiry to be held under the provisions of section 13 in the locality concerned.

(2) If the Minister is satisfied after holding such inquiry that any such change as aforesaid is desirable, he may with the prior approval of the Governor-in-Council by an amending Instrument give effect to such change.

(3) The Minister may by Instrument make such incidental, consequential or supplemental provisions with respect to administrative arrangements as may appear to be necessary or proper for the purposes of carrying out such change or for giving full effect thereto and without prejudice to the generality of the foregoing may by such Instrument:

(*a*) provide for the abolition or establishment, or the restriction or extension of the jurisdiction of any council in or over any part of the area affected by such Instrument;

(*b*) provide for the name of any altered area;

(*c*) provide for the adjustment or alteration of the boundaries of any area affected by such change or of the area of the authority of any council wholly or in part situate within such affected area, or for the union of the area of the authority of any councils;

(*d*) transfer, extend or limit the functions of any council within the area affected;

(*e*) provide for the constitution and election of a council in any such area or for the amendment, alteration, extension or exclusion of any constitution or system of election of any existing council with respect to such altered area;

· (*f*) provide for the transfer of any writs, process, records or documents relating to or to be executed in any part of the area affected by such change and for determining questions arising from such transfer; or

(*g*) provide for the adjustment of any property, debt, right or liability affected by such change.

Failure to hold meetings or properly to apply revenues, etc. [see p.19]
(First Schedule)

9. (1) If any council shall at any time fail on three consecutive occasions, to meet with the minimum frequency required by the provisions of section (1) of the First Schedule the Minister shall cause an inquiry to be held under the provisions of section 13, at which inquiry the council concerned shall be given an opportunity of being heard.

(2) If at any time it shall appear that the revenues of a council are not being properly used in the best interests of the area as a whole, or that the administration of the affairs of the council is inefficient or corrupt or that the council has failed or failed sufficiently to carry out the provisions of this Law relating to the levy of rates or to act in conformity with the provisions of this Law or any other written law, the Minister shall cause an inquiry to be held under the provisions of section 13 at which inquiry the council concerned shall be given an opportunity of being heard.

(3) The Minister upon considering the report of such an inquiry may with the prior approval of the Governor-in-Council:

(a) declare all the seats of the members of the council to be vacant and order a fresh election; or

(b) issue an amending Instrument dissolving the council.

(4) In exercising his powers under paragraph (b) of subsection (3) the Minister shall by the same Instrument by which the council is dissolved establish a new council under the provisions of this Law or may appoint other fit and proper persons, not being less than three in number to form a new council for the purposes of this Law.

(5) The provisions of section 8 shall have no application to the exercise of any power by the Minister under subsection (4) of this section.

Effect of issue of amending Instrument

10. An Instrument issued under the provisions of sections 7, 8 or 9 shall not unless the contrary intention appears affect the validity of any decision taken or act done by the council existing at the time of the issue of such Instrument and shall not affect any right, privilege, obligation or liability accrued or incurred or existing at the time of the issue of such Instrument.

Failure to carry out work or to make or to enforce bye-laws [see p. 44]

11. If any council shall fail to do or carry out any work or thing which it is or may be empowered under the provisions of this Law or of any other written Law to do or carry out, or shall fail to make, amend, revoke or enforce any bye-laws on any matters upon which it is empowered to make, amend, revoke or enforce bye-laws, and such failure on the part of the council constitutes in the opinion of the

Minister, a grave danger and menace to the health, safety or welfare of the public within or without the area, the Minister may give notice to the council in default, requiring it to take measures within its powers under the provisions of this Law or of any other written Law to abate and remove such danger; and if the council shall fail to take and properly carry out the required measures, the Minister, upon being satisfied that the council has so failed without reasonable cause, may, notwithstanding the provisions of section 88:

(*a*) make such bye-laws as may be necessary to abate and remove such danger, and such bye-laws shall, until revoked by the Minister, have the force and effect of law within the area concerned;

(*b*) authorise any person or persons to do or carry out any works or things and to spend such moneys in so doing or carrying out works or things as to him may seem necessary and such person or persons shall be deemed to have vested in him or them all of the powers of the council in respect of the doing or carrying out of the particular work or thing; and any moneys so expended under the authority of the Minister shall be a debt due to the Minister charged on the revenue of the council concerned.

Revocation of Instrument [see pp.19-20]

12. (1) The Minister may on the application of any persons concerned, with the prior approval of the Governor-in-Council, revoke the Instrument establishing any council if he considers it in the interests of the persons living within the area to do so.

(2) The Minister shall give an opportunity to the council concerned to make representations to him in writing before he exercises his powers under this section.

Power to hold inquiries

13. (1) The Minister may cause such inquiries to be held at such times and in such places as he may consider necessary or desirable for the purposes of this Law.

(2) The Minister may appoint in writing any person to conduct any such inquiry who may sit with or without assessors as the Minister shall direct.

(3) The Minister or person appointed by him under subsection (2) shall cause a notice of the time and place of the inquiry to be given to any council or person appearing to him to be interested in the subject matter of the inquiry.

(4) The person conducting any inquiry under this section shall submit a report to the Minister at the conclusion of such inquiry.

(5) Where the Minister causes an inquiry to be held the costs of such inquiry shall be defrayed by such council as he may direct and the Minister may certify the amount and the amount so directed by him to be paid by such council shall be a debt due to the Minister from that council.

Powers of Minister or person appointed to hold inquiry

14. The Minister and any person appointed by him in writing under section 13 shall have the following powers:

(*a*) to procure all such evidence, written or oral, and to examine all such persons as witnesses as the Minister or person appointed by him may think necessary;

(*b*) to require the evidence of any witness to be made on oath or affirmation, such oath or affirmation to be that which could be required of the witness if he were giving evidence in a Magistrate's Court;

(*c*) to summon any person in the Eastern Region to attend any inquiry to give evidence, and to examine him as a witness or require him to produce any document or other thing in his possession;

(*d*) to issue a warrant to compel the attendance of any person who, after having been summoned to attend, fails to do so and does not excuse such failure to the satisfaction of the Minister or person appointed by him, and to order him to pay all costs which may have been occasioned in compelling his attendance or by reason of his refusal to obey the summons, and also to fine such a person a sum not exceeding fifty pounds, such fine to be recoverable in the same manner as a fine imposed by a Magistrate's Court;

(*e*) to enter upon any land, including Crown land, for the purposes of obtaining information or evidence.

Summons and Warrant (Forms A & B Second Schedule)

15. (1) A summons issued under the provisions of paragraph (*c*) of section 14 shall be as in Form A in the Second Schedule.

(2) A warrant issued under the provisions of paragraph (*d*) of section 14 shall be as in Form B in the Second Schedule.

Obligation of witness at inquiry to answer

16. A person called as a witness in any inquiry held under the provisions of section 13 shall not be excused from answering any question on the ground that the answer thereto may criminate or tend to criminate himself or on the ground of privilege:

Provided that an answer by a person to a question put by or before the person presiding at the inquiry shall not, except in the case of criminal proceedings for perjury in respect of such evidence, be in any proceedings, civil or criminal, admissible in evidence.

Appointment of Local Government Commissioners [see p. 42]

17. (1) The Minister may by notice in the *Regional Gazette* appoint suitable persons to be Local Government Commissioners who shall be termed County Commissioners, Municipal Commissioners or District Commissioners, and may delegate to them such of his functions as he may think fit other than the functions conferred upon him under the provisions of sections 3, 7, 8, 9 and of this section.

(2) Any delegation made under the provisions of subsection (1) shall be revocable at will and no delegation shall prevent the exercise of any function by the Minister.

PART IV. GENERAL PROVISIONS AS TO MEMBERS AND MEETING OF COUNCILS AND ELECTORAL REGULATIONS

Constitution of councils [see p. 23]

18. (1) A council shall consist of a chairman, a vice-chairman and such number of councillors as is laid down in the Instrument by which it is established.

(2) A Municipality shall consist of a Mayor, a Deputy Mayor and such number of councillors as is laid down in the Instrument by which it is established.

Qualifications of councillors [see pp. 31-2]

19. Subject to the provisions of section 20 a person shall be qualified to be elected as a councillor, if:

(*a*) he is a British subject or a British protected person of the age of twenty-one years or more; and

(*b*) (i) was born in the area of the authority of the council in which he seeks election or his father was born in such area; or

(ii) he has resided in the area of the authority of the said council for a period of twelve months immediately preceding the date of the election; and

(*c*) his name appears on the register of electors for the said council.

Disqualifications for office and loss of qualifications for office [see pp. 32-4]

20. A person shall be disqualified from being elected or appointed, or co-opted, or, being a member of a council shall cease to be a member of such council if he:

(*a*) is, by virtue of his own act, under any acknowledgment of allegiance, obedience or adherence to any foreign power or state; or

(*b*) is an undischarged bankrupt having been adjudged or otherwise declared bankrupt under any law in force in any part of Her Majesty's dominions; or

(*c*) has been sentenced by a court in any part of Her Majesty's dominions to death, or to imprisonment (by whatever name called), and has not either suffered the punishment to which he was sentenced, or such other punishment as may by competent authority have been substituted therefor, or received a free pardon; or

(*d*) holds or is acting in any paid office or other place of profit in the gift or disposal of the Crown; or

(*e*) holds or is acting in any paid office or other place of profit (other than that of Mayor or chairman) in the gift or disposal of any council or of any committee thereof; or

(*f*) is, under any law in force in the Eastern Region, adjudged to be a lunatic or otherwise declared to be of unsound mind; or

(*g*) has within five years before the date of election or since his election been surcharged under the provisions of this law to an amount exceeding five hundred pounds; or

(*h*) is a police officer; or

(*i*) is disqualified by virtue of section 47 or 54 of this Law; or

(*j*) holds an appointment to be a member of a Native Court established under the provisions of the Native Courts Ordinance (Cap. 142).

Disqualification for office by reason of non-disclosure of contract with council [see p. 34]

21. A person shall be disqualified from being elected or appointed to be a member of a council if he is a party to any subsisting contract with the council concerned for and on account of the public service, and has not published within one month before the date of election to the electors in the area concerned a notice setting out the nature of such contract and his interest therein or informed the person or body of persons by whom he is to be appointed as the case may be:

Provided that a person shall not be disqualified from being a councillor by reason only of his holding the office of returning officer for that council unless he has directly or indirectly by himself or his partner received any profit or remuneration in respect of that office.

Vacation of seats of members

22. In addition to the provisions of sections 20 and 21 the seat of a member of a council shall become vacant:

(*a*) upon his death; or

(*b*) if he shall without leave of the council previously obtained fail to attend for a period of six consecutive months any meeting of the council;

Provided that:

(i) attendance as a member of a meeting of any committee of the council, or at a meeting of any joint committee, shall be deemed for the purposes of this section to be attendance at a meeting of the council;

(ii) a member of any branch of Her Majesty's naval, military, or air forces when employed during war or any emergency on any naval, military or air force service, and a person whose employment in the service of Her Majesty in connection with war or any emergency is such as, in the opinion of the Minister, to entitle him to relief from disqualification on account of absence, shall not cease to be a member of a council by reason only of failure to attend meetings of a council if the failure is due to that employment.

Validity of acts done by unqualified person

23. The acts and proceedings of any person elected to any office under this Law and acting in that office shall notwithstanding his disqualification be as valid and effectual as if he had been qualified.

Chairman [see pp. 23-4]

24. (1) Unless appointed in the Instrument the Chairman of a council shall be elected annually by the council, such election to be by secret ballot.

(2) The chairman shall unless he resigns or ceases to be qualified or becomes disqualified continue in office until his successor becomes entitled to act as chairman.

(3) During his term of office the chairman shall be a member of the council notwithstanding any provision of this Law or of anything contained in the Instrument of the council concerned.

(4) No person shall be elected or appointed to be chairman of a council without his consent to be so elected or appointed.

(5) A person elected or appointed to be chairman of a council shall not be eligible to be elected or appointed to the office of chairman of another council.

Election of chairman

25. Save and except as shall be provided in the Instrument the election of the chairman shall be the first business transacted at the annual meeting of a council.

Resignation of chairman

26. A person elected or appointed to be chairman of a council may at any time resign his office by notice of resignation delivered to the council concerned.

Filling of casual vacancy in office of chairman

27. (1) On a casual vacancy occurring in the office of an elected chairman an election to fill the vacancy shall be held not later than the next meeting of the council held after the date on which the vacancy occurs, or if that meeting is held within fourteen days after that date then not later than the next following meeting of the council and shall be conducted in the same manner as an ordinary election.

(2) On a casual vacancy occurring in the office of a chairman appointed under the Instrument the person or body of persons entitled to appoint under the Instrument shall appoint a person to fill such vacancy within fourteen days.

(3) A person elected or appointed under this section to fill a casual vacancy shall hold office until the date upon which the person in whose place he is elected or appointed would ordinarily have retired and he shall then retire.

Allowances to chairman

28. (1) The Minister may by order fix the maximum amount or the rate of any allowance or out-of-pocket expenses payable to a chairman by a council.

(2) Subject to the provisions of any order made under subsection (1) a council may by resolution make provision for the payment of reasonable allowances or out-of-pocket expenses to the chairman of such council.

Vice-chairman

29. (1) A council shall elect or appoint in each year a councillor to be the vice-chairman of the council.

(2) The vice-chairman shall, unless he resigns, ceases to be qualified or becomes disqualified, hold office until immediately after the

election of a chairman at the next annual meeting of the council, and during that time shall continue to be a member of the council notwithstanding any provision of this Law or of anything contained in the Instrument of the council concerned.

(3) No person shall be elected or appointed to the office of vice-chairman without his consent.

Election of councillors

30. Without prejudice to the powers of appointment exercisable under this Law and unless otherwise specified in the Instrument councillors shall be elected by the local government electors for the area concerned in the manner provided by this Law.

Term of office of councillors

31. (1) The term of office of elected councillors shall be three years.

(2) The term of office of any councillor elected at an election of a council held in accordance with paragraph (a) of subsection (2) of section 5 before the date stated in the Instrument for the establishment of the council shall commence from the date of the establishment of such council and not from the date of the election for the purposes of this section.

(3) No person appointed to be a councillor under the provisions of this Law shall be appointed for a term of office for more than three years.

(4) No person shall be elected or appointed to be a councillor without his consent.

Councillors, etc., may be re-elected or re-appointed

32. A person ceasing to hold any office to which he is elected or appointed under the provisions of this Law shall, unless he is not qualified or is disqualified, be eligible for re-election or re-appointment.

Resignation

33. A person elected or appointed to be a councillor or to any office other than that of chairman under the provisions of this Law may at any time resign his office by a notice of resignation delivered to the chairman of the council concerned.

Declaration by council of vacancy in office

34. Where a councillor ceases to be qualified to be a member of the council, or becomes disqualified from being a member of the

council, the council shall forthwith declare his office to be vacant and signify such vacancy by notice signed by the chairman of the council.

Filling casual vacancies in the case of councillors

35. (1) A council shall notify the Minister of any casual vacancy occurring in the number of its elected councillors and an election to fill such vacancy shall be held within sixty days of such notification on a day to be fixed by the council.

(2) An election held under the provisions of this section shall be conducted in the same manner as is prescribed for elections for such council under the provisions of the Instrument establishing such council.

(3) Where a casual vacancy occurs within one year of the retirement of an elected councillor an election under this section shall not be held to fill the vacancy; but in such a case a council may co-opt a person to fill the vacancy.

(4) No person shall be co-opted without his consent.

(5) On a casual vacancy occurring in the number of councillors appointed under the Instrument the person or body of persons entitled to appoint under the Instrument shall appoint a person to fill such vacancy within sixty days of its occurrence.

(6) A person elected or appointed or co-opted under this section to fill a casual vacancy shall, subject to the provisions of this Law, hold office until the date upon which the person in whose place he is elected, appointed or co-opted would ordinarily have retired, and he shall then retire.

Councillors' expenses

36. (1) The Minister may by order fix the maximum amount or the rate of any allowance or out-of-pocket expenses payable by a council to the members of that council.

(2) Subject to the provisions of any order made under subsection (1), a council may, by resolution, make provision for the payment of reasonable allowances or out-of-pocket expenses to the members of such council whether elected, appointed or co-opted when engaged on the business of the council or of a committee thereof.

Standing rules (First Schedule) [see p. 75]

37. The provisions of the First Schedule to this Law shall have effect as respects the proceedings and business of councils of joint committees of councils and of committees of councils and subject to the provisions of such Schedule a council may make standing rules for the regulation of its proceedings and business and for the business and proceedings of committees thereof and may vary or revoke such rules.

Disability of members of councils and committees for voting on account of interest in contracts, etc. [see p. 73]

38. If a chairman, vice-chairman, person presiding or other member of a council or any committee thereof has any pecuniary or other interest, direct or indirect, in any contract or proposed contract or other matter, and is present at a meeting of the council or the committee at which the contract or other matter is the subject of consideration, he shall at the meeting disclose the fact and shall not take part in the consideration or discussion of or vote on any question with respect to the contract or other matter:

Provided that this section shall not apply to an interest in a contract or other matter which a member of a council or committee may have as a rate-payer or as an inhabitant of the area, or to an interest in any matter relating to the terms in which the right to participate in any service, including the supply of goods, is offered to the public.

Electoral Regulations [see p. 30]

39. (1) Subject to the provisions of this Law the Minister with the prior approval of the Governor-in-Council may by regulation make provision for the election of persons as councillors including (without prejudice to the generality of the foregoing power) the following matters:

(*a*) the registration of electors throughout the Region or in any area of authority of a council or councils;

(*b*) the holding of elections and the conduct of elections;

(*c*) the division of the area of the authority of a council for any purposes connected with elections;

(*d*) the method of nominating candidates;

(*e*) the procedure to be followed when two or more candidates have received an equal number of votes in an election.

(2) The Minister may by regulation prescribe the officer to be charged with the conduct of elections, his duties and powers including the power to appoint assistants.

PART V. ELECTION OFFENCES [see pp. 36-7]

This part to apply to all elections

40. The provisions of this Part shall apply to any election held under the provisions of this Law.

41. (1) If any corrupt practice is committed by any candidate elected at an election held under the provisions of this Law, the election of such candidate shall be invalid.

(2) The expression 'corrupt practice' as used in this Law means any of the following offences:

(a) personation;

(b) treating;

(c) undue influence;

(d) bribery; and

(e) aiding, abetting, counselling or procuring the commission of personation.

(3) A corrupt practice shall be deemed to be committed by a candidate if it is committed with his knowledge and consent, or with the knowledge and consent of a person who is acting under the general or special authority of such candidate with reference to the election.

Personation and punishment for personation

42. (1) Any person who at an election applies for a voting paper in the name of some other person whether that name be the name of a person living or dead, or of a fictitious person, or who, having voted once at any such election, applies at the same election for a voting paper in his own name, shall be guilty of the offence of personation.

(2) Any person who is guilty of personation, or of aiding, abetting, counselling or procuring the commission of the offence of personation, shall be liable on conviction to a fine of fifty pounds or to imprisonment for six months.

(3) A person charged with the offence of personation shall not be convicted except on the evidence of not less than two credible witnesses.

(4) Any person found committing the offence of personation or who is reasonably suspected of having committed or of being about to commit the offence of personation may be immediately arrested without a warrant by any police officer or person whose duty it is to conduct an election under the provisions of this Law or by any person whom he may call to his assistance.

Persons to be deemed guilty of treating

43. The following persons shall be deemed guilty of treating:

(i) any person who corruptly, by himself or by any other person, either before, during or after the election, directly or indirectly gives or provides or pays, wholly or in part, the expense of giving or providing, any food, drink, entertainment, or provision to or for any person for the purpose of corruptly influencing that person, or any other person, to vote or refrain from voting at such election, or on account of such person or any other person having voted or refrained from voting at such election; and

(ii) any voter who corruptly accepts or takes any such food, drink, entertainment, or provision.

Undue influence

44. Any person who directly or indirectly by himself or by any other person on his behalf makes use of or threatens to make use of any force, violence, or restraint, or inflicts or threatens to inflict by himself or by any other person any temporal or spiritual injury, damage, harm, or loss upon or against any person, in order to induce or compel such person to vote or refrain from voting, or on account of such person having voted or refrained from voting, at any election, or who by abduction, duress, or any fraudulent device or contrivance impedes or prevents the free use of the vote by any voter or thereby compels, induces, or prevails upon any voter either to give or refrain from giving his vote at any election shall be guilty of undue influence.

Unlawful Oaths

45. Any person who administers or is present at and consents to the administration of any oath or engagement in the nature of an oath purporting to bind the person who takes it to vote for a candidate or to refrain from voting for a candidate or to refrain from voting at all at any election shall be guilty of undue influence.

Persons to be deemed guilty of bribery

46. The following persons shall be deemed to be guilty of bribery:

(*a*) any person who directly or indirectly, by himself or by any other person on his behalf, gives, lends or agrees to give or lend, or offers, promises, or promises to procure or to endeavour to procure, any money or valuable consideration to or for any voter, or to or for any person on behalf of any voter, or to or for any other person, in order to induce any voter to vote or refrain from voting, or corruptly does any such act as aforesaid on account of such voter having voted or refrained from voting, at any election;

(*b*) any person who directly or indirectly, by himself or by any other person on his behalf, gives or procures, or agrees to give or procure, or offers, promises, or promises to procure or to endeavour to procure, any office, place or employment to or for any voter or to or for any person on behalf of any voter, or to or for any other person, in order to induce such voter to vote or refrain from voting, or corruptly does any such act as aforesaid on account of any voter having voted or refrained from voting, at any election;

(*c*) any person who directly or indirectly by himself or by any other person on his behalf makes any such gift, loan, offer, promise, procurement, or agreement as aforesaid to or for any person, in order to induce such person to procure, or to endeavour to procure, the return of any person as councillor or the vote of any voter at any election;

(*d*) any person who, upon or in consequence of any such gift, loan, offer, promise, procurement, or agreement, procures, or engages, or promises or endeavours to procure, the return of any person as councillor or the vote of any voter at any election;

(*e*) any person who advances or pays, or causes to be paid, any money to or for the use of any other person, with the intent that such money, or any part thereof, shall be expended in bribery at any election, or who knowingly pays, or causes to be paid, any money to any person in discharge or repayment of any money wholly or in part expended in bribery at any election;

(*f*) any voter who, before or during any election, directly or indirectly, by himself or by any other person on his behalf, receives, agrees, or contracts for any money, gift, loan or valuable consideration, office, place, or employment, for himself or for any other person, for voting or agreeing to vote or for refraining or agreeing to refrain from voting at any such election;

(*g*) any person who, after any election, directly or indirectly, by himself or by any other person on his behalf, receives any money or valuable consideration on account of any person having voted, or refrained from voting, or having induced any other person to vote or to refrain from voting at any such election:

Provided that the aforesaid provisions shall not extend or be construed to extend to any money paid or agreed to be paid for or on account of any legal expenses *bona fide* incurred at or concerning any election.

47. (1) Any person who is guilty of bribery, treating, or undue influence shall be liable on conviction to a fine of one hundred pounds or to imprisonment for two years.

(2) Any person who is convicted of bribery, treating, undue influence, or personation, or of aiding, abetting, counselling, or procuring the commission of the offence of personation, shall (in addition to any other punishment) be incapable, during a period of five years from the date of his conviction:

(*a*) of being registered as a voter or voting at any election of a councillor;

(*b*) of being elected as a councillor, or, if elected before his conviction, of retaining his seat as such councillor.

Offences in respect of nomination papers, voting papers, etc., and ballot boxes

48. (1) Any person who:

(*a*) forges or fraudulently defaces or fraudulently destroys any nomination paper, or delivers to the officer to whom nomination papers are required by this Law to be delivered any nomination paper, knowing the same to be forged; or

(*b*) forges or counterfeits or fraudulently destroys any voting paper or the official mark on any voting paper; or

(*c*) without due authority supplies a voting paper to any person; or

(*d*) without due authority destroys, takes, opens, or otherwise interferes with any ballot box or packet of voting papers then in use for the purposes of the election,

shall be guilty of an offence, and be liable to a fine of one hundred pounds or to imprisonment for two years.

(2) Any attempt to commit any offence specified in this section shall be punishable in the manner in which the offence itself is punishable.

(3) In any prosecution for an offence in relation to the nomination papers, ballot boxes, or voting papers, at an election held under this Law, the property in such boxes and papers, as well as the property in the counterfoils, may be stated to be in the officer charged with the conduct of such election.

Requirement of secrecy. Application

49. (1) The officer charged with the conduct of elections and his assistants and every counting agent, candidate and candidate's agent in attendance at a polling station or at the counting of the votes shall maintain and aid in maintaining the secrecy of the voting.

(2) No such officer, assistant and counting agent, candidate or candidate's agent shall except for some purpose authorised by law, communicate before the poll is closed to any person any information as to the name or number on the voters' lists of any voter who has or has not applied for a voting paper, or voted at the polling station.

(3) No person shall:

(*a*) interfere with a voter when recording his vote; or

(*b*) otherwise obtain or attempt to obtain in a polling station information as to the candidate for whom a voter in that station is about to vote or has voted; or

(*c*) communicate at any time to any person any information obtained in a polling station as to the candidate for whom a voter in that station is about to vote or has voted; or

(*d*) directly or indirectly induce a voter to display his voting paper after he has marked it so as to make known to any person the name of the candidate for or against whom he has so marked his vote.

(4) If any person acts in contravention of the provisions of this section he shall be guilty of an offence and liable upon conviction to imprisonment for a period not exceeding six months or to a fine not exceeding fifty pounds.

Offence. Voting by unregistered person

50. Any person who wilfully and knowingly votes in an election in respect of which his name is not so registered shall be guilty of an offence and shall be liable on conviction to imprisonment for a term not exceeding twelve months or to a fine of one hundred pounds.

Disorderly conduct at elections

51. Any person who at an election acts or incites others to act in a disorderly manner for the purpose of preventing or obstructing the conduct of such election shall be guilty of an offence and shall be liable on conviction to imprisonment not exceeding six months or to a fine not exceeding fifty pounds.

Offences at polling stations

52. (1) No person shall on the date on which a poll is taken at any polling station commit any of the following acts within such place, namely:

268

(*a*) canvassing for votes; or

(*b*) soliciting the vote of any elector; or

(*c*) persuading any elector not to vote for any particular candidate; or

(*d*) persuading any elector not to vote at the election; or

(*e*) operating or permitting the use of any megaphone, amplifier or public-address apparatus for announcements (other than official announcements) concerning the elections; or

(*f*) shouting slogans concerning the election.

(2) Any person who contravenes the provisions of this regulation shall be guilty of an offence and shall be liable on conviction to a fine of one hundred pounds or to imprisonment for one year for each offence.

Offences as to registration

53. Any person who:

(*a*) without lawful authority destroys, mutilates, defaces or removes or makes any alteration in any notice or any document required to be made for the purposes of registration; or

(*b*) wilfully or knowingly gives false information or makes a false statement in reference to any application to have his name placed on or any objection to the retention of the name of a person on a register of electors; or

(*c*) makes in any record, register or document which he is required to prepare, publish or keep for the purpose of registration any entry or statement which he knows to be false or does not believe to be true,

shall be guilty of an offence and shall be liable to a fine of one hundred pounds or to imprisonment for a term not exceeding twelve months.

Punishment of persons guilty of certain illegal practices

54. Every person who:

(*a*) votes, or induces or procures any person to vote at any election, knowing that he or such other person is prohibited by this Law or by any regulations made thereunder, or by any other Law, from voting at such election; or

(*b*) before or during an election, knowingly or recklessly publishes any false statement of the withdrawal of a candidate at such election for the purpose of promoting or procuring the election of another candidate; or (*c*) before or during an election, knowingly or recklessly publishes any false statement of fact in relation to the personal character or conduct of a candidate calculated to prejudice the chance of such candidate to be elected at such election for the purpose of promoting or procuring the election of another candidate,

shall be guilty of an illegal practice, and, being convicted thereof, shall be liable to a fine of fifty pounds or to imprisonment for six months and shall be incapable, during a period of five years from the date of his conviction, of being registered as a voter or of voting at any election of a member of a council.

PART VI. LEGAL PROCEEDINGS IN RESPECT OF QUALIFICATION AND ELECTIONS

Proceedings in respect of qualification

55. (1) Proceedings may be instituted in the Supreme Court against any person acting or claiming to be entitled to act as chairman or councillor on the ground of his being disqualified within the meaning of this section from so acting:

Provided that proceedings under this section on the ground of a person acting as aforesaid shall not be instituted after the expiration of six months from the date on which he so acted.

(2) If in proceedings under this section it is proved that the defendant acted as chairman or councillor while disqualified from so acting, then the court may:

(i) make a declaration to the effect that the defendant acted as aforesaid while disqualified from so acting and declare that the office in which he acted is vacant;

(ii) grant an injunction restraining him from so acting;

(iii) order that he shall forfeit to Her Majesty such sum as the court thinks fit not exceeding fifty pounds for each occasion on which he so acted while disqualified.

(3) If in proceedings under this section it is proved that the defendant claims to be entitled to act as chairman or councillor, and is disqualified from so acting, the court may make a declaration to the effect that the defendant claims to be entitled so to act and is disqualified from so acting and declare that the office in which the defendant claims to be entitled to act is vacant, and grant an injunction restraining him from so acting.

(4) No proceedings shall be instituted under this section by any person other than a local government elector.

(5) For the purposes of this section a person shall be deemed to be disqualified from acting as chairman or councillor:

(*a*) if he is not qualified to be, or is disqualified from being, a councillor, or for holding the office of chairman; or

(*b*) if by reason of resignation or failure to attend meetings of the council, he has ceased to be a councillor or to hold the office of chairman.

Presentation of election petition

56. A petition complaining of an undue return or undue election of a councillor (hereinafter called an election petition) may within one month from the date of the publication of the result of the election be presented to the Supreme Court in its civil jurisdiction by any one or more of the following persons, that is to say:

(*a*) some person who voted or had a right to vote at the election to which the petition relates; or

(*b*) some person who claims to have had a right to be returned or elected at such election; or

(*c*) some person who alleges himself to have been a candidate at such election.

Grounds for election petition

57. An election may be questioned on the following grounds:

(*a*) that the Electoral Officer's decision that a candidate for election had not been validly nominated was wrong;

(*b*) that the person whose election is questioned was at the time of the election not qualified or was disqualified from being elected as a councillor;

(*c*) that an election was avoided by corrupt practices or offences against this Law; or

(*d*) that the person whose election is questioned was not duly elected by a majority of lawful votes at the election.

Security for costs

58. (1) At the time of presenting an election petition, or within such time as the Court may order, the petitioner shall give security for the payment of all costs, charges and expenses which may become payable by him to any witness summoned on his behalf or to any respondent.

(2) The security shall be of such amount and shall be given in such a manner as the Court may order, and in the event of any failure to comply with such order no further proceedings shall be held on the petition.

59. (1) Every election petition shall be tried by the Supreme Court, in open court.

(2) At the conclusion of the trial, the Court shall determine whether the councillor whose return or election is complained of, or any other person and what person was duly returned or elected, or whether the election of the person whose return or election was complained of was void, and shall certify such determination to the council; and, upon such certificate being given, such determination shall be final; and the election shall be confirmed, or a new election shall be held, as the case may require, in accordance with such certificate.

Procedure (*Rules of Court* 3 *of* 1951) (*Cap.* 211)

60. An election petition shall be presented to the Supreme Court in accordance with the Supreme Court (Election Petitions) Rules, 1951, and subject to the provisions of this Part, and without prejudice to any power to make rules under the Supreme Court Ordinance, the Chief Justice may from time to time make, amend, or revoke rules for regulating the practice and procedure to be observed in relation to proceedings under this Part, and subject to any such rules, the procedure in proceedings under this Part shall, as near as circumstances will admit, be the same, and the Court shall have the same powers, jurisdiction, and authority, as if it were trying a civil action; and witnesses shall be subpoenaed and sworn in the same manner, as near as circumstances will admit, as in the trial of a civil action in the Supreme Court and shall be subject to the same penalties for perjury.

Obligation of witness to answer, and certificate of indemnity

61. (1) A person called as a witness in any proceedings under this Part shall not be excused from answering any question on the ground that the answer thereto may criminate or tend to criminate himself or on the ground of privilege:

Provided that:

(*a*) a witness who answers truly all questions which he is required by the court to answer shall be entitled to receive a certificate of indemnity under the hand of the presiding judge stating that such witness has so answered; and

(*b*) an answer by a person to a question put by or before the court shall not, except in the case of criminal proceedings for perjury in respect of such evidence, be in any proceedings, civil or criminal, admissible in evidence.

(2) Where a person has received a certificate of indemnity in relation to an election, and any legal proceedings are at any time instituted against him for any offence against the provisions of Part V of this Law committed by him, previously to the date of the certificate, at or in relation to the said election, the court having cognisance of the case shall on proof of the certificate stay the proceedings, and may in its discretion award to the said person such costs as he may have been put to in the proceedings.

PART VII. COMMITTEES

Finance committees [see p. 52]

62. Every County Council, every Municipality and every District Council shall appoint a Finance Committee for regulating and controlling the finances of the Council.

Medical and Health committees [see pp. 52-3]

63. (1) Unless otherwise provided in the Instrument every County Council, Municipality and every District Council shall appoint a Medical and Health Committee for the purpose of carrying out any functions concerning public health conferred upon such council by this Law or any other written Law.

(2) The Minister may by Instrument specify the composition of such committee including the number and qualifications of any members who are not members of the council.

Joint committees

64. A council may concur with any one or more councils in appointing from among their respective members a joint committee of such councils for any purpose in which they are jointly interested and may delegate to such committee with or without restrictions or conditions any powers or functions of the council relating to the purpose for which the joint committee is formed except the power of making bye-laws, or levying a rate or issuing a precept or of borrowing money.

Other committees

65. A council may appoint a committee for any such general or specific purpose as in the opinion of the council would be better regulated and managed by means of a committee.

Provided that this section shall not authorise the appointment of a Finance Committee or a committee for any purpose for which a council is required to appoint a committee by its Instrument.

General provisions as to all committees

66 (1) The number of the members of any committee appointed by a council, their term of office and the area within which the committee is to exercise its authority shall be specified by the council.

(2) A committee may include members who are not members of the council:

Provided that at least two-thirds of the members of every committee shall be members of the council.

(3) A committee may co-opt persons who are not members of the council to be members of such committee but persons so co-opted shall not be entitled to vote on any question before such committee, and shall not count as members of such committee for the purposes of subsection (2).

(4) No person shall be appointed or co-opted to be a member of a committee except with his own consent.

(5) Every committee or joint committee shall report its proceedings to the council or councils appointing such committee.

Power of delegation by council [see p. 56]

67. A council may delegate to any committee with or without restrictions or conditions any functions exercisable by the council either with respect to the whole or any part of the area of the authority of the council except the power of making bye-laws, levying a rate, issuing a precept or of borrowing money.

Standing Orders for committees

68. Subject to the provisions of this Law, a council appointing a committee and councils who concur in appointing a joint committee may make, vary and revoke standing orders respecting the quorum, proceedings and the place of meeting of the committee or joint committee, but subject to any such standing orders the quorum, proceedings and place of meeting shall be such as the committee or joint committee may determine.

General functions [see p. 26]

69. (1) It shall be the duty of every council established under this Law to discharge the functions conferred by this or any other written law and generally to maintain order and good government within the area of its authority; and for these purposes a council, within such limits as may be prescribed by the Instrument by which it is established, may either by its own officers or by duly appointed agents do all such things as are necessary or desirable for the discharge of its functions and for the maintenance of the health, safety and well-being of all persons living within the area of its authority.

(2) Any functions conferred upon a council shall be exercisable over all persons within the area of its authority save as is otherwise expressly provided in this Law.

Prevention of crime [see p. 26]

70. (1) It shall be the duty of every council and Village Council together with the individual members thereof to interpose for the purpose of preventing and to the best of their ability to prevent the commission of any offence within the area of their authority by any person.

(2) A council or Village Council or any individual member thereof, knowing of the occurrence of any act which is likely to result in a serious breach of the peace within the area of the authority of the council, shall report the matter to the nearest police officer, court or administrative officer immediately, and failure to report such an act shall be an offence and shall render any individual member of the council or of the Village Council concerned to a fine not exceeding one hundred pounds.

(3) Any member of council or Village Council within the area in which he resides shall, if called upon by a superior police officer or administrative officer to do so, take any reasonable action necessary for the prevention of the commission of any offence, and failure to take such action shall be an offence and shall render the individual liable to a fine not exceeding one hundred pounds.

Powers of a council to order strangers to leave its area

71. (1) A council may order any person who is not a member of a native community living in the area of its authority and who fails, when so required by the council to produce reasonable proof to the council that his means and legitimate labour are sufficient for the adequate support of himself and his dependents, to leave such area within such time after the order has been communicated to him, not being less than fourteen days, as the council may direct:

Provided that any person so ordered to leave such area may within fourteen days of the order being communicated to him appeal against the order to a Magistrate's Court, but the court shall not set aside the order unless such person satisfies the court that his means and legitimate labour are sufficient for the adequate support of himself and his dependents.

(2) Any person who fails to obey an order made under this section, or who, having left the area which he was directed by the order to leave, returns to such area without the consent of the council, shall be liable to a fine of twenty-five pounds or to imprisonment for six months.

Power to accept gifts

72. A council may accept, hold and administer any gift of property for any public purpose, or for the benefit of the inhabitants of the area of its authority or any part thereof, and may execute any works (including works of maintenance and improvement) incidental to or consequential on the exercise of the powers conferred by this section.

Fees, charges, licences

73. (1) A council may charge fees for any service or facility provided by the council or for any licence or permit issued by such council under the provisions of this Law or of any bye-law, regulation or rule made hereunder.

(2) A council may for good cause authorise the remission of any fees or other charges imposed under the provisions of this Law or any bye-law, regulation or rule made hereunder.

Power to contract Regulations [see p.13]

74. (1) Subject to the provisions of this section a council may enter into any contract necessary for the despatch of its functions under this or any other written law.

(2) A council shall not enter into a contract which by its terms will involve a council in the expenditure of more than one hundred pounds without the approval of the Minister in accordance with any regulations made under the provisions of this section.

(3) Any contract made by a council which by its terms will involve the council in the expenditure of more than fifty pounds but not exceeding one hundred pounds shall in the case of contracts for the supply of goods and materials or for the execution of works require notice of the intention of the council to enter into the contract to be published and tenders invited.

(4) The Minister may make regulations for giving effect to the provisions of this section and may by such regulations provide for:

(*a*) the establishment and constitution of tenders boards;

(*b*) the organisation of the work of such boards and the manner in which they shall perform their functions; and

(*c*) the payment by councils of any allowances to the members of such board.

Insurance

75. A council may insure all or any of its property against risks of any type.

Provision of offices, etc., by councils

76. (1) Subject to the provisions of section 74 a council may:

(*a*) build, acquire or provide and furnish buildings within the area of the authority of such council to be used for the purpose of transacting the business of the council and for public meetings and assemblies; or

(*b*) combine with any other council for the purpose of acquiring or providing and furnishing any such buildings; or

(*c*) contribute towards the expense incurred by any other council in acquiring or providing and furnishing any building within the area of the authority of such council suitable for use for any of the aforesaid purposes.

(2) A council may build, provide and maintain quarters or houses for any officer or employee of the council.

Medical Officers of Health in area of authority of District or Local Councils (Cap. 183)

77. The Minister, after consultation with the Minister of Health, may appoint any person who fulfils the duties of a Health Officer under the provisions of the Public Health Ordinance to carry out in respect of the area of authority of any District or Local Council the duties of a Medical Officer of Health as laid down in subsection (2) of section 92 and any person so appointed may give any order or direction necessary in the exercise of the performance of his duties to any person employed by such council for the purposes of any health or sanitary duties and any such order or direction shall be obeyed by such employee.

Newspapers and publications

78. A council may publish newspapers or periodicals and may provide information services.

Local Government Associations [see p. 47]

79. A council may contribute to Local Government Associations and incur expenditure incidental to the holding of meetings thereof.

Functions [see pp. 22-3]

80. The Minister may by Instrument declare that, subject to such limitations and conditions as he may impose, a council either shall perform or may perform all or any of the following functions in respect of the area for which it is established:

Agriculture

(1) provide services for the improvement of agriculture;

(2) control methods of husbandry;

Animals

(3) prohibit, restrict or regulate the movement in or through the area of the council of any livestock;

(4) establish, maintain and control pounds, seize and impound any stray animal, and provide for the payment of compensation for damage done by such animal;

(5) prohibit cruelty to animals, and any specified acts of cruelty to animals;

(6) prohibit, restrict and regulate the keeping of livestock of any description;

(7) prevent and control the outbreak or the prevalence of any disease among animals;

(8) provide services for the improvement of livestock;

Buildings

(9) prescribe the conditions subject to which the erection and construction, demoltition, re-erection and construction, conversion and re-conversion, alteration, repair, sanitation and ventilation of public and private buildings and structures may be undertaken and carried out;

(10) provide for the layout of buildings;

(11) provide for building lines;

(12) make advances upon such conditions as shall be thought fit for the purpose of enabling rate-payers to build or to buy dwelling houses;

(13) prepare and undertake and otherwise control schemes for improved housing layout and settlement;

(14) prescribe the conditions to be satisfied by a site for any building or for any class of building;

(15) prohibit the construction of any new building unless and until the plans thereof have been submitted to and approved by the council;

(16) provide for the demolition of dangerous buildings if necessary at the expense of the owner, or occupier, and provide for the recovery of such expenses;

(17) prohibit or regulate the use in any defined area of any inflammable material in the construction or repair of any building;

(18) build, equip and maintain social centres, public libraries, communal feeding centres, restaurants, catering and other rest houses, or buildings designed and used for public purposes;

(19) build, equip, maintain and let shops;

(20) prohibit or regulate the making of borrow pits or other excavations;

(21) control and regulate the siting of advertisements and hoardings or other structures designed for the display of advertisements;

Education

(22) build, equip or maintain any school or other educational institution;

(23) grant sums of money towards the establishment, equipment or maintenance of any school or other educational institution;

(24) grant and maintain scholarships or bursaries to suitable persons to attend any school or other educational institution in Nigeria or elsewhere;

(25) provide for the compulsory education of children or of specified categories of children between the ages of five and fourteen years;

(26) grant sums of money for the education of adults;

(27) grant sums of money towards the establishment or maintenance of any public library, museum or to any association existing for the promotion of arts, and crafts, or recreation and sport;

279

Forestry

(28) establish and maintain tree nurseries, forest plantations and forest reserves and sell the produce thereof;

Liquor

(29) prohibit restrict regulate or license the manufacture, sale, distribution, supply, possession and consumption of palm wine and any kind or description of fermented liquor usually made by Nigerians;

Markets

(30) build, equip, open, close and maintain markets and prohibit the erection of stalls in places other than markets;

(31) regulate and control markets, including the fixing of and collection of stallages, rents and tolls;

(32) fix the days and hours during each day on which a market may be held and prevent the sale and purchase of goods in markets on any day or at any hours except those fixed;

Public Health

(33) safeguard and promote public health including the prevention of and the dealing with any outbreak or the prevalence of any disease;

(34) build, equip, and maintain, or grant sums of money towards the establishment, equipment or maintenance of any hospital, maternity home, dispensary, asylum for the aged, destitute or infirm or for orphans or asylums and settlements for lepers;

(35) exterminate and prevent the spread of tsetse fly, mosquitoes, rats, bugs and other vermin;

(36) establish and operate ambulance services;

(37) establish, install, build, maintain, and control drains, latrines, public lavatories and wash places and any sewage systems;

(38) establish, maintain, and carry out sanitary services for the removal and destruction of and otherwise dealing with night-soil and all kind of refuse;

(39) provide, erect and maintain a public water supply, regulate or prohibit the sinking of wells and provide for the closing of wells;

(40) prevent the pollution of the water in any river, stream, water-course, water hole or drain and prevent the obstruction of any river, stream or water-course;

(41) build, manage, license and control slaughter houses;

(42) regulate the slaughter of and provide for the inspection of animals intended for the food of man;

(43) regulate the preparation and sale of meat;

(44) establish, maintain and control cemeteries and burial grounds;

(45) provide for the control and registration of bake houses, dairies, aerated water manufactories, food preparing and preserving establishments, laundries and wash-houses;

Public Order

(46) prohibit, regulate or restrict the carrying and possession of weapons;

(47) prohibit, restrict and regulate the migration of persons from or to the area of the council;

(48) prevent fires and control grass-fires;

(49) establish and maintain fire brigades and provide for the use and custody of any appliance for the extinguishing of fires;

(50) prohibit or regulate gambling;

(51) license and regulate guides, porters and carriers;

(52) control the movement of beggars in streets and public places;

(53) suppress brothels, disorderly houses, and take measures to prevent prostitution;

(54) prohibit, restrict or control the hawking of wares;

(55) regulate and control public collections in streets and public places;

(56) prohibit, regulate or restrict drumming;

(57) provide for the prohibition, regulation or registration of any customary plays.

(58) provide for the prohibition, regulation or registration of any customary clubs;

Registration of Persons

(59) provide for the registration of persons residing within the area of the authority of the council or in any part thereof;

(60) require the marriage, birth or death of any person within the area of the authority of the council to be reported to or registered with the council and to appoint registration offices and registrars for such purposes;

Roads, Streets, etc.

(61) make, alter, divert and maintain roads, streets, paths, culverts, bridges, street-drains and water courses;

(62) provide or arrange for lighting in public places;

(63) regulate all traffic in the area;

(64) license bicycles and vehicles other than motor vehicles including motor bicycles;

(65) establish, provide and maintain parks for motor and other vehicles;

(66) require persons to carry lights during certain hours in certain areas;

(67) establish, acquire and maintain transport services by land or water including ferries;

(68) regulate or prohibit the planting, cutting, tapping or destruction of any trees or vegetation growing along any street, road or path or any public place;

(69) provide that the owner or occupier of any land or tenements maintain, clear and keep free from vegetation the roads, streets or paths adjoining their land or tenements;

(70) regulate the naming of roads and streets and the numbering of houses;

Trade and Industry

(71) prescribe the conditions under which any offensive trade or industry may be carried on;

(72) prescribe the conditions of employment in factories, workshops, bakehouses, eating houses and laundries;

(73) fix the maximum price which may be demanded in the sale by retail for any article of food in any market;

(74) establish, erect, maintain and control public weighing machines and other instruments of measurements; or establish and operate secondary industries;

(75) provide for the control and registration of hotels and catering establishments;

Various Matters

(76) protect, preserve and prohibit the removal from any place of any African antique work of art;

(77) regulate child betrothals;

(78) establish, control and manage recreation grounds, open spaces and parks;

(79) licence and regulate the carrying of passengers and goods by canoes and other small craft and provide for safety precautions;

(80) provide for the maintenance of any traditional office or customary title which is on the date of the commencement of this Law receiving such maintenance, or which is recognised by a vote of three-quarters of the total membership of the council in the area;

(81) provide for the licensing of any suitable building or other place for the performance of stage plays or other public entertainment and to prescribe the conditions under which such plays or entertainments may be shown;

(82) provide for the celebration of any traditional or customary ceremony;

(83) prescribe the duties of any person employed by the council in connexion with any function of such council;

(84) prohibit, restrict or regulate the capture, killing or sale of fish or any specified kind of fish;

(85) erect, extend or alter any pier owned or erected by the Council subject to the provisions of the Piers Ordinance and the Ports Ordinance, 1954 (Cap. 170) (No. 27 of 1954);

(86) grant sums of money to the Department of Social Welfare of the Regional Government or Associations existing for the benefit and welfare of children and young persons or of infirm or aged persons;

(87) the prohibition of the practice of nudity;

(88) perform any function for the provision of the peace, good order and welfare of the persons within the area of the authority of the council which may be sanctioned by the Minister, whether such function is similar to those enumerated in this section or not;

(89) provide for the building of rural postal agencies and for the maintenance of rural postal services which have been approved by the Director of Posts and Telegraphs.

(90) provide for or grant sums of money to organisations existing to assist in the repatriation of destitute adults and young persons or children who are not members of a native community living in the area of its authority and for the repatriation to the area of the authority of the council from other parts of Nigeria of members of native communities living in the area of the authority of the council;

(91) provide for the entertainment of and hospitality to guests of the council.

Bye-laws for use and alienation of land

81. (1) The Minister may by Instrument declare that subject to such limitations and conditions as he may impose a council may make bye-laws for all or any of the following purposes:

(a) regulate and control the use and alienation of land including land communally owned or of any interest therein;

(b) control the borrowing of money or money's worth secured upon standing crops;

(*c*) prevent and control soil erosion;

(*d*) provide for the fencing of land and for the maintenance and repair of such fences;

(*e*) require any person to cultivate land to such extent and with such crops as will secure an adequate supply of food for the support of such person and of those dependent upon him; or

(*f*) establish a registry or a system of registration for the recording or filing of documents and plans relating to the alienation of land or any interest therein.

(2) For the purposes of this section 'land' means all land including everything attached to the earth in the Eastern Region other than freehold land, Crown land and land which is the subject either of a lease under the Crown Lands Ordinance (Cap. 45) or the Native Lands Acquisition Ordinance (Cap. 144).

Delegation of powers and functions by County Councils to District Councils

82. (1) A County Council may, with the concurrence of a District Council within the area of its authority, delegate to such District Council, with or without restrictions or conditions, any of its functions under this Law except:

(*a*) functions for the discharge of which the County Council is required to appoint a committee; and

(*b*) the power of borrowing money or issuing a precept.

(2) A District Council shall act as agents for a County Council in the exercise of any functions delegated by a County Council to it under the provisions of this section.

Complaint by County Council of District Council

83. If it appears to a County Council that any District Council within the area of its authority has made default in performance of any function conferred upon it by an Instrument which specifies that it is the duty of such Council to perform such function, the County Council shall complain to the Minister.

Power of Minister to enforce certain functions of councils in default [see p. 44]

84. (1) If the Minister is satisfied that any council has made default in the performance of any function conferred upon it by an Instrument which specifies that it is the duty of such council to perform such function, he may:

(*a*) make an order declaring the council to be in default, directing it for the purpose of removing the default to perform such of its functions and in such manner and within such time or times as may be specified within the order; or

(*b*) make an order transferring to another council such of the functions of the council in default, as may be specified in the order; or

(*c*) make an order transferring to the Minister such of the functions of the council in default as may be so specified.

(2) If a council with respect to which an order has been made under paragraph (*a*) of subsection (1) fails to comply with any requirement thereof within the time limited thereby for compliance with that requirement, the Minister may make an order under paragraph (*b*) or (*c*) or subsection (1).

Expenses of the Minister or council upon transfer of functions

85. Where any function of a council is transferred to the Minister or to another council under the provisions of subsection (1) of section 84, the expenses incurred by the Minister or the council in discharging such function shall, except in so far as they may be met by any grant made by the Minister or the council, be a debt due from the council in default to the Minister or the council to which the function is transferred as the case may be.

PART IX. BYE-LAWS

Bye-laws [see p.121]

86. (1) A council may make bye-laws for the carrying into effect and the purposes of any function conferred upon it by this Law or any other Law or Ordinance and may in such bye-laws specify a fine not exceeding twenty-five pounds or in default of payment imprisonment not exceeding six months for the breach of any such bye-law and, in the case of a continuing offence, a further penalty not exceeding five pounds for each day after written notice of the offence has been served on the offender.

(2) Such bye-laws may make provision for the payment of such fees or charges as shall to the council seem fit.

(3) A council may authorise the remission of any fee or charge imposed under the provision of any bye-law made under the provisions of this section.

(4) Any bye-law made by a council under the provisions of this section shall be read and construed subject to the provisions of this Law and any other written law.

(5) A bye-law made by a District Council shall not be inconsistent with any bye-law made by a County Council which is in force within the area of the authority of such District Council.

(6) A bye-law made by a Local Council shall not be inconsistent with any bye-law made by a District Council or County Council which is in force within the area of the authority of such Local Council.

Method of making bye-laws [see pp.123-4]

87. (1) Bye-laws shall be made under the common seal of the council or in the case of a Local Council under the hand of two members of the Council and shall not have effect until they are approved by the Minister.

(2) The Minister may amend any bye-law submitted to him for approval before he approves such bye-law.

(3) No bye-law shall be made by a council unless reasonable notice, in such manner as the Minister shall determine, of the intention of the council to make such bye-law has been given to the inhabitants of the area to be affected thereby.

(4) The Minister may approve or refuse to approve any bye-law submitted and may fix the date on which the bye-law is to come into operation upon the date of its confirmation.

(5) All bye-laws shall be published in the *Regional Gazette* or in such manner as the Minister shall determine.

Minister may make bye-laws [see p.125]

88. The Minister may at any time after having given to a council reasonable notice and having considered the representations of the council thereon make or amend any bye-law which such council is empowered by this Law to make, or revoke any bye-law made by such council.

Copy of bye-law to be deposited at council offices [see pp.124-5]

89. (1) A copy of any bye-law when confirmed shall be deposited at the offices of the council by whom the bye-law was made and shall at all reasonable times be open to public inspection without payment, and a copy thereof shall on application be furnished to any person on payment of such sum as the council may determine.

(2) A County Council shall send a copy of every bye-law made by such Council, and confirmed, to every District Council situate within the area of its authority.

(3) A District Council shall send a copy of every bye-law deposited at their offices under the provision of subsection (2) of this section to every Local Council to which they apply.

(4) A District Council shall send a copy of every bye-law made by such Council and confirmed to the County Council in the area of the authority of which such District Council is situate and to every Local Council to which they apply.

(5) Any council which receives a copy of a bye-law under the provisions of this section shall deposit such copy at its offices.

(6) The copy so deposited shall be open to inspection by the public without payment.

District Council may enforce bye-laws of County Council [see p.125]

90. A District Council shall have power to enforce bye-laws made by a County Council which are for the time being in force in the area of its authority.

Local Council may enforce bye-laws of District and County Councils

91. A Local Council shall have power to enforce bye-laws made by a District Council or by a County Council which are for the time being in force in the area of its authority.

PART X. PROVISIONS AS TO OFFICERS AND STAFF AND LOCAL
GOVERNMENT STAFF BOARD [see p.115]

County Councils and Municipalities to employ Medical Officers of Health.
Duties of Medical Officer of Health

92. (1) Subject to the approval of the Minister and the provisions of this Part, every County Council and every Municipality shall appoint a fit person to be the Medical officer of Health for the area of its authority.

(2) It shall be the duty of any Medical Officer of Health appointed under the provisions of subsection (1):

(*a*) to give effect to and to enforce any bye-laws or rules relating to public health made under the provisions of this Law or any other written law which are in force within the area of the authority of such council;

287

(*b*) to cause to be made from time to time inspections of the area of the authority of the council with a view to ascertain what nuisances exist calling for abatement under the provisions of the Public Health Ordinance (Cap. 183) and to ensure that the provisions of that Ordinance to abate the same are enforced; and

(*c*) to take all such steps as may be desirable under the provisions of any written law to improve and maintain the standard of health of the persons living within the area.

Native Court Staff

93. (1) It shall be the duty of a council to engage and pay adequate staff (including clerks) for any Native Court for the maintenance of which it is made responsible under the provisions of the Instrument by which it is established.

(2) Notwithstanding the provisions of subsection (1) the Minister may require such council to remove any clerk employed in a Native Court from any particular court, who in his opinion is unsatisfactory, and upon receipt of such request the council shall cause such clerk to be removed from such court forthwith and it shall be the duty of such council to replace such clerk forthwith.

General powers to engage staff

94. A council may with the approval of the Minister appoint such officers, engage such staff and employ such persons as it shall think necessary for the efficient discharge of the functions of such council.

Control and dismissal of staff by Minister [see p.115]

95. No person appointed, engaged or employed by a council in any capacity shall be dismissed by a council for any reason without the approval of the Minister in writing.

Remuneration of staff

96. Subject to the provisions of this Part and to any regulations made by the Minister under the provisions of section 104 a council may pay to any person appointed, engaged or employed such reasonable remuneration as it may determine.

Joint appointment of officers and employment of staff

97. Subject to the provisions of section 94 a council may agree with any one or more councils, whether situated in the same area or not, in the employment of any staff or the appointment of any officer other than a town clerk, the clerk or secretary to the council or a treasurer.

Age of compulsory retirement

98. Without prejudice to other powers of terminating the employment of any officer, it shall be lawful for a council to require an officer to retire from the service of a council when he attains the age of sixty-five years or at any time thereafter, and, unless a council by resolution in a particular case or with regard to any particular class of officers otherwise determines, all officers shall retire on attaining that age.

Officers not to be interested in contract

99. Any officer of a council who is in any wise concerned or interested directly or indirectly by himself or his partner (otherwise than as a minority share-holder in a company) in any contract or work made with or executed for the council shall be incapable of holding any office or employment under this Law.

Appointment of seconded Government Officers

100. Notwithstanding the other provisions of this Part the council may with the approval of the Governor and of the Minister appoint to any office in its service a Government officer seconded to the service of the council for that purpose, for such period and on such terms and conditions as the Governor may approve.

Security may be demanded by council of its officers and others

101. A council may in the case of any officer, other than a Government officer appointed under the provisions of section 100, in its employment, whether under this or any other written law, and whether employed jointly with another council or not, or in the case of a person not in its employment but who is likely to be entrusted with the custody or control of money or property belonging to the council, either require him to give, or itself take, such security for the faithful execution of his office and for his duly accounting for all money or property which may be entrusted to him as the council thinks sufficient.

Accountability of officers

102. (1) Every officer, other than a Government officer appointed under section 100, employed by a council, whether under this or any other written law, shall at such times during the continuance of his office, or within three months after his ceasing to hold it, and in such manner as the council directs, make out and deliver to the council, or as it directs, a true account in writing of all money and property committed to his charge, and of his receipts and payments, with vouchers and other documents and records supporting the entries therein, and a list of persons from whom or to whom money is due in connexion with his office, showing the amount due from or to each.

(2) Every such officer shall pay all money due from him to the council, or otherwise as such council may direct.

(3) If any such officer:

(*a*) refuses or wilfully neglects to make any payment which he is required by this section to make; or

(*b*) after three days' notice in writing signed by the chairman of the council or by three members thereof, and given or left at his usual or last known place of residence, refuses or wilfully neglects to make out or deliver to the council, or as it directs, any account or list which he is required by this section to make out and deliver, or any voucher or other document or record relating thereto, or to give satisfaction respecting it to the council or as it directs;

a Magistrate's Court having jurisdiction where the officer is or resides may, on complaint, by order require him to make such payment or delivery or to give such satisfaction.

(4) Nothing in this section shall affect any remedy by action against any such officer or his surety, except that the officer shall not be both sued by action and proceeded against under the provisions of this section for the same cause.

Power of interdiction

103. A council may interdict any officer, other than a Government officer appointed under section 100, or employee of the council from the duties and emoluments of his office or employment for incapacity, neglect or misconduct pending the decision of the council as to his removal, and in the event of his removal such officer or employee shall be deemed to have been removed from office or employment as from the date of such interdiction.

'Staff Regulations' (Cap. 99) [see p.115]

104. (1) Subject to the provisions of the Labour Code Ordinance the Minister may from time to time make and, when made, amend, add to or rescind regulations to be known as 'Staff Regulations' for any or all of the following purposes relating to the officers or to any class or grade of the officers of local government councils generally or of groups of councils or of individual councils:

(*a*) maintaining discipline;

(*b*) regulating appointments, remuneration, increments, promotion, termination of appointments, dismissals and leave;

(*c*) regulating the payment of allowances, the grant of advances, and the terms and conditions of service generally;

(*d*) providing for the transfer of staff or any employee from the service of one council to that of another and regulating the conditions of such transfer; and

(*e*) such other matters relating to departmental procedure and the duties and responsibilities of officers as the Minister considers can be best regulated by such regulations.

(2) Any such regulations in so far as they relate to discipline may in particular provide for:

(*a*) withholding or deferring of increments, or reduction in rank or salary either permanently or for a stated period; and

(*b*) the deduction from salary due or about to become due of such sum as may be appraised in respect of damage to property of a council by misconduct or breach of duty on the part of an officer.

(3) Any regulations made under the provisions of this section may provide for the delegation of any power of the Minister.

Provident fund

105. (1) It shall be lawful for the Minister by regulation to establish and maintain a local government officers' contributory provident fund or to establish and maintain schemes for the payment of retiring benefits to persons who have been employed by any council, to the legal personal representatives, estates or dependants of persons who die while so employed and to the widows and children of deceased persons who have been so employed, and such schemes may be altered, varied, amended or wound up from time to time, due regard being had to the existing rights of any person coming within the scope of any such scheme.

(2) In the exercise of his powers under subsection (1) the Minister may provide that any retiring benefit or any proportion thereof be charged on the revenues of the council or councils by which he has been employed.

(3) It shall be lawful for a council to require any officer, member of the staff or person appointed or engaged or employed by it to make contributions to any fund or scheme so established.

Gratuities, and allowances

106. A council may, subject to the approval of the Minister, grant gratuities and allowances to persons who have been employed by the

council and who are not qualified for benefit under the provisions of section 105, or to the legal personal representatives, estates or relatives of such persons.

Gratuities, etc., not liable to attachment

107. No retiring benefit or gratuity or other allowance granted in pursuance of the provisions of this Part, and no rights acquired by any officer in respect of contributions made in pursuance of provisions for the grant of retiring benefits to widows and children of deceased officers, shall be assignable or transferable, or liable to be attached or sequestered, or levied upon, for or in respect of any debt or claim whatsoever:

Provided that the provisions of this section shall not affect the right of the council or the Government to recover from any sums due or payable to or in respect of any officer any amount owing to the council or the Government by such officer.

Establishment of Local Government Service Board

108. As soon as may be after the commencement of this Law there shall be established a Local Government Service Board, which shall consist of a chairman and four members to be appointed by the Minister.

Functions of Local Government Service Board Regulations

109. (1) The Minister or any council may (either generally or specifically) refer to the Local Government Service Board for their advice in any matter relating to the appointment of, engagement of, or the employment of any person by a council or the dismissal or disciplinary control of any person appointed, engaged, or employed by a council, or any other matter that affects the appointment, engagement or employment of the staff of a council.

(2) It shall be the duty of the Local Government Service Board to advise the Minister or the council as the case may be on any question referred to it in accordance with the provisions of this section but the Minister or council shall not be obliged to act in accordance with the advice given by the Local Government Service Board.

(3) The Minister may authorise any person to act on his behalf for the purposes of this section.

(4) Subject to the provisions of this Law the Minister may make regulations for giving effect to the provisions of this section and may by such regulations provide for:

(*a*) the appointment, tenure of office and terms of service of members of the Local Government Service Board;

(*b*) the organisation of the work of the Board and the manner in which it shall perform its functions;

(*c*) consultation by the Board with persons other than the members of the Board; and

(*d*) the appointment, tenure of office, and terms of service of staff to assist the Board in the performance of its functions.

PART XI. GENERAL FINANCIAL PROVISIONS

Declaration of revenue and funds of councils [see p. 94]

110. (1) The revenues and other funds of a council are hereby declared to be as follows:

(i) all sums of money or funds as are granted to a council by the Minister under the provisions of sections 221 and 230.

(ii) Revenue accruing to a council from the following sources:

(*a*) moneys derived from licences, permits, dues, charges or fees, specified by any bye-law made by a council;

(*b*) moneys payable to a council under the provisions of any other written law;

(*c*) receipts derived from any public utility concern, service, or any undertaking belonging to or maintained by a council either in whole or in part;

(*d*) rents derived from the letting or leasing of any building or land belonging to a council;

(*e*) grants-in-aid out of the general revenue of the Eastern Region, or other public revenue;

(*f*) any particular public revenue which may lawfully be assigned to a council;

(*g*) any sums of money which may lawfully be assigned to a council by any public corporation;

(*h*) interest on the invested funds of a council;

(*i*) receipts from the sale of lands; and

(*j*) fees, fines and penalties payable in respect of or as a result of proceedings in any Native Court which a council is required to maintain and the proceeds of sale of any forfeitures ordered by such Native Court.

(2) In addition to the revenue and funds specified in subsection (1) such sums of money as are payable to a County Council by a District Council in satisfaction of a precept issued by such County

Council under the provisions of section 160 shall form a part of the revenue and funds of such County Council.

(3) In addition to the revenue and funds specified in subsection (1) any general or special rates imposed by a Municipality or District Council by virtue of the provisions of this Law shall form part of the revenue and funds of such Municipality or District Council.

(4) In addition to the revenue and funds specified in subsection (1) such sums of money as are payable to a Local Council by a District Council in satisfaction of a precept issued by such Local Council under the provisions of section 162 shall form part of the revenue and funds of such Local Council.

(5) Any other moneys lawfully derived by a council from any other source whatsoever not hereinbefore specifically mentioned shall be and form part of the revenue and funds of such council.

Expenditure

111. Subject to the approval by the Minister of any estimates submitted by a council in accordance with the provisions of section 118 a council may incur all expenditure necessary for, and incidental to, the carrying out of any functions conferred upon it under this or any other Law or Ordinance, or by the Instrument by which it is established.

Power to borrow [see p.100]

112. (1) A council may from time to time raise loans within the Eastern Region of such amounts, from such sources, in such manner and upon such conditions as the Minister may approve.

(2) Such loans shall be secured upon the property and the revenues of the council.

(3) Where any interest or any payment of capital due on any loan remains unpaid for three months after a demand therefor has been served on the council in writing by the person entitled thereto, the Minister may:

(*a*) order that a rate necessary to produce the sum due shall be levied upon and collected from the rate-payers of the area of the authority of the council either immediately or at such date as he shall order, and for the purpose of raising such sum the Minister shall in addition have the same power as the council concerned of making and levying a general or special rate or of issuing a precept; or

(*b*) order the sale of any property including land on which the loan is secured.

Powers of Minister

113. The power of the Minister under section 112 of making and levying a general or special rate may be exercised at any time.

Overdraft

114. It shall be lawful for a County Council or Municipality or a District Council to obtain advances from banks by overdraft upon the credit of such County Council or Municipality or District Council:

Provided that no such overdraft shall at any time in any circumstances exceed the income of the prior year of such County Council or Municipality or District Council.

Investment of funds

115. A council may invest all or any portion of the moneys of the council in such manner as may be approved by the Minister.

Accounts

116. A council shall keep such accounts (including deposit and suspense accounts) within such limits and in such form as the Minister shall from time to time direct.

Financial memoranda [see p. 91]

117. The Minister may issue written instructions (to be called Financial Memoranda), not inconsistent with any of the provisions of this Law, for the better control and management of the financial business of councils, and for the regulation of the procedure of Finance Committees; and such instructions may be issued either generally or with respect to any particular council or with respect to the councils in any particular area.

Annual and supplementary estimates [see pp.104-6]

118. (1) Subject to the provisions of subsections (8), (9) and (10) of this section, every County Council, every Municipality and every District Council shall prepare and approve by resolution a detailed estimate of its revenue and expenditure for the next ensuing financial year and shall submit such estimate together with a covering copy of such resolution to the Minister on or before the thirty-first day of December in each year.

(2) The Minister may at any time require a Local Council to submit a detailed estimate of its revenue and expenditure for the next ensuing financial year.

(3) The Minister shall consider such estimate as submitted and may either approve or disapprove such estimate as a whole or disapprove of any item or items contained therein and shall notify the council accordingly:

Provided that if such estimate is not approved or disapproved by the Minister before the commencement of the financial year for which such estimate is prepared, such estimate shall be deemed to be an approved estimate for the purposes of this section.

(4) The Minister may impose such conditions upon the giving of his approval under the provisions of subsection (3) as he shall think fit, and until any such condition is satisfied by the council to which it is addressed such estimate or such item or items in such estimate shall be deemed to be disapproved by the Minister for the purposes of this section.

(5) Where the Minister approves the estimate as a whole the council may incur the expenditure, collect the revenue, and generally put into operation the provisions of the approved estimate, but where the estimate is disapproved as a whole no expenditure shall be incurred, no revenue collected nor shall any of the provisions of the estimate be put into operation without the prior approval of the Minister.

(6) Where the Minister disapproves of any item or items in an estimate submitted for approval, the remainder of any such estimate excluding such item or items so disapproved shall be deemed to be an approved estimate but the council shall not incur any expenditure or collect revenue as the case may be in respect of the item or items disapproved.

(7) Where the Minister has disapproved of an estimate as a whole or has disapproved of any item or items in an estimate and subsequently approves such estimate or such item or items or subsequently approves an amended or varied estimate or amended or varied item or items then such estimate or such item or items shall be deemed to be and to have been an approved estimate or an approved item or items from the beginning of the financial year to which such estimate or item or items relate.

(8) A council may by resolution authorise the expenditure of money appropriated for any one purpose in an approved estimate on any other purpose therein contained, but no such expenditure shall be incurred for any purpose in respect of which provision has not been made in such approved estimate without the prior consent of the Minister, and no expenditure shall in any case be so incurred in

respect of any purpose where the item in the estimate relating thereto has been disapproved by the Minister.

(9) Where it appears to a council in any financial year that expenditure for any specified purpose is desirable and no or insufficient provision therefor has been made in the estimate for such year, a council may submit a supplementary estimate to the Minister for approval and the provisions of subsections (5), (6), (7) and (8) of this section shall apply to such supplementary estimate.

(10) Notwithstanding the provisions of this section a council may by resolution authorise expenditure in any financial year up to five *per centum* of its estimated revenue for that year without the approval of the Minister upon any item or items appearing in the estimates which have been approved by the Minister, but no such expenditure shall be incurred for any purpose in respect of which provision has not been made in such estimate without the prior consent of the Minister:

Provided that a council shall not incur any expenditure under this subsection on any item or items disapproved by the Minister under this section.

(11) Notwithstanding the provisions of section 110, to arrive at the estimated revenue of a District Council for the purposes of this subsection any sum payable by such District Council to a council in satisfaction of a precept shall first be deducted.

(12) The Minister may consider and approve estimates for the first year of the operation of a council notwithstanding that the provisions of this section have not been complied with.

Writing off irrecoverable arrears of revenue

119. (1) A council may, from time to time, authorise the writing off as irrecoverable debts in regard to which no further proceedings need be taken any sum due or payable to the council from or by any person, on the ground of the poverty of such person or for other sufficient cause:

Provided that no such sum shall be written off as an irrecoverable debt without the prior approval of the Minister if it exceeds twenty pounds in any one case, or, if by so writing it off, the total sum written off in any financial year will exceed the sum of two hundred pounds.

(2) A council may from time to time authorise the writing off of deficiencies of cash or stores:

Provided that no such deficiency be written off without the prior approval of the Minister if it exceeds twenty pounds in value in any one case, or, if, by so writing it off, the total value of such deficiencies written off in any financial year will exceed the value of two hundred pounds.

Appointment of Examiners of Accounts [see p. 44]

120. (1) The Minister may by notice in the *Regional Gazette* appoint suitable persons to be Examiners of the Accounts of local government councils in such areas as shall be specified in such notice.

(2) Any persons appointed under the provisions of subsection (1) shall have a right of access to all council and committee meetings within the area specified in such notice and shall have access within office hours to the records and accounts of any council situate within such area for the purpose of advising the Minister or any such council either generally or specifically.

PART XII. RATES AND RATING

Municipalities and District Councils to be rating authorities [see p. 91]

121. For the purposes of this Law every Municipality and District Council shall be the rating authority for the area of its authority and, save and except as is provided in sections 11, 112 and 171, no authority, council or person other than a Municipality or a District Council shall for the purposes of this Law have power to make or levy any rate in the area of the authority of such Municipality or District Council, notwithstanding any local customary law to the contrary.

Power and duty to make sufficient rates

122. Every council shall make such rates or issue such precepts as will be sufficient to provide for such part of the total estimated expenditure to be incurred by the council during the period in respect of which the rate is made or precept is issued as is to be met out of moneys raised by rates, including in that expenditure any sums payable to any other council under precepts issued by that council, together with such additional amount as is in the opinion of the council required to cover expenditure previously incurred, or to meet contingencies or to defray any expenditure which may fall to be defrayed before the date on which the moneys to be received in respect of the next subsequent rate or precept will become available.

System of rating and liability for the payment of rates where Assessment Ordinance applies (Cap. 16)

123. (1) In any area in which the Assessment Ordinance applies a Municipality or a District Council shall have power to impose an annual rate on any tenements within its area which are assessed in accordance with that Ordinance and such rate shall be a uniform amount per pound of the annual value of such tenements.

(2) The owner and occupier of every tenement not exempt from the rate shall be liable for the payment of the rate, which shall be deemed to be an owner's rate and as between the occupier and the owner of any tenement shall, in the absence of any agreement to the contrary, be borne by the owner, and the amount thereof if paid by the occupier may be recovered by him from the owner in an action for money paid to his use or may be deducted from any rent due or to become due in respect of the tenements.

(3) For the purposes of this section the terms, 'annual value', 'occupier', 'owner' and 'tenement' have the meanings assigned to them from time to time in the Assessment Ordinance respectively.

System of rating when Part XIII applies (Cap. 16) [see pp. 97-8]

124. (1) In any area to which the Assessment Ordinance does not apply, if it is so stated in the Instrument by which it is established, a Municipality or a District Council may impose an annual rate on any tenements within the area of its authority which are assessed in accordance with the provisions of Part XIII of this Law and such rate shall be a uniform amount per pound of the annual value of such tenements.

(2) The owner and occupier of every tenement not exempt from the rate shall be liable for the payment of the rate, which shall be deemed to be an owner's rate and as between the occupier and the owner of any tenement shall, in the absence of any agreement to the contrary, be borne by the owner, and the amount thereof if paid by the occupier may be recovered by him from the owner in an action for money paid to his use or may be deducted from any rent due or to become due in respect of the tenement.

(3) For the purposes of this subsection the terms 'annual value', 'occupier' and 'owner' have the meanings assigned to them from time to time in the Assessment Ordinance (Cap. 16) respectively, and the term 'tenement' means any land with buildings which is held or occupied as a distinct or separate holding or tenancy or any wharf or pier but shall not include any land without buildings.

125. (1) In any area to which the Assessment Ordinance (Cap. 16) does not apply, a Municipality or a District Council, if it is so stated in the Instrument by which it is established, may make and levy an annual rate upon the annual income of any person who is liable for the payment of tax under the Direct Taxation Ordinance (Cap. 54) and who resides within the area of its authority, and such rate shall be a uniform amount per pound of the income of such person:

Provided that any person who is taxed in respect of any cattle in lieu of any other tax under the provisions of section 10 of the Direct Taxation Ordinance (Cap. 54) shall not for that reason be liable for the payment of rates under this subsection.

(2) In addition, such Municipality or District Council may by resolution make and levy an annual rate upon any other person who, or class of person which, is taxable within the area of its authority by virtue of the provisions of the Direct Taxation Ordinance (Cap. 54), and such rate shall be a uniform amount per person:

Provided that the amount of such rate shall not exceed the lowest amount of rate payable by any person rated under the provisions of subsection (1) of this section.

(3) The annual income of any person who is rateable under the provisions of this subsection shall be presumed to be the annual income of such person ascertained under the provisions of section 7 of the Direct Taxation Ordinance (Cap. 54), for the purposes of taxation under that Ordinance.

System of capitation rating [see pp. 97-9]

126. In any area to which the Assessment Ordinance (Cap. 16) does not apply, a Municipality or a District Council if it is so stated in the Instrument by which it is established may make and levy an annual rate upon any person or class of persons over the age of sixteen years ordinarily resident within the area of its authority.

General and special rates

127. (1) For the purpose of raising revenue a Municipality or a District Council may by resolution make and levy a general rate.

(2) In addition to a general rate a Municipality or a District Council may by resolution make and levy a special rate for the purposes of raising revenue for any special purposes, or from any particular part of the area of its authority. Such rate shall be termed a 'special rate'.

(3) If it is so stated in the Instrument by which it is established a Municipality or a District Council may, subject to the provisions of this Part, apply one system of rating for making and levying a general rate and a different system of rating for making and levying a special rate.

Publication of rate

128. (1) Notice of every rate shall be given by the Municipality or District Council within ten days after the passing of the resolution making such rate, and the rate shall not be valid unless notice thereof is duly given in the manner for the time being required by law.

(2) Notice may be given in such manner as the Municipality or District Council may resolve and may, if the Municipality or District Council think fit, be given either by affixing a copy of the resolution or a notice at any time within the said period of ten days in some public or conspicuous place or situation in the area of the authority of any Local Council affected, or by publishing a copy of the resolution or a notice in one or more newspapers circulating in the area of the authority of the Municipality or District Council, and different methods of publication may be used as respects different parts of the area of the authority of the Municipality or District Council.

Date and place of payment

129. The rate shall be paid at the office of the Municipality or District Council or at such other place, at such time and in such manner as may be specified by such Municipality or Council from time to time.

Power to remit rate

130. (1) A Municipality or a District Council shall have power to reduce or remit the payment of any rate on account of the poverty of any person liable for the payment thereof.

(2) A Municipality or a District Council may with the approval of the Minister reduce or remit the payment of any rate by any person or class of persons liable for the payment thereof.

Exemptions from assessment and rating

131. Notwithstanding the provisions of this Law the following tenements shall be exempt from all the provisions relating to assessment and rating under this Law:

(a) all lands and buildings appropriated exclusively for the purposes of public worship;

301

(*b*) cemeteries and burial grounds;

(*c*) schools and buildings, including teachers' houses, within such school premises used exclusively for the purposes of conducting such schools; and

(*d*) private hospitals registered under the Private Hospitals Ordinance (Cap. 178), and hospitals and similar institutions exempt from such registration by reason of being maintained or owned by a local government council.

Claim for amount of rate

132. (1) The claim for the amount of any rate payable under the provisions of this Law shall be prior to all other claims against the person liable to pay the same, except claims by the Crown or the Government.

(2) If any person fails to pay any rate for which he is liable on or before the date on which it is payable the Municipality or the District Council as the case may be may recover the same as a civil debt with costs and interest at the rate of ten *per centum per annum* from the day when such rate ought to have been paid until the date of payment.

Penalty for refusal to pay rates

133. Any person who without lawful justification or excuse, the proof of which shall lie on the person charged, shall refuse to pay any rate payable by him under this Law on or before the date on which it is payable, or who shall wilfully misrepresent in any way his rateable capacity, shall be liable to a fine not exceeding fifty pounds or to imprisonment for six months.

Penalty for inciting a person to refuse to pay rates, etc.

134. Any person who without lawful justification or excuse, the proof of which shall lie on the person charged, shall incite any person to refuse to pay any rate payable by him under this Law on or before the day on which it is payable, or who shall incite or assist any person to misrepresent in any way his rateable capacity, shall be liable to a fine not exceeding one hundred pounds or to imprisonment for two years.

Penalty for unauthorised collection of rates

135. Any person who not being authorised under this Law or by a Municipality or a District Council or a rate-collector to do so shall collect or attempt to collect any rate shall be liable to a fine of one hundred pounds or to imprisonment for two years.

Duty to give information

136. Any person whose authority and control is recognised by a section of a community or any employer or any head of a family or any householder or any person who may be required so to do shall give all such information as may be required of him by any Municipality, any District Council or rate-collector with a view to obtaining information for the assessment or collection of the rate.

Penalty for refusing to give information

137. Any person having been required to give information under the provisions of section 136 who shall neglect or refuse to give such information or who shall wilfully mislead or attempt to mislead any Municipality, any District Council or rate-collector or their agents on any matter connected with the collection of the rate shall be liable to a fine of one hundred pounds or to imprisonment for two years.

Appointment of rate-collectors

138. (1) A Municipality or a District Council may in writing appoint any Village Council, district headman or other suitable person or group of persons to be a rate-collector in respect of any specified area.

(2) It shall be the duty of every rate-collector:

(*a*) to furnish orally or in writing to the Municipality or District Council a nominal roll of all rateable persons or tenements as the case may be in the area to which he has been appointed;

(*b*) to collect and receive from each person liable for the payment of rates in the area to which he has been appointed the rates payable by each such person;

(*c*) to pay all amounts so collected to the Municipality or the District Council; and

(*d*) to report to the Municipality or the District Council the name of any person who has failed to pay the amount due from him for rates.

Penalty in respect of offences by rate-collectors

139. Any rate-collector or individual member of a rate-collector who:

(*a*) fails to deposit with the Municipality or the District Council any sum of money collected by him as rates;

(*b*) demands from any community or any person an amount in excess of the duly assessed rates;

(*c*) renders false returns, whether orally or in writing, of the number of the rate-payers or the amounts of rates collected or received by him;

(*d*) fails to carry out any duty imposed upon him, either individually or as a member of a rate-collector,

shall be liable to a fine of one hundred pounds or to imprisonment for two years.

Proceedings may be taken against members of a rate-collector collectively or separately

140. When a group of persons is collectively appointed to be a rate-collector proceedings may be taken against such group or any member of such group, either together or separately, in respect of any act or default punishable under section 139 and upon proof of the commission of an offence by such group every member thereof shall individually be liable to the penalties prescribed unless he shall satisfy the court that he was in no way responsible for or a party to the commission of the offence.

Legal Proceedings

141. Proceedings either to enforce the payment of any rate payable under the provisions of this Part or for the imposition of penalties under the provisions of this Part may be taken by a Municipality or a District Council as rating authority or by a rate-collector as the case may be, before a Magistrate's Court.

PART XIII. ASSESSMENT

Part XIII not to apply where Assessment Ordinance applies

142. The provisions contained in this Part shall not apply in any area to which the Assessment Ordinance (Cap. 16) applies.

Appointment of Assessment Committee

143. The Minister may in any area before or after the establishment of any council appoint a committee of not less than four or more than eight members to be called the 'Assessment Committee' for the hearing of objections to the valuation list made under this Law.

Standing Orders

144. The Minister may make, vary and revoke standing orders respecting the quorum, proceedings and place of meeting of such committee but subject to any such standing orders the quorum, proceedings and place of meeting shall be such as the committee may determine.

Appointment of appraisers

145. The Minister may before or after the establishment of any council appoint any suitable persons to be appraisers for the purposes of this Law.

Minister may delegate powers

146. (1) The Minister may delegate all or any of his powers under sections 143, 144 or 145 to any person or council.

(2) Any such delegation shall be revocable at will and no delegation shall prevent the exercise of any power by the Minister.

Duties of appraisers

147. (1) Subject to the provisions of this section, it shall be the duty of appraisers to ascertain and assess the annual value of the tenements in such place and at such time as may be directed by the Minister, a Municipality, or a District Council as the case may be.

(2) It shall be the duty of appraisers to ascertain to the best of their ability the average annual value of all the tenements in the area of the authority of the Municipality or District Council other than those already assessed under subsection (1), or, when so directed, to ascertain the average annual value of any specified number or class of such tenements, and such average annual value shall be deemed to be the annual value of each of such tenements for the purposes of assessment under this Law.

(3) It shall be the duty of appraisers from time to time to ascertain and assess the annual value of any tenement which having been assessed under the provisions of this section in the opinion of the appraisers requires reassessment, and of any tenement which being rateable or about to become rateable has not been already assessed.

(4) For the purposes of this section the terms 'annual value' and 'tenement' shall have the meanings assigned to them in subsection (3) of section 124.

Allowances

148. The Minister, a Municipality or a District Council as the case may be shall pay such reasonable allowances to the members of the Assessment Committee and appraisers not being Government officers or officers in the employment of any council as shall be considered fit.

New Assessment, reassessment

149. A Municipality or a District Council may in any year direct that a new assessment or a reassessment shall be made in respect of all the tenements or of any class of tenements within the area of its authority or part thereof.

Power of appraisers

150. Any appraiser may:

(*a*) on any day, except a Sunday or a public holiday, between the hours of seven o'clock in the morning and six o'clock in the afternoon enter into and upon any tenement for the purpose of making a valuation thereof and take such measurements and other particulars as he may deem necessary for the purpose;

(*b*) call upon the occupier for his name or, if the occupier is not the owner, the name and address of the owner of the tenement;

(*c*) call upon the owner or occupier of any tenement to exhibit to him any receipt for rent, rent book or other documents whatever connected with the rent or value of the tenement;

(*d*) require the owner or occupier of any tenement actually rented to make a declaration in writing as to the yearly rent paid or payable for the same;

(*e*) require the owner or occupier to inform him as to the boundaries of the tenement;

(*f*) generally require the owner or occupier to furnish any information which in the opinion of the appraiser may affect the annual value of the tenement; and

(*g*) appoint in writing deputies who may exercise all the powers of an appraiser under this section.

Penalty for refusing information

151. (1) Any person who, when required by an appraiser or his deputy to exhibit anything or to make any declaration or give any information which the appraiser or his deputy is authorised to require of him under the provisions of section 150, shall refuse or neglect to exhibit such thing or to make such declaration or to give such information or shall knowingly make a false declaration or shall knowingly give false information shall be liable to a fine of twenty-five pounds, or to imprisonment for six months.

(2) Any person who prevents or hinders an appraiser or his deputy from entering, inspecting or measuring any tenement shall be liable to a fine of twenty-five pounds, or to imprisonment for six months.

Assessment of annual value of a tenement actually rented at a fair rent

152. Subject to the provisions of subsection (2) of section 147, when any tenement is actually rented and a declaration in writing is made as to the yearly rent of such tenement or as to the amount of rent paid or payable for the same, the appraiser shall, if he is of opinion that the yearly rent so stated is the fair annual value of the tenement, assess the annual value on it.

Assessment of annual value in other cases

153. Subject to the provisions of subsection (2) of section 147, the appraiser shall, according to the best of his ability, assess the annual value of any tenement:

(*a*) where such tenement is not actually rented;

(*b*) where no declaration has been made with respect to such tenement;

(*c*) where the appraiser is of opinion that the rent stated in the declaration is not the fair annual value of such tenement.

Valuation List

154. (1) As soon as any assessment is made or an existing assessment is altered the appraiser shall make out and sign a list of the several tenements assessed and of their respective valuation and shall deliver the same to the Minister, the Municipality or the District Council as the case may be.

(2) The Minister, the Municipality or District Council as the case may be shall give notice of the fact that a valuation list has been prepared and as to the place at which it may be inspected, and the list or an examined copy thereof shall be open for inspection at the place mentioned during ordinary office hours.

(3) A valuation list shall, for the purpose of any rate to be levied in respect of the tenements assessed, be the valuation list for the year in which it is published and for the next following year.

Notice of objection

155. (1) Any owner or occupier of a tenement who may be dissatisfied with the valuation of such tenement as appearing in the valuation list may lodge a notice of objection with the Assessment Committee within thirty days of the publication of the valuation list by the Minister, the Municipality or the District Council:

Provided that in the case of a tenement assessed in accordance with the provisions of subsection (2) of section 147 no objection shall be entertained by reason only of the fact that the annual value of such tenement is less than is stated in the valuation list.

(2) The notice of objection shall state fully the grounds on which the objection is made, and the objector shall cause a copy thereof to be served on the Municipality or the District Council.

(3) The person lodging an objection shall deposit with the Assessment Committee such fee as shall be prescribed by the Minister, the Municipality or the District Council as the case may be. Such fee may at the discretion of the committee be forfeited to the Minister or Municipality or District Council as to the whole or a part thereof if the objection is disallowed but shall otherwise be refunded when the objection has been heard.

Notice of hearing of objection

156. Upon a notice of objection being lodged and the prescribed fee being paid within the prescribed period, the Assessment Committee shall give notice to the objector and to the appraiser of the date and place at which the objection will be heard.

Power of Assessment Committee

157. (1) The Assessment Committee:

(a) may, by summons, require the attendance of any person and may examine him for the purpose of any objection before them and may require answers to any questions which they think fit to put touching the matter before them;

(b) may require and enforce the production of all books, papers and documents which they may consider necessary; and

(c) may administer oaths or affirmations.

(2) If any person summoned refuses to attend as a witness or refuses or neglects to make any answer, or to produce any books, paper or document in his possession he shall be guilty of an offence, and for each offence shall be liable to a fine of ten pounds.

Order of Assessment Committee

158. (1) The Assessment Committee, after hearing the objector and the appraiser and any evidence which may be produced and which the Committee may consider necessary, shall either make an order directing the alteration of the assessment or shall refuse to make any order.

(2) When an order is made under this section the Assessment Committee shall cause a certified copy thereof to be served on the Municipality or the District Council, who shall make the alteration directed in the valuation list.

Appeal

159. Any person who has lodged an objection with the Assessment Committee and who is dissatisfied with the decision of the Committee thereon may appeal to a Magistrate's Court subject to the following conditions:

(*a*) the appellant shall within fourteen days after the decision of the Committee give notice in writing to the Assessment Committee of his intention to appeal and of the grounds thereof; and

(*b*) the appellant shall within the like period enter into a recognisance before a Magistrate with two sufficient sureties conditioned to pay any costs which may be awarded against him on such appeal.

PART XIV. PROVISIONS AS TO PRECEPTS

County Councils may precept [see p. 91]

160. (1) A County Council shall have power to issue precepts for the purpose of meeting liabilities in respect of expenditure for which the whole of the area of the authority of the council is liable or for the purpose of meeting liabilities in respect of expenditure for which only part of the area of its authority is liable.

(2) A precept issued by a County Council for the purpose of meeting liabilities in respect of expenditure for which the whole area of its authority is liable shall be addressed to all the District Councils situate in the area of the authority of such County Council.

(3) A precept issued by a County Council for the purpose of meeting liabilities in respect of expenditure for which party only of the area of its authority is liable shall be addressed to such District Councils as are situate within the area chargeable with such expenditure.

(4) Any such precept shall be expressed as a lump sum and shall be satisfied by the District Council to which it is addressed.

(5) Where a County Council issues a precept to more than one District Council under the provisions of this section, the sum required from a District Council shall bear to the total sum required by the County Council the same proportion as the number of persons resident in the area of the District Council bears to the number of persons resident in the area of the County Council.

Information to be contained in precepts issued by County Council

161. A County Council shall on issuing a precept inform the District Council of the purpose for which such precept is issued and give such other information as is reasonably necessary to enable the District Council to satisfy such precept and to ascertain if the precept shall be satisfied by a general rate or by a special rate.

Local Councils may precept

162. (1) Subject to the provisions of section 163 a Local Council shall have power to issue precepts for the levying of rates to the District Council in the area of authority in which it is situate to meet all liabilities falling to be discharged by such Local Council.

(2) Any precept issued by a Local Council shall be satisfied by the District Council by the levying of a rate.

Precepts by Local Council

163. (1) Any precept issued by a Local Council shall be passed by the council by a resolution of three-fourths of the councillors present and voting at a meeting of the council, and approved by the Minister unless the Instrument by which the council is established otherwise provides.

(2) A precept may be issued by a Local Council for the purposes of meeting liabilities in respect of expenditure for which the whole of the area of the authority of the council is liable or for the purpose of meeting liabilities in respect of part of the area of its authority.

(3) A precept issued by a Local Council shall be so issued as to secure that any rate is levied:

(*a*) in the case of a rate to meet liabilities in respect of expenditure for which the whole area of the authority of the council is chargeable, on the whole of the area of the authority of such Local Council; and

(*b*) in the case of a rate to meet liabilities in respect of expenditure for which part of the area of the council is chargeable, on that part of the area of the authority of the council chargeable therewith.

(4) A precept issued by a Local Council shall indicate the purpose for which the precept is issued and may indicate the rate-payers or classes of rate-payers upon whom the rate is to be levied by the District Council.

(5) In an area in which the Assessment Ordinance (Cap. 16) applies a precept issued by a Local Council shall not require the District Council to make and levy in any one year:

(*a*) a general rate in excess of ten *per centum* of the annual value of any rateable tenement; and (*b*) a special rate in excess of ten *per centum* of the annual value of any rateable tenement.

(6) In an area in which the Assessment Ordinance (Cap. 16) does not apply a precept issued by a Local Council shall not require the District Council to make and levy in any one year a general rate in excess of:

(*a*) ten *per centum* of the annual value of any rateable tenement, rated under the provisions of section 124; or

(*b*) threepence in the pound of a rateable income rated under the provisions of subsection (1) of section 125;

(*c*) the lowest sum of money payable by a rate-payer under paragraph (*b*) rated under the provisions of subsection (2) of section 125; or

(*d*) a capitation rate of four shillings per person rated under the provisions of section 126.

(7) In addition to the provisions of subsection (6) in an area to which the Assessment Ordinance (Cap. 16) does not apply a Local Council may issue precepts to the District Council requiring it to make and levy a special rate in any one year not in excess of the amounts of rate specified in subsection (6).

(8) The Minister may from time to time increase, reduce, revoke or vary the amounts of rate specified in subsections (5) and (6) of this section.

Precepts may include general and special contributions

164. A precept issued by a County Council or by a Local Council may include as separate items a contribution for purposes for which the whole area of its authority is chargeable and a contribution for special purposes.

Date on which payment required to be stated in precept

165. A precept shall state the date or dates on or before which payments are required to be made.

Time of issuing precepts

166. (1) Unless otherwise stated in the Instrument, any precept issued by a County Council shall be served on the District Council concerned before the 1st day of November in the year preceding the financial year in which the demand is to be satisfied.

(2) Any precept issued by a Local Council shall be served on the District Council concerned before the 28th day of February in the

year in which the demand is to be satisfied or at such later date as is ordered by the Minister.

Minister may vary precept by County Council

167. (1) Upon an application being made to him by a District Council to whom a precept has been issued by a County Council under the provisions of section 160 the Minister may direct that such precept shall not be satisfied, or that it be reduced or that a precept for some other amount shall issue in its stead.

(2) An application by a District Council under this section shall not be made after two months of its receipt of the precept which is complained of.

(3) Before giving a direction under this section the Minister shall give the Councils concerned an opportunity of being heard.

(4) Upon a direction being made under this section the amount due under the precept shall be the amount stated in such direction notwithstanding any provision in this Law to the contrary.

District Council to furnish information to County and Local Councils

168. It shall be the duty of a District Council to furnish to every County and Local Council concerned such information as to its rateable value and the amount of tax collected under the provisions of the Direct Taxation Ordinance (Cap. 54) within the area of its authority together with such other information as may be required by such County or Local Council in order to enable them to issue a precept upon such District Council.

Amount due under a precept to County and Local Councils

169. (1) The amount due under a precept to a County Council by which it is issued shall be the total sum of money specified therein.

(2) The amount due under a precept to a Local Council by which it is issued shall be the amount produced by the levy of the rate specified therein.

(3) For the purposes of estimating and ascertaining the amount due under a precept the cost of collection and losses in collection shall not be considered.

Interest on unsatisfied precepts

170. Where the amount due under a precept or any part of that amount is not paid on or before the date specified in the precept for payment, the council by which the precept was issued may if it thinks fit require the District Council to pay interest at five *per* *centum per annum* on that amount or part of that amount, and any interest so payable shall be paid by the District Council to the council by which the precept was issued in like manner as if it were due under the precept.

Power for securing payment of precepts

171. (1) Where in pursuance of a precept issued by a County or Local Council (in this section referred to as 'the precepting council') any amount is payable directly or indirectly by a District Council to the precepting council, and, on application for a certificate by the precepting council made after twenty-one days' notice given to the District Council, the Minister is satisfied that the District Council has refused or through wilful neglect or wilful default failed to pay the amount due under the precept, the Minister may issue a certificate to that effect, and thereupon the precepting council, instead of or in addition to bringing an action or actions, shall have the power of applying for a receiver and a receiver may, upon such application being made, be appointed by the Minister.

(2) Any receiver appointed under the provisions of this section shall from time to time raise by or out of the revenues and funds of the District Council sufficient money to pay the amount of the payment which is so in default and all sums due while he is a receiver in respect of such amounts, together with all costs, charges and expenses incurred in or about the appointment of such receiver and the execution of his duties under this section including a proper remuneration for his services, and shall render to the defaulting District Council the balance if any remaining in his hands after making the said payments.

(3) The receiver may raise the money he is authorised to raise under this section by means of a rate, and for this purpose he shall have the same power as the defaulting District Council of making and levying a general or special rate and may make and levy a special rate for the purpose of raising such sum, and the receiver shall have access to and the use of the documents of the defaulting District Council as he may require.

(4) The receiver may raise the money he is authorised to raise under this section by the receipt of the rents and profits of the property of the defaulting District Council and, with the approval of the Minister, by the sale of the property in such manner and subject to such conditions of sale and otherwise as the Minister may direct.

(5) The Minister may remove a receiver appointed under this section and appoint another in his stead from time to time; and may

make such orders and give such directions as to the powers and duties of the receiver and otherwise as to the disposal of the money received by him as may be thought fit for carrying this section into effect.

Appointment of auditors [see p.108]

172. The Minister may appoint auditors to audit the accounts of councils or of a council.

Audit of Accounts [see p.108]

173. (1) Every council shall cause to be kept true accounts in accordance with such instructions as may from time to time be issued by the Minister.

(2) Within such period after the end of each financial year as may be prescribed by the Minister every council shall cause its accounts for the preceding financial year to be compiled and a statement or abstract of such accounts to be prepared.

(3) Such accounts, together with all books, vouchers and papers relating thereto, together with such annual statement or abstract and a copy thereof, shall be laid before an auditor appointed by the Minister.

(4) The auditor shall make and sign a report on such accounts and statements or abstract, and a duplicate copy of such report, together with such statement or abstract, shall be sent to the Minister.

(5) Every council shall permit the auditor to check any cash in its possession and to have access at all times to all its accounts and all books, vouchers and papers relating thereto and will provide him with any explanation or information that he may require with regard to the accounts.

(6) A copy of the annual statement or abstract and of the auditor's report shall be furnished by the council to any inhabitant of the area of the authority of the council, upon the payment of such fee as may be specified by the council:

Provided that this section shall not apply to any Local Council unless so directed by the Minister.

Liability for payment of remuneration of auditors

174. The remuneration and expenses of any auditor appointed under this Law, including the staff of such auditor, to such amount as may be sanctioned by the Minister, shall be paid by the council concerned.

Powers and duties of auditor [see pp.109-10]

175. (1) An auditor appointed by the Minister at every audit held by him may:

(*a*) disallow any item of account which is contrary to law;

(*b*) surcharge the amount of any expenditure contrary to law upon the individual responsible for incurring or authorising the expenditure;

(*c*) surcharge any sum which has not been duly brought into account upon the individual by whom that sum ought to have been brought into account;

(*d*) surcharge the amount of any loss or deficiency upon any individual by whose negligence or misconduct the loss or deficiency has been incurred:

Provided that no item of expenditure incurred by a council shall be disallowed or surcharged by the auditor, if it has been approved by the Minister.

(2) For the purpose of this Part a member of a council shall be deemed to be responsible for incurring or authorising expenditure if being present at the resolution of the council or Committee of the Council incurring or authorising such expenditure he voted in favour thereof or does not cause his vote against the resolution to be recorded in the minutes.

(3) It shall be the duty of any such auditor:

(*a*) to certify the amount due from any person upon whom he has made a surcharge; and

(*b*) certify at the conclusion of the audit his allowance of the accounts, subject to any disallowances or surcharges which he may have made.

Special relief for officers and servants [see pp.111-12]

176. Notwithstanding any of the provisions of section 175, no liability to surcharge shall be incurred by an officer or servant of the council who can prove to the satisfaction of the auditor that he acted in pursuance of, and in accordance with, the terms of a resolution of the council or of a committee duly appointed by the council, or on the written instructions of any senior officer of the council.

Auditor may take evidence [see p.110]

177. (1) For the purpose of any examination under the provisions of this Part, the auditor may take evidence and examine witnesses upon oath or affirmation (which oath or affirmation the auditor is hereby empowered to administer) and may by summons under his hand require all such persons as he may think fit to appear personally before him at a time and place to be stated in such summons and to produce all such books and papers, including the minutes of the proceedings of the council or of any committee thereof, as he may consider necessary for such examination.

(2) Any person who, when so required, without reasonable excuse:

(*a*) neglects or refuses to comply with the terms of such summons;

(*b*) having appeared, refuses to be examined on oath or affirmation or to take such oath or affirmation; or

(*c*) having taken such oath or affirmation, refuses to answer such questions as are put to him;

shall be guilty of an offence and shall be liable, on conviction therefor, for every such neglect or refusal, to a fine not exceeding twenty-five pounds or to imprisonment for a term not exceeding six months.

Payment of sums certified to be due

178. Every sum certified by the auditor to be due from any person shall be paid by that person to the treasury of the council concerned within sixty days after it has been so certified or, if an appeal with respect to that sum has been made, within thirty days after the appeal is finally disposed of or abandoned or fails by reason of the non-prosecution thereof.

Recovery of sums certified to be due

179. (1) Any sum which is certified by the auditor to be due and has become payable shall, on complaint made or action taken by or under the direction of the Minister, be recoverable as a civil debt.

(2) In any proceedings for the recovery of such a sum, a certificate signed by the auditor shall be conclusive evidence of the facts certified, and a certificate signed by the chairman of the council concerned or other officer whose duty it is to keep the accounts that the sum certified to be due has not been paid to him shall be conclusive evidence of non-payment, unless it is proved that the sum certified to be due has been paid since the date of the certificate.

(3) Unless the contrary is proved, a certificate purporting to be signed by the auditor, or by the chairman of the council or other officer whose duty it is to keep the accounts, shall be deemed to have been signed by such auditor, chairman or other officer, as the case may be.

Appeals against decisions of auditors [see p.110]

180. (1) Any person who is aggrieved by a decision of the auditor on any matter with respect to which he made an objection at the audit, and any person aggrieved by a surcharge made by the auditor may, within thirty days from the notification to him of such surcharge or other decision, where the surcharge or other decision relates to an amount not exceeding two hundred pounds, appeal to the Minister and may in any other case appeal either to the Minister or to the Supreme Court.

(2) The notification referred to in subsection (1) shall be served by delivering the same to, or by sending it by registered post addressed to the person to whom it relates, or to the chairman of the council at the principal office of the council.

(3) The Court or Minister on such appeal shall have power to confirm, vary or quash the decision of the auditor and to remit the case to the auditor with such directions as the Court or Minister thinks fit for giving effect to the decision on appeal, and if the decision of the auditor is quashed, or is varied so as to reduce the amount of the surcharge to two hundred pounds or less, the appellant shall not be subject to the disqualification by reason of the surcharge imposed by section 20 of this Law.

(4) Where an appeal is made to the Minister under this section, he may at any stage of the proceedings and shall, if so directed by the Court, state in the form of a special case for the opinion of the Court any question of law arising in the course of the appeal, but save as aforesaid the decision of the Minister shall be final.

Rules of Court

181. Without prejudice to any power to make rules of court under the Supreme Court Ordinance and subject to the provisions of this Part, the Chief Justice may make rules of court for regulating the pleading, practice and procedure of the Supreme Court in any matter brought before such court under the provisions of this Part.

PART XVI. ACQUISITION OF AND DEALING IN LAND

Power to acquire [see p.127]

182. A council for the purpose of any of its functions under this or any other written law may by agreement acquire, whether by way of purchase, lease or exchange, any land, whether situate within or without the area of the authority of the council.

Power to let land

183. Subject to the provisions of any written law, a council may let any land which it may possess:

(a) with the consent of the Minister for any term;

(b) without the consent of the Minister for a term not exceeding seven years.

Transfer of Crown land to Council

184. (1) Notwithstanding the provisions of the Crown Lands Ordinance (Cap. 45), the Governor with the approval of the Secretary of State may, on the payment of such consideration (if any) as may be agreed with a council, transfer to a council any Crown land occupied by a council for the purpose of its functions under this or any other law, or which may be required for any such purpose.

(2) On the transfer of any such land the Commissioner of Lands shall issue a certificate under his hand and seal to the effect that such land has been made over to the council, and such certificate shall confer on the council the estate or interest referred to therein against all persons, free from all adverse or competing rights, titles, interests, trusts, claims and demands whatsoever.

Power to sell land

185. A council may with the consent of the Minister sell or exchange or mortgage any land which it may possess.

Application of money

186. Money received by a council in respect of a transaction under section 185 shall be applied in such manner or for such purposes as the Minister may approve.

Compulsory acquisition of land [see p.127]

187. (1) The Minister may authorise a council to acquire compulsorily any land whether situated within or without the area of its authority for an estate in fee simple or for a term of years for the purpose of any of its functions under this Law or any other written law including such functions as are exercised through any committee.

(2) The council shall pay such consideration including rent or compensation for such land as may be agreed upon or determined under the provisions of this Law.

318

Preliminary investigation [see p.128]

188. (1) Whenever it appears to a council that any land in any locality is likely to be needed for any purpose referred to in subsection (1) of section 187, it shall be lawful for any person either generally or specially authorised by the council in this behalf, and for his servants and workmen, to do all or any of the following things:

(*a*) to enter upon and survey and take levels of any land in such locality;

(*b*) to dig or bore under the sub-soil;

(*c*) to do all other acts necessary to ascertain whether the land is adapted for such purpose; and

(*d*) to clear, set out and mark the boundaries of the land proposed to be taken, and the intended line of work (if any) proposed to be made thereon:

Provided that no person shall enter into any building or upon any enclosed court or garden attached to a dwelling house (except with the consent of the occupier thereof) without previously giving the occupier at least seven days notice of his intention to do so.

(2) As soon as conveniently may be after any entry made under subsection (1) the person so authorised as aforesaid shall pay for all damage done, and in the case of a dispute as to the amount to be paid the person aggrieved may refer such dispute to the Magistrate's Court or to the Supreme Court.

Notice of intention to acquire land compulsorily [see p.128]

189. (1) A council which intends to acquire land compulsorily under the provisions of section 187 shall publish a notice of its intention:

(*a*) in a prominent position on the land it is intended to acquire; and

(*b*) outside the offices of the council; and

(*c*) in such manner as is customary within the area.

(2) A copy of the notice shall be served on the persons interested or claiming to be interested in such land or to such of them as shall, after reasonable enquiry, be known to the council.

(3) A copy of the notice shall be supplied free of charge to any person applying for the same.

Contents of notice. (*Third Schedule*)

190. The notice may be in the form in the Third Schedule or to the like effect and shall contain:

319

(*a*) a description of the land it is intended to acquire;

(*b*) a statement that the council intends to request the Minister to make an order empowering it to acquire the land compulsorily;

(*c*) a statement whether the land is to be acquired for an estate in fee simple or for a term of years;

(*d*) a statement of the terms and conditions on which the council intend to hold the land when it is intended to acquire for a term of years; and

(*e*) a statement as to the purposes for which the land is required.

Service of notice under section 189 *not an admission of interest*

191. The fact that notice has been served upon any person under section 189 shall not be taken as an admission by the council that the person on whom such notice is served or any other person has any estate or interest in the land or any part of the land specified in the notice, or debar the council from alleging in any proceedings under this Law or otherwise that such land is the property of the council.

Person having claim to inform council

192. Any person claiming to have an interest in the land described in the notice shall within sixty days of the publication of such notice deliver to the council a written statement showing the exact nature of the claim in respect of which compensation is claimed and no such claim shall be entertained by the council after such period.

Copy of notice and claims to be sent to the Minister

193. After the expiration of sixty days and within six months from the date of the publication of such notice, the council shall send a copy of the notice to the Minister and of any claim or claims in relation thereto with a request that an order be made empowering them to acquire such land compulsorily.

Order of Minister

194. The Minister upon receipt of the notice aforesaid may make an order authorising the council to acquire compulsorily the land therein described and such land shall vest in the council for the estate or interest specified in such notice against all persons free from all adverse or competing rights, titles, interests, trusts, claims and demands whatsoever.

Notice, order, etc., to be filed

195. (1) A copy of the notice, a copy of the order of the Minister together with a plan of the land shall be filed in the appropriate office of the Land Registry by the council concerned.

(2) Any plan so filed shall be of sufficient accuracy to enable the boundaries of the land to be accurately identified.

Abandonment of acquisition

196. A council at any time before the vesting in the council under section 194 of land intended to be compulsorily acquired may declare that the acquisition of such land is abandoned:

Provided that the owner of the land and all persons entitled to any estate or interest in the land shall be entitled to receive from the council all such costs as may have been reasonably incurred by them by reason or in consequence of the proceedings for acquisition and compensation for the damage which they may have sustained by reason or in consequence of the notice of intended acquisition but shall not be entitled to compensation for loss of bargain or for damages for breach of contract.

Where purpose for which lands are required has failed

197. Where any lands are or have been acquired under the provisions of this Law by a council such lands shall to the extent of the interest acquired therein be and be deemed to have been the property of the council from the date of such acquisition notwithstanding that the purpose for which such lands were acquired has failed or that all or any such lands are no longer required for the purpose for which they were acquired or being used.

Rent or compensation to be paid

198. If there is no dispute as to the amount of rent or compensation payable the council shall pay to the person or persons entitled thereto the rent or compensation agreed upon.

Disputes as to compensation (Cap. 122)

199. Notwithstanding any provision of the Magistrates' Courts Ordinance, if a person who has lodged a claim has not given satisfactory evidence of such claim, or if there is a dispute as to the amount of rent or compensation payable, or if separate or conflicting claims are made in respect of the same lands, the amount of compensation due and every such case of disputed interest or title shall be settled in the Magistrate's Court to the extent of its jurisdiction or the Supreme Court as the case may be upon a summons taken out by the council or any persons holding or claiming any estate or interest in any lands described in the notice.

Summons to state the amount council willing to pay

200. Every summons taken out by a council for the purpose of determining the amount of rent or compensation to be paid shall state the amount of rent or compensation the council is willing to pay for the lands to which the summons relates.

Principles of assessment of compensation

201. In estimating the compensation to be given for any lands or any estate or interest therein or for any mesne profits thereof the court shall act on the following principles:

(*a*) no allowance shall be made on account of the acquisition being compulsory;

(*b*) the value of the land, estate, interest or profits shall subject to the provisions of this section be taken to be the amount which such land, estate, interest or profits if sold in the open market by a willing seller might be expected to realise;

(*c*) where part only of the land, estate, interest or profit belonging to any person is acquired under the provisions of this Part the court may take into account any enhancement of the value of the residue by reason of the proximity of any improvements or works made or constructed or to be made or constructed by the council acquiring such part;

(*d*) the court may have regard not only to the value of the land, estate, interest or profits to be acquired but also to any damage which may be sustained by the owner by reason of the severance of such lands from other lands belonging to such owner or other injurious circumstances affecting such other land by such acquisition:

Provided that the court in estimating such compensation shall assess the same according to what it finds to have been the value of land, estate, interest or profits at the time when notice of intention to acquire was served and without regard to any improvement :or works made or constructed or to be made or constructed thereafter on such land.

Council exonerated upon payment

202. The payment to any person to whom any consideration, rent or compensation shall be paid or the payment into court of any compensation upon a decision of the court shall effectually discharge the council from seeing to the application or being answerable for the misapplication thereof.

Costs

203. (1) Where the acquiring council has made an unconditional offer of any sum as compensation or rent to any claimant and the sum awarded by the court to that claimant does not exceed the sum offered, the court shall, unless for special reasons it thinks proper not to do so, order the claimant to bear his own costs.

(2) Where the claimant has made an unconditional offer in writing to accept any sum as compensation or rent and the sum awarded by the court is equal to or exceeds that sum the court shall, unless for special reasons it thinks proper not to do so, order the acquiring council to bear their own costs and to pay the costs of the claimant so far as such costs were incurred after the offer was made.

(3) Where the court orders the claimant to pay the costs or any part of the costs of the acquiring council, the acquiring council may deduct the amount so payable by the claimant from the amount of the compensation or rent payable.

(4) Without prejudice to any other method of recovery, the amount of costs ordered to be paid by a claimant shall be recoverable from him by the acquiring council as a civil debt.

PART XVII. LEGAL PROCEEDINGS: NOTICES, ETC.

Power to sue and be sued

204. Where a council deems it expedient for the promotion or the protection of the interests of the inhabitants of its area it may prosecute or defend any legal proceedings.

Notice of suit to be given to council by intending plaintiff

205. (1) No suit shall be commenced against a council until one month at least after written notice of intention to commence the same has been served upon the council by the intending plaintiff or his agent.

(2) Such notice shall state the cause of action, the name and place of abode of the intending plaintiff and the relief which he claims.

Limitation of suits against council

206. When any suit is commenced against any council for any act done in pursuance or execution or intended execution of a Law or Ordinance or of any public duty or authority, or in respect of any alleged neglect or default in the execution of any such Law or Ordinance, duty or authority, such suit shall not lie or be instituted unless it is commenced within six months next after the act, neglect or default complained of, or in the case of a continuance of damage or injury, within six months next after the ceasing thereof.

Mode of service on council

207. The notice referred to in section 205, and any summons, notice or other document required or authorised to be served on a council in connexion with any suit by or against such council, shall be served by delivering the same to, or by sending it by registered post addressed to, the chairman of the council at the principal office of the council:

Provided that the court may with regard to any particular suit or document order service on the council to be effected otherwise, and in that case service shall be effected in accordance with the terms of such order.

Appearance of council in legal proceedings

208. Subject to the provisions of section 24 of the Native Courts Ordinance (Cap. 142):

(1) in the case of a prosecution by or on behalf of a council, a council may be represented by an officer or employee of the council duly authorised in that behalf by the council;

(2) in any civil cause or matter in which a council is a party, a council may be represented by an officer or employee duly authorised in that behalf.

Preservation of jurisdiction of native courts in certain matters

209. No Native Court shall be precluded from trying an offence under this Law by reason of the fact that such offence, if committed, was a breach of order, resolution, bye-law, direction or rule issued or made by any member of the court as a member of a council or by reason of the fact that the proceedings have been instituted by or on behalf of any member of the court as a member of or agent for a council.

Description of property of council

210. Wherever in any criminal process or proceedings it is necessary to refer to the ownership or description of property belonging to or under the management of a council such property may be described as the property of the council.

Onus of proof in certain cases

211. Where in any proceedings under this Law any person is summoned or otherwise dealt with as the occupier of any tenement or building and such person shall allege that he is not the occupier the proof of such allegation shall be upon such person.

Name of council need not be proved

212. In any proceedings instituted by or against a council it shall not be necessary to prove the corporate name of the council or the constitution and limits of its area.

Power of councillors and servants to enter premises

213. Subject to the provisions of this Law, any member of a council, officer or servant of a council duly authorised in writing for the purpose by the council may, at all reasonable times, enter into or upon any land, buildings or premises within the area in which such council is established for the purpose of carrying out any inspection, inquiry or the execution of works under the provisions of this Law.

Publication of notice

214. Save as in this Law is otherwise expressly provided, the publication of any notice or other document required by this Law to be published shall be deemed to be duly made if it is fixed for a reasonable time in some conspicuous place on or near the outer door of the office of the council during office hours, and also in some other conspicuous place or situation within the area of the authority of the council.

Compulsory publication of notices to other councils

215. Save as in this Law is otherwise expressly provided:

(1) a copy of every notice required to be published by this Law by a County Council shall be sent to every District Council within the area of the authority of such County Council;

(2) a copy of every notice required to be published by this Law by a District Council shall be sent to every Local Council within the area of the authority of such District Council.

Service of notice by the council

216. (1) Subject to the provisions of this section, any notice, order or other document required or authorised by this Law, or by any other written law, to be served by or on behalf of the council, or by an officer of the council, on any person shall be deemed to be duly served:

(*a*) where the person to be served is a company, if the document is addressed to the secretary of the company at its registered office or at its principal office or place of business, and is either:

(i) sent by post or in a prepaid letter; or

(ii) delivered at the registered office, or at the principal office or place of business, of the company;

(*b*) where the person to be served is a partnership, if the document is addressed to the partnership at its principal place of business, identifying it by the name of the style under which its business is carried on, and is either:

(i) sent by post in a prepaid letter, or

(ii) delivered at that office;

(*c*) where the person to be served is a public body, a local or native authority, or a corporation, society or other body, if the document is addressed to the clerk, president, secretary, treasurer or other principal officer of that body, authority, corporation or society at its principal office and is either:

(i) sent by post in a prepaid letter, or

(ii) delivered at that office;

(*d*) in any other case, if the document is addressed to the person to be served, and is either sent to him by post in a prepaid letter or delivered at his residence or place of business.

(2) Any document which is required or authorised to be served on the owner or occupier of any premises may be addressed 'the owner' or 'the occupier', as the case may be, of those premises (naming them) without further name or description, and shall be deemed to be properly served:

(*a*) if the document so addressed is sent or delivered in accordance with paragraph (*d*) of subsection (1); or

(*b*) if the document so addressed, or a copy thereof so addressed, is delivered to some person on the premises or, where there is no person on the premises to whom it can be delivered, is affixed to some conspicuous part of the premises.

(3) Where a document is served on a partnership in accordance with this section, the document shall be deemed to be served on each partner.

(4) For the purpose of proving the service by post of any document, it shall (except where the document is sent by registered post)

326

be sufficient to prove that it was properly addressed and was put into the post.

(5) For the purpose of enabling any document to be served on the owner of any premises, the council may by notice in writing require the occupier of the premises to state the name and address of the owner thereof, and if the occupier refuses or wilfully neglects to do so, or wilfully mis-states the name and address of the own er, he shall unless in the case of a refusal he shows cause to the satisfaction of the court for his refusal, be liable on summary conviction in respect of each offence to a fine not exceeding five pounds.

(6) In this section the word 'document' means any notice, order or other document which is required or authorised to be served as specified in subsection (1) of this section.

(7) For the purposes of this section, a notice, order or other document shall be deemed to be a notice, order or other document which is required or authorised to be served on a person, if it is required or authorised to be notified, given or transmitted, or (in the case of a demand) if it is required or authorised to be made, to that person, and in this section the expression 'served' and 'service' shall be construed accordingly.

Inspection of documents

217. A document directed by this Law to be open to inspection shall be so open during ordinary office hours, and without payment unless otherwise provided.

Instrument executed or issued by council

218. (1) Any contract or instrument which, if entered into or executed by a person not being a body corporate, would not require to be under seal, may be entered into or executed on behalf of a council by any person generally or specially authorised by such council for that purpose.

(2) Any document purporting to be a document duly executed or issued under the seal of a council or on behalf of a council shall, unless the contrary is proved, be deemed to be a document so executed or issued, as the case may be.

PART XVIII. MISCELLANEOUS

Crown rights

219. Save as is otherwise expressly provided nothing in this Law shall affect prejudicially any estate, right, power, privilege or exemption of the Crown.

Transfer to a council of powers and duties of Government officers

220. A council may exercise any powers and may perform any duties for the time being vested in or imposed upon any Government Officer which the Governor may by order declare to be transferred to such council.

Property of local and native authorities to vest in Minister for reallocation [see pp.17, 91-2]

221. Upon the establishment of a council all sums of money, street, open places, lands, buildings, waterworks, bridges, piers, ferries, vehicles, goods and all other property whatsoever vested in, belonging to, held by, or purporting to belong to or to be held by any local authority or native authority formerly constituted within the area of the authority of such council shall be transferred to and vest in a like interest in the Minister, and all such property so vested shall thereafter be allocated by way of free grant to any council established under the provisions of this Law in such proportions and upon such terms and conditions as the Minister may determine.

Subsisting contracts, etc., of local and native authorities and pending proceedings, etc [see p.18].

222. (1) Upon the establishment of a council upon a direction under the hand of the Minister given in that behalf whereof notice in writing shall be given to all interested parties, the rights, interests, obligations and liabilities of any local authority or native authority formerly constituted within the area of the authority of such council under any contract or instrument whatsoever (including contracts of service) subsisting immediately before the date of such directions shall be deemed to be and by virtue of this provision shall be assigned to the council specified in such direction as from such date as may be specified; and any such contract or instrument in respect to which such direction as aforesaid is given shall be as of full force and effect against or in favour of the council so specified and shall be enforceable as fully and effectually as if, instead of the local authority or native authority concerned, the council so specified had been named therein or had been a party thereto.

(2) Any proceeding or cause of action, pending or existing, immediately before the date specified in any direction given pursuant to the provisions of subsection (1) of this section, by or against any such local authority or native authority as is referred to in such subsection in respect of any right, interest, obligation or liability under any such contract or instrument as is specified in such direction may

be continued and enforced by or against the council specified in such direction as it might have been against the local authority or native authority concerned if this Law had not been passed.

(3) For the purposes of this section the term 'obligations and liabilities' shall include the obligation and liability of any such local or native authority as is referred to in subsection (1) to pay any retiring allowance to any person who was formerly an officer of or in the employment of such local or native authority in pursuance of its customary practice or under the provisions of any superannuation scheme for native administration servants.

Notices, regulations, bye-laws, etc., made by the Governor of Nigeria, the Governor and certain local government bodies to remain in force (Fourth Schedule) (No. 16 of 1950) [see p.126]

223. (1) Any rule or order made by the Governor of Nigeria or the Governor and any notice, order, rule, regulation or bye-law made by any local or native authority under the provisions of any law or Ordinance including any Ordinance listed in the Fourth Schedule and any bye-law made by any local government council under the provisions of the Eastern Region Local Government Ordinance, 1950, shall remain effective and in force until such time as it is revoked or replaced by a bye-law or notice made or issued under the provisions of this Law by any council established in the area of such local authority, native authority or local government council and which has the power to make or issue such bye-law or notice.

(2) Any such notice, order, rule, regulation or bye-law made by the Governor of Nigeria or the Governor or such local authority, native authority or local government council may be enforced by such council as though made by such council.

(3) Any licence, registration or permit issued, made or granted under the provisions of any written law shall continue in force for the period specified in such licence, registration or permit unless the same is sooner suspended or cancelled under or in pursuance of any bye-law lawfully made under the provisions of this Law.

Native Court sitting fees

224. It shall be the duty of any council required by the Instrument by which it is established to maintain a Native Court to pay such sitting fees to any member of such Native Court as are laid down from time to time by the Minister.

225. Notwithstanding any provisions of the Native Courts Ordinance (Cap. 142), or of any warrant issued thereunder, all fees, fines and penalties payable in respect of or as a result of proceedings in any Native Court and the proceeds of sale of any forfeiture ordered by such Native Court shall be paid to and form part of the revenue of any council responsible for the maintenance of such Court by virtue of the provisions of the Instrument establishing such council.

Certain Ordinances and Laws not to have effect (Fourth Schedule) [see p. 8]

226. (1) Upon the establishment of a council the Ordinances and Laws set out in the first column of the Fourth Schedule shall cease to have effect in the area of such council to the extent set out in the second column thereof until the Instrument by which such council is established is revoked under the provisions of section 12.

(2) Such revocation shall not affect:

(*a*) anything lawfully done or suffered under this Law;

(*b*) any right, privilege, obligation or liability which has lawfully accrued or been incurred under this Law;

(*c*) any penalty, forfeiture or punishment lawfully incurred in respect of any offence committed against this Law;

(*d*) any investigation, legal proceeding or remedy in respect of any such right, privilege, obligation, liability, penalty, forfeiture or punishment as aforesaid; and any such investigation, legal proceeding or remedy may be instituted, continued or enforced and any such penalty, forfeiture or punishment may be imposed as if such Instrument had not been so revoked.

Property, subsisting contracts and pending proceedings of council
upon revocation of instrument

227. Upon the revocation of an Instrument establishing a council under the provisions of section 12:

(*a*) all sums of money, streets, open places, lands, buildings, waterworks, bridges, piers, ferries, vehicles, vessels, goods and all other property whatsoever vested in, belonging to, held by or purporting to belong to or to be held by the council concerned shall be transferred to and vest in a like interest in the Minister;

(*b*) the rights, interests, obligations and liabilities of such council under any contract or instrument whatsoever subsisting immediately before the date of the said revocation shall be deemed to be and by virtue of this section shall be assigned to the Minister and any such contract or instrument shall be as of full force and effect against or in favour of the Minister and shall be enforceable as fully and effectually as if, instead of a council concerned, the Minister had been named therein and had been a party thereto;

(c) any proceeding or cause of action pending or existing immediately before the date of such revocation by or against such council in respect of any right, interest, obligation of liability under any such contract or instrument as is referred to in paragraph (b) of this section may be continued and enforced by or against the Minister as it might have been against the council concerned as if such revocation had not been effected.

Regulations

228. The Minister may make regulations with respect to the following matters:

(a) the collection of rates and the form of any precept, demand note, valuation list, or any other document;

(b) the submission of reports and returns;

(c) the display and publication of notices;

(d) generally for the proper and orderly conduct of the business of a council;

(e) the form of conditions in any contract of service;

(f) the borrowing of money by councils;

(g) the provision of machinery for negotiating conditions of service, salaries and wages between councils, their staffs, officers and employees;

(h) the procedure for the allocation of market stalls; and

(i) generally for the better carrying out of the provisions of this Law.

Amendments (Fifth Schedule)

229. The Parts or sections set out in the second column of the Ordinances and Law referred to in the first column of the Fifth Schedule are hereby amended to the extent and in the manner set out in the third column of the said Schedule opposite to the said provisions in the second column.

Repeal of Ordinance No. 16 of 1950 and saving

230. (1) Subject to the provisions of this Part, and of this section, the Eastern Region Local Government Ordinance, 1950, is hereby repealed.

(2) Any Instrument establishing a local government council under the provisions of the Eastern Region Local Government Ordinance, 1950, shall remain of full effect and shall be read and

construed as one with this Law and shall be of the same force and effect as if it had been made under the provisions of this Law, and any council established by such an Instrument shall be deemed to be a council established by Instrument under the provisions of this Law.

(3) Any such Instrument may be amended in accordance with the provisions of this Law.

(4) A council established by Instrument made under the provisions of the Eastern Region Local Government Ordinance, 1950, shall have power to perform such functions (including the making of bye-laws) and to do such other acts as are conferred upon it by virtue of such Instrument as though such functions and powers had been conferred upon it by an Instrument made under the provisions of this Law.

(5) The Minister may by an Instrument establishing a council under the provisions of this Law revoke any Instrument establishing a local government council under the provisions of the Eastern Region Local Government Ordinance, 1950, in the area of such council.

(6) Upon the revocation of an Instrument under the provisions of subsection (5):

(*a*) all sums of money, streets, open places, lands, buildings, waterworks, bridges, piers, ferries, vehicles, goods, and all other property whatsoever vested in, belonging to, held by, or purporting to belong to or to be held by the local government council the Instrument establishing which is revoked shall be transferred to and vest in a like interest in the Minister, and all such property so vested shall thereafter be allocated by way of free grant to any council established under the provisions of this Law in such proportions and upon such terms and conditions as the Minister may determine;

(*b*) upon a direction under the hand of the Minister given in that behalf whereof notice in writing shall be given to all interested parties, the rights, interests, obligations, and liabilities of any local government council the Instrument establishing which is revoked under any contract or instrument whatsoever (including contracts of service) subsisting immediately before the date of such direction shall be deemed to be and by virtue of this provision shall be assigned to the council named in such direction as from such date as may be so specified; and any such contract or instrument in respect to which such direction as aforesaid is given shall be as of full force and effect against or in favour of the council so specified and shall be as enforceable as fully and effectively as if the council so specified had been named therein or had been a party thereto; and

(c) any proceedings or cause of action pending or existing immediately before the date specified in any direction given pursuant to the provisions of paragraph (b) of this subsection by or against any such council as is referred to in such paragraph in respect of any right, interest, obligation, or liability under any such contract or instrument as is specified in such direction may be continued and enforced by or against the council specified in such direction as it might have been against the council concerned if this Law had not been passed.

(7) In this section the expression 'obligations and liabilities' includes the obligation and liability of any council to pay any retiring allowance to any person who was formerly an officer of or in the employment of such council granted in pursuance of any written law.

FIRST SCHEDULE

MEETINGS AND PROCEEDINGS OF COUNCILS
(Section 37)

Number of meetings [see p. 66]

1. (1) A council shall in every year hold an annual meeting and at least three other meetings, which shall be as near as may be at regular intervals, for the transaction of general business.

(2) The annual meeting shall be held in April in every year upon such date as the council may fix.

(3) The other meetings shall be held on such other days before the annual meeting next following as the council at the annual meeting decides or determines by standing orders.

(4) All meetings of a council shall be held within the area of the authority of such council.

Convening meetings [see p. 67]

2. (1) The chairman of a council may call a meeting of the council at any time.

(2) If the chairman of a council refuses to call a meeting of the council after a written requisition for that purpose signed by one-third of the councillors has been presented to him, or if, without so refusing, such chairman does not call a meeting within ten days after such requisition has been presented to him, the persons presenting the requisition, on that refusal or on the expiration of ten days as the case may be, may forthwith call a meeting of the council.

333

Notice of meetings [see p. 67]

3. (1) Except as is provided in subsection (2), at least ten clear days before a meeting of a council a notice shall be published at the offices or the regular place of meeting of the council stating the time and place of the meeting and the business proposed to be transacted thereat.

(2) The Mayor of a Municipality or the Chairman of an Urban District Council may call an emergency meeting upon giving forty-eight hours notice thereof published in the manner specified in the preceding subsection.

(3) Every notice shall be signed by the chairman except where the meeting is called by councillors in accordance with subsection (2) of section 2 of this Schedule, when such notice shall be signed by a councillor on behalf of such councillors.

Summons to councillors to attend [see p. 68]

4. A summons to attend the meeting of any council other than a Local Council, specifying the business proposed to be transacted thereat, shall be left at or sent by post to the usual place of residence of every councillor:

Provided that want of service of the summons on any councillor shall not affect the validity of a meeting.

Only business specified to be transacted at meeting [see p. 68]

5. Except in the case of business required to be transacted under this Law at the annual meeting of a council, no business shall be transacted at a meeting of the council other than that specified in the summons relating thereto.

Chairman of meeting [see p. 73]

6. (1) At a meeting of a council the chairman of the council, if present, shall preside.

(2) If the chairman of the council is absent from a meeting of the council the vice-chairman of the council, if present, shall preside.

(3) If both the chairman and vice-chairman are absent from a meeting of the council, such councillor as the members of the council present shall choose shall preside.

Quorum [see p. 70]

7. Save and except as is otherwise provided in the Instrument:
(i) no business shall be transacted at a meeting of a council other

334

than a Local Council unless at least one-third of the whole number of the members of the council are present thereat;

(ii) no business shall be transacted at a meeting of a Local Council unless at least one-half of the whole number of the members of the council are present thereat.

Meetings to be public [see p. 71]

8. (1) Every meeting of a council shall be open to the public.

(2) This section shall not apply to any Standing Committee, any other committee appointed by a council or a committee of the whole council.

Decision on question [see pp. 71-2]

9. (1) Subject to the provisions of this Law or of the Instrument by which it is established all acts of a council other than a Local Council and all questions coming or arising before such council shall be done and decided by a majority of the councillors present and voting thereon at a meeting of the council.

(2) Subject to the provisions of the Instrument by which it is established all acts of a Local Council and all questions coming or arising before it shall be done and decided by a majority of three-fourths of the councillors present and voting thereon at a meeting of the Local Council.

(3) In the case of an equality of votes the person presiding at the meeting shall have a second or casting vote.

Breaches of order at meeting of council [see p. 74]

10. (1) At any meeting of a council or of a committee thereof if a councillor or other member of a committee shows disregard for the authority of the chairman or abuses the standing rules or orders of such council or committee by persistently and wilfully obstructing the business of the council or otherwise, the person presiding at the meeting shall direct the attention of the meeting to the incident mentioning by name the person concerned, and may, by writing under his hand, suspend such person from the exercise of his functions as a councillor or member of a committee for a period of not more than thirty days.

(2) In the case of grave disorder arising in any meeting of a council or of a committee thereof the person presiding may, if he thinks it necessary to do so, adjourn the meeting or committee without question put, or suspend any meeting for a time to be specified by him.

Names of members to be recorded

11. The names of the councillors or members of a committee thereof present at a meeting of a council or of a committee thereof shall be recorded.

Minutes [see p. 69]

12. (1) Minutes of the proceedings of a meeting of a council or of a committee thereof shall be regularly entered in books kept for that purpose, and shall be read, confirmed and signed by the person presiding at the same or next ensuing meeting of the council or committee as the case may be, and any minute purporting to be so signed shall be received in evidence without further proof.

(2) Until the contrary be proved, a meeting of a council or of a committee thereof in respect of the proceedings whereof a minute has been so made and signed shall be deemed to have been duly convened and held, and all the members present at the meeting shall be deemed to have been qualified, and where the proceedings are proceedings of a committee the committee shall be deemed to have been duly constituted and to have had power to deal with the matter referred to in the minutes.

Minutes open to inspection

13. The minutes of the proceedings of a council shall at all reasonable times be open to inspection by any inhabitant of the area for which the council is established and any such inhabitant may obtain a copy thereof or an extract therefrom upon payment of such fee as may be specified by the council.

Vacancy, etc., not to invalidate proceedings

14. The proceedings of a council or of a committee thereof shall not be invalidated by any vacancy among its members or the want of qualification of any councillor.

SECOND SCHEDULE
(Section 14)

Form A

SUMMONS TO WITNESS UNDER SECTION 14 OF THE EASTERN REGION LOCAL GOVERNMENT LAW, 1955

To A. B. (Name of person summoned and his calling and residence, if known).

You are hereby summoned to appear before (here name the person before whom the inquiry is to be held) appointed by the Minister of Internal Affairs to inquire (state briefly the subject of the inquiry) at (place)   upon the   day of   , 195   , at   o'clock and to give evidence respecting such inquiry: (if the person summoned is to produce any documents, add) and you are required to bring with you (specify books and documents required).

THEREFORE fail not at your peril.

GIVEN under my hand this   day of   , 195   .

Signed...

Form B
(Section 14)

WARRANT OF ARREST

To P.C................................and any member of the Nigeria Police Force.

WHEREAS a summons under section 14 of the Eastern Region Local Government Law, 1955, has been served upon one
(name of witness) of
(address) to attend and give evidence before (here name the persons appointed to hold the inquiry) appointed by the Minister of Internal Affairs to inquire (state briefly the subject of the inquiry) at (place) upon the   day of   , 195   ;

AND WHEREAS the said (name of witness) has neglected to be or appear at the time and place as aforesaid and it has been proved to me upon oath that the said summons has been duly served upon the said (name of witness) and who has not excused such failure to my satisfaction;

I have to command you forthwith to apprehend the said (name of witness) and to bring him before me.

GIVEN under my hand at   this   day of   , 195

Signed......................................

THIRD SCHEDULE [see p.128]

(Section 190)

THE EASTERN REGION LOCAL GOVERNMENT LAW, 1955

NOTICE is hereby given that the following lands (describe the lands, giving measurement and showing boundaries wherever practicable).

....

....

are required by the   Council for the following purposes

....

....

....

(state purpose for which land is required)

TAKE NOTICE that the   Council intends to ask the Minister of Internal Affairs for an order authorising the Council to acquire the said lands absolutely or for a term of   years subject to the following terms and conditions.

ANY person claiming to have any right or interest in the said land is required within sixty days from the date of this notice to send to the   Council a statement of his right and interest and of the evidence thereof and of any claim made by him in respect of such right or interest.

THE   Council is willing to treat for the acquisition of the said land.

THE amount of compensation or rent which the   Council is willing to pay is £

The   day of   , 195 ·

Seal of the   Council.

FOURTH SCHEDULE [see p.8]

(Section 226)

Ordinance or Law	Section or Part
1. The Markets Ordinance (Cap. 127).	The whole Ordinance.
2. The Native Authority Ordinance (Cap. 140).	The whole Ordinance.
3. The Public Health Ordinance (Cap. 183).	Sections 17; 18; 41; 42; and 43.
4. The Townships Ordinance (Cap. 216).	The whole Ordinance.
5. The Port Harcourt Township Ordinance No. 38 of 1948).	The whole Ordinance.

338

Ordinance or Law	Section or Part
6. The Port Harcourt Town Council (Power of Surcharge) Law, 1952 (No. 4 of 1952).	The whole Law.

FIFTH SCHEDULE
(Section 229)

Ordinance	Part or Section	Amendment
1. The Appointment and Deposition of Chiefs Ordinance (Cap. 12)	5	*Insert* immediately after the expression 'Eastern Region Local Government Ordinance, 1950' where it appears in subsection (2) the expression 'or Eastern Region Local Government Law, 1955'
2. The Births, Deaths and Burials Ordinance (Cap. 20)	38	*Insert* immediately after the expression 'Eastern Region Local Government Ordinance, 1950' the expression 'or the Eastern Region Local Government Law, 1955'
3. The Building Lines Regulation Ordinance (Cap. 24)	3	*Insert* immediately after the expression 'Eastern Region Local Government Ordinance, 1950' the expression 'or under paragraph 11 of section 80 of the 'Eastern Region Local Government Law, 1955'
4. The Criminal Procedure Ordinance (Cap. 45)	89	*Delete* paragraph (*d*) and *substitute* the following paragraph therefor: (*d*) 'If on a Local Government Council established under the provision of the Eastern Region Local Government Ordinance, 1950, in accordance with section 219 of that Ordinance, and if on a Local Government Council established under the provisions of the Eastern Region Local Government Law, 1955, in accordance with the provisions of section 207 of that Law'

Ordinance	*Part or Section*	*Amendment*
5. The Direct Taxation Ordinance (Cap. 54)	2	(a) *Insert* in the definition 'District Council' immediately after the expression 'Eastern Region Local Government Ordinance, 1950' the expression 'or the Eastern Region Local Government Law, 1955' (b) *Insert* in the definition 'Local Council' immediately after the expression 'Eastern Region Local Government Ordinance, 1950' the expression 'or the Eastern Region Local Government Law, 1955' (c) *Insert* immediately after the definition 'Local Council' the following new definition: 'Municipality' means any Municipality established under the provisions of the Eastern Region Local Government Law, 1955;'
	12	*Insert* immediately after the expression 'District Council' wherever it appears in subsection (2) the expression 'or a Municipality'
	13	*Insert* immediately after the expression 'District Council', wherever it occurs in the proviso to subsection (1) which commences 'Provided further that in the Eastern Region' and in subsection (2), the expression 'or a Municipality'
	15A	*Insert* immediately after the expression 'District Council' wherever it occurs the expression 'or Municipality'
	16	*Delete* the expression 'of a District Council' in subsection (2) and *substitute* the expression 'of a District Council or a Municipality in the Eastern Region'

Ordinance	Part or Section	Amendment
5. (Continued)	17	*Delete* the expression 'the District Council' and *substitute* the expression 'the District Council or Municipality in the Eastern Region'
	19	*Insert* immediately after the expression 'a District Council' wherever it occurs the expression 'or a Municipality'
	20	*Insert* immediately after the expression 'District Council' where it occurs the expression 'or a Municipality'
	21	*Insert* immediately after the expression 'District Council' the expression 'or Municipality'
6. The Ex-Native Office Holders Removal Ordinance (Cap. 68)	2	*Insert* immediately after the expression 'Eastern Region Local Government Ordinance, 1950' the expression 'or the Eastern Region Local Government Law, 1955'
7. The Labour Code Ordinance (Cap. 99)	2	*Insert* immediately after the expression 'Eastern Region Local Government Ordinance, 1950' in the definition 'Local Council' the expression 'or the Eastern Region Local Government Law, 1955;'
8. The Land Development (Provision for Roads) Ordinance (Cap. 106)	2	(a) *Insert* in the definition 'District Council' after the expression 'Eastern Region Local Government Ordinance, 1950' the expression 'or the Eastern Region Local Government Law, 1955;' (b) *Insert* immediately after the definition 'land' the following new definition: 'Municipality means any Municipality established under the provisions of the Eastern Region Local Government Law, 1955;'

341

Ordinance	Part or Section	Amendment
8. (Continued)	7, 8, 10, 11	*Insert* immediately after the expression 'District Council' wherever it occurs the expression 'or Municipality'
9. The Magistrates' Courts Ordinance (Cap. 122)	19	*Insert* immediately after the expression 'Eastern Region Local Government Ordinance, 1950' in paragraph (*e*) of subsection (1) the expression 'or the Eastern Region Local Government Law, 1955'
10. The Magistrates' Courts (Appeals) Ordinance (Cap. 123)	2	*Insert* immediately after the expression 'Eastern Region Local Government Ordinance, 1950' in the definition 'civil proceedings' the expression 'or the Eastern Region Local Government Law, 1955'
11. The Magistrates' Courts (Civil Procedure) Ordinance (Cap. 124)	2	*Insert* immediately after the expression 'Eastern Region Local Government Ordinance, 1950' in the definition 'civil proceedings' the expression 'or the Eastern Region Local Government Law, 1955'
	19	*Insert* immediately after the expression 'Eastern Region Local Government Ordinance, 1950' in paragraph (*d*) of subsection (1) the expression 'or the Eastern Region Local Government Law, 1955'
12. Native Courts Ordinance (Cap. 142)	10	*Insert* the following new paragraph immediately after paragraph (*d*) of subsection (1); '(*e*)the provisions of the Eastern Region Local Government Law, 1955, together with all rules, regulations, orders or bye-laws made thereunder'

Ordinance	Part or Section	Amendment
13. Native Lands Acquisition Ordinance (Cap. 144)	2	(a) *Insert* in paragraph (b) (iii) of the definition 'alien' immediately after the expression 'Eastern Region Local Government Ordinance, 1950' the expression' or the Eastern Region Local Government Law, 1955' (b) *Insert* in paragraph (c) of the definition 'native' immediately after the expression 'Eastern Region Local Government Ordinance, 1950', the expression 'or the Eastern Region Local Government Law, 1955'
14. The Nigeria Town and Country Planning Ordinance (Cap. 155)	49	*Insert* immediately after the expression 'Eastern Region Local Government Ordinance, 1950' where it occurs in paragraph (c) of subsection (1) the expression 'or by Part XVII of the Eastern Region Local Government Law, 1955 as the case may be.
15. The Eastern Region Loans Law, 1954 (E.R. No. 4 of 1954)	2	*Insert* immediately after the expression 'Eastern Region Local Government Ordinance, 1950' the expression 'or the Eastern Region Local Government Law, 1955'

This printed impression has been carefully compared by me with the Bill which has passed the Eastern House of Assembly and is found by me to be a true and correctly printed copy of the said Bill.

L. O. OKORO

Clerk of the Eastern House of Assembly

INDEX

E = Eastern Region Law; w = Western Region Law. Figures following E and w are references to the sections in the text of the Laws

347

convening of inaugural meeting, 67; w § 35 (3)
Service Board, Local Government, 120; E § 109, 110
Sovereignty, 12
Surcharge, disqualification by,
112; E § 20 (G); w § 24 (B)
officials and, 111, 112; E § 176;
w § 143
Summons to a council meeting,
67, 68;
First Schedule, Para 4;
w § 38
Staff, associations, 119, 120
control by chief officers, 117,
118
control by council, 116
control by departmental committees, 116, 117
control of by Minister in
Eastern Region, 44, 45, 115,
116; E § 94, 95
control of by Regional Authority in Western Region, 44,
45, 115, 116; w § 84
records of service of, 119

regulations, 115
Standing Orders, 75;
E § 37; w § 48

Tender, acceptance of, 133
invitation to, 131, 132
opening of, 132-3
receipt of, 132
Townships Ordinance, 7, 8
Treasuries, establishment of, 91-
93

Urgency, certificate of, 106

Vote, officer controlling, 106-7
Voting, at committee meetings,
72-3
at council meetings, 71-3;
E First Schedule, Para 9;
w § 43

Warrant Chiefs, 4
Warren, Mr J. H., 70
Wraith, Mr Ronald, 28

Yorubas, 3